The Modes of Scepticism

D0498972

The Modes of Scepticism

Ancient Texts and Modern Interpretations

Julia Annas

Professor of Philosophy,
University of Arizona, Tucson

and

Jonathan Barnes

Professor of Ancient Philosophy
in the University of Oxford

CAMBRIDGE
UNIVERSITY PRESS

Published by the Press Syndicate of the University of Cambridge
The Pitt Building, Trumpington Street, Cambridge CB2 1RP
40 West 20th Street, New York, NY 10011-4211, USA
10 Stamford Road, Oakleigh, Melbourne 3166, Australia

© Cambridge University Press 1985

First published 1985
Reprinted 1986, 1991, 1994, 1997

Library of Congress catalogue card number: 84–20053

British Library Cataloguing in Publication Data
Annas, Julia
The modes of scepticism: ancient texts and
modern interpretations.
1. Skepticism   II. Barnes, Jonathan
186 B525

ISBN 0 521 25682 8 hard covers
ISBN 0 521 27644 6 paperback

Transferred to digital printing 2003

CE

Contents

Preface

This book, like most jointly written works, has arisen from a shared interest which we have developed together with mutual benefit and pleasure. We are especially grateful for the invention of the word-processor, which has stimulated continuous exchanges and criticisms by making correction pleasing rather than tedious, and which has, we think, resulted in a book which is a product of joint labour throughout, even in parts where one or other of us was originally responsible for more of the ingredients.

We have discussed the modes in several seminars and lectures, and we are grateful to our audiences for their patience and their helpful comments. We hope that the book will encourage further discussion, and that others may succeed in elucidating opaque argumentation where we have failed – and may even discover what Pericles' slave really was doing on the roof-top.

Julia Annas
Jonathan Barnes

Oxford, April 1984

Introduction

Those who investigate any subject are likely either to make a discovery, or to deny the possibility of discovery and agree that nothing can be apprehended, or else to persist in their investigations. That, no doubt, is why of those who undertake philosophical investigations some say that they have discovered the truth, others deny the possibility of apprehending it, and others are still pursuing their investigations. Those who are properly called dogmatists – such as the Aristotelians and the Epicureans and the Stoics and others – think they have discovered the truth; Clitomachus and Carneades and other Academic philosophers have said that the truth cannot be apprehended; and the sceptics persist in their investigations.

With this paragraph Sextus Empiricus, the Greek sceptical philosopher, begins his introductory handbook to sceptical thought, the *Outlines of Pyrrhonism*. He portrays sceptics as perpetual students or researchers, as people who 'persist in their investigations', and the Greek adjective *skeptikos* derives from a verb meaning 'to inquire' or 'to consider'. Now inquirers persist in their inquiries because they have neither discovered the object of their search nor concluded that it lies beyond all discovery: they have, as yet, no opinion on the matter. Hence the word *skeptikos* or 'sceptical' acquires its familiar connotation. Sceptics are doubters: they neither believe nor disbelieve, neither affirm nor deny.

To be sceptical on any given matter is to suspend judgement on it, to subscribe to no positive opinion either way. A sceptical philosophy recommends doubt and suspension of judgement over a substantial range – perhaps even over the whole range – of human investigations. Everyone is a sceptic on some issues, for there are numerous questions on which, temporarily at least, we cannot make up our minds and over which we suspend judgement. Sceptical philosophers extend, generalise, and systematise that ordinary attitude.

The ancient sceptics labelled their opponents 'dogmatists'. The word 'dogmatist' in contemporary English has a pejorative tone – it hints at an irrational rigidity of opinion, a refusal to look impartially at the evidence. In its ancient sense the word lacked that tone: a dogmatist was simply someone who subscribed to dogmas or doctrines. We shall use the word in the ancient sense. The disadvantage of this practice is off-set by the convenience of having a short label for all those who are not sceptical philosophers.

This book is an introduction to sceptical philosophy. We intend, for reasons which will become apparent in the first chapter, that it may also serve as an introduction to philosophy itself. We approach the subject through the works of certain Greek thinkers; for scepticism, like most other forms of philosophical thought, was first elaborated in ancient Greece. The texts with which we are primarily concerned describe what were known as the ten 'modes' of suspension of judgement: they present ten ways in which one can be induced to suspend judgement and to become a sceptic. These texts contain only a small part of the works of the Greek sceptics, but they must surely count among the most influential pages in the history of Western philosophy.

We have tried to be elementary. We hope that our book will be read, understood, and even enjoyed, by readers who are new to philosophy and to Greek thought.

In the first two chapters we sketch the history of sceptical philosophy and endeavour to exhibit its importance both in ancient and in modern thought. The third chapter offers a general survey of the nature and the history of the Ten Modes themselves. The following chapters, which form the main body of the book, are ten in number, one for each mode.

The modes are preserved for us by three separate sources, Philo of Alexandria, Sextus Empiricus, and Diogenes Laertius. Each of Chapters 3 to 13 begins with a translation of the relevant paragraphs in those three authors, and then continues with some pages of commentary. The modes occur in different orders in our different sources. We have chosen to follow Sextus' ordering. Thus Sextus' exposition of the modes can be read in the order in which it was written by anyone who goes consecutively through the first sections of each of our chapters. We have not preserved the original order of the texts of Diogenes and Philo: the reader who wishes to follow them through in their entirety will find them set out in Appendix A.

Other ancient authors occasionally mention the Ten Modes. The most important passages are translated in the course of Chapter 3. Thus our book can claim to present all the significant ancient material on the Ten Modes of suspension of judgement.

The translations aim at fidelity in substance and, to a lesser extent, in style. We have tried to translate Greek prose into English prose. But on occasion we have sacrificed literary to philosophical virtue, and our prose descends into barbarism when we can find no easy way of expressing in English the precise force of a Greek phrase. Certain terms of a technical or semi-technical nature present difficulties of translation: those terms are included in the Glossary.

For Sextus we have translated the Teubner text of Mutschmann, revised by Mau; for Diogenes, Long's edition in the Oxford Classical Texts series; for Philo, the standard edition of Cohn and Wendland. Where we have departed from the readings of those editions – and at certain other textually disputed points – we have placed an asterisk in the translation. Appendix E contains notes on all the asterisked passages.

The commentary is discursive in form, not a sequence of line by line notes. It is both exegetical and critical. We want to understand, so far as we can, exactly what Sextus and his colleagues mean, and we are interested in the history of the thoughts they present. Although we have not attempted a minute analysis of every passage in the texts, we have not altogether shunned detailed matters of scholarship. We are equally concerned with the philosophical value of the Ten Modes and have tried to determine, or at least to suggest ways of determining, the extent to which the modes do or should induce suspension of judgement and scepticism.

In recent years there has been a renaissance of interest in Hellenistic philosophy in general, and in ancient scepticism in particular. The scholars who have contributed to that revival have, on the whole, published learned papers in learned journals. We owe much to their work, without which we would not have thought to write this book. They have reopened a rich and fascinating territory to the specialist in Greek philosophy. We hope that this book may help non-specialists to enjoy the treasures of that lost world.

1   Sceptical Philosophy

What can we know about the world? How can we think and talk about it? Those two large questions determine two main areas of philosophy. Epistemology discusses questions of cognition: What is knowledge? How much can we know? Of what can we be certain? In what circumstances are our beliefs justified? Logic or philosophy of language is devoted to questions of meaning: What is it for us or our utterances to mean something? How can we refer to things in the external world? By what inferential processes can we legitimately move from one statement to another?

Among Anglo-Saxon philosophers, logic is now often taken to be the fundamental part of philosophy, and questions of meaning are accorded a certain priority: until we understand how we can talk and think about things we can make no progress. Such an attitude to philosophy is young. It traces its origins to the work of the German mathematician and logician, Gottlob Frege, whose active life spanned the period from 1880 to 1925.

Before the age of logic came the age of epistemology. For such thinkers as Descartes and Locke, Hume and Kant, the basic questions of philosophy concerned not language and thought but rather the nature and scope of human understanding. The first task of the philosopher was to determine in what ways and to what extent we can gain knowledge of the world. The triumph of logic has given a distinctive colouring to modern Anglo-Saxon philosophy: in style and approach, in method and argument, it differs noticeably from the philosophy of earlier epochs. In just the same way the reign of epistemology affected the character of three centuries of European philosophical thought.

It is easy to see how epistemological questions might come to occupy a primary place in philosophical speculation. If we are concerned as philosophers to gain some general understanding of the nature of reality, we might find it natural to turn first to that most familiar part of reality, ourselves. And our attempt to follow the old maxim 'Know yourself' will surely include an analysis of our own cognitive powers. Or again, the very nature of philosophical inquiry and its concern with large and abstract issues will lead to epistemological worries: how, after all, can we hope to know, or to be justified in believing, the heady theses which philosophy suggests? John Locke explains the origins of his *Essay concerning Human Understanding* as follows:

Five or six Friends meeting at my Chamber, and discoursing on a subject very remote from this, found themselves quickly at a stand, by the Difficulties that rose on every side. After we had a while puzzled our selves, without coming any nearer a Resolution of those Doubts which perplexed us, it came into my Thoughts, that we took a wrong course; and that, before we set our selves upon Enquiries of that Nature, it was necessary to examine our own Abilities, and see, what Objects our Understandings were, or were not fitted to deal with. This I proposed to the Company, who all readily assented; and thereupon it was agreed, that this should be our first Enquiry. (*Epistle to the Reader*)

Locke's original inquiries led necessarily to epistemology.

It is easy, too, to see how scepticism will become an issue of the greatest importance once epistemology is regarded as the primary part of philosophy. Before embarking on their further inquiries, epistemologists ask how much they can expect to know. To this question the sceptic has an uncompromising answer: little or nothing. At the gates of knowledge the sceptic stands guard: before we can enter the citadel we must answer his challenge.

Epochs of thought are not neatly determined, but the reign of epistemology can be given an inaugural year and we can cite a specific event which, more than anything else, made epistemology the fundamental concern of philosophers. In 1562 the French scholar and publisher Henri Etienne brought out the first modern edition of Sextus Empiricus' *Outlines of Pyrrhonism*. Etienne, or Stephanus in the Latinised version of his name, published a Latin translation of the work (Latin being the international language of the learned world), and Sextus' hitherto obscure book rapidly rose to become the dominant philosophical text of the age. It was the rediscovery of Sextus and of Greek scepticism which shaped the course of philosophy for the next three hundred years.

Before the *Outlines* were published scholars had, it is true, possessed some knowledge of ancient sceptical thought. In Diogenes Laertius' *Lives of the Philosophers* the biography of Pyrrho, one of the founders of Greek scepticism, is accompanied by a brief survey of the sceptical approach to philosophy. Diogenes' work had been available in Latin since 1430 – indeed it was the Latin translation of Diogenes which introduced the word *scepticus* into modern European thought. Some account of sceptical ideas could also be found in the philosophical writings of Cicero, notably in his *Academics*. But Cicero does not purport to offer a complete sceptical philosophy, and Diogenes' account is crabbed and in parts barely intelligible. Sextus, by contrast, gives an exposition which is systematic, lucid, lively and sympathetic. His text is a *tour de force* and its impression was stunning.

The triumph of Sextus was swift. Its first major literary manifestation is Montaigne's remarkable essay entitled *A Defence of Raymond Sebond*. This long, rambling composition, written in about 1575, assembles a mass of sceptical arguments, most of them lifted from the text of Sextus. From a philosopher's point of view, the most spectacular testimony to Sextus' influence is to be found in the writings of Descartes. In his *Reply* to the seventh set of *Objections*, published in the second edition of the *Meditations* in 1642, Descartes says:

> We must not think that the sect of sceptics is long extinct. It flourishes today as much as ever, and nearly all who think that they have some ability beyond that of the rest of mankind, finding nothing that satisfies them in the common philosophy, and seeing no other truth, take refuge in scepticism.

Descartes saw scepticism as a disease of epidemic magnitude: his whole philosophical activity was given to the search for a cure.

A century later the disease was still rife. As a young man, David Hume went down with it:

> The *intense* view of these manifold contradictions and imperfections in human reason has so wrought upon me, and heated my brain, that I am ready to reject all belief and reasoning, and can look upon no opinion as even more probable or likely than another. (*Treatise of Human Nature* I iv 7)

Hume's attitude to scepticism is complex. It is at best misleading simply to label him a sceptic; but there is no doubt that his philosophy is informed by and founded upon the sceptical arguments which derive from Sextus.

Hume's sceptical puzzlings worried Kant. Kant was, in the ancient sense, a dogmatist through and through. But he was a critical dogmatist, and he held that the sceptical method was an indispensable propaedeutic to critical dogmatism. It was scepticism, after all, which had roused reason from its 'sweet, dogmatic dreams'. And, in a different metaphor the sceptic is ... the taskmaster who constrains the dogmatic reasoner to develop a sound critique of the understanding and reason ... While ... the sceptical procedure cannot of itself yield any *satisfying* answer to the questions of reason, none the less it *prepares the way* by arousing reason to circumspection, and by indicating the radical measures which are adequate to secure it in its legitimate possessions. (*Critique of Pure Reason*, A769)

Scepticism, for Kant, continued to pose the problems, and to point the way to their non-sceptical solution.

Those quotations from Descartes, Hume and Kant could be matched by a thousand others from philosophers of humbler talents. Scepticism was the philosophical disease of the age, and the disease had been transmitted by Sextus Empiricus' *Outlines of Pyrrhonism*.

Even if scepticism is no longer the first problem for a philosopher, it is still an issue which no philosopher will avoid. But if scepticism remains important, does its ancient history concern us? No doubt it will be instructive and entertaining, from a purely historical point of view, to follow back its career; but is there any other, non-historical, interest in going beyond Kant and Hume and Descartes to their Greek sources?

The arguments which Descartes and his successors expound and criticise are almost all to be found in the ancient texts. But there is much more in the pages of Sextus than Descartes indicates, and a philosophical reader who troubles to go back to Sextus will find, at the very least, a greater abundance of sceptical argumentation than modern discussion would lead him to imagine.

But there is another and more interesting difference between ancient and modern scepticism. The Greeks took their scepticism seriously: the moderns do not.

Modern scepticism frequently represents itself as issuing a challenge to *knowledge*. The sceptic argues that, under pressure from his arguments, we must abandon many, or indeed all, of our claims to knowledge and confess that in truth we know very little. At first, that conclusion may seem heady and sparkling; but on repetition it may come to appear flat. For the sceptical challenge leaves all our *beliefs* intact: provided only that we do not claim to *know* anything, we may continue with our usual assertions and persist in our usual beliefs. We shall allow that our beliefs do not amount to knowledge, but we shall insist that we are still justified in holding them. A scepticism of that sort may actually seem a charade. (For is not the sceptic merely stipulating knowledge out of existence by insisting that no degree of justification, however high, is quite enough for knowledge?) It will certainly seem idle. It does not affect our behaviour or our mode of life, and it is to that extent unserious.

The ancient sceptics did not attack knowledge: they attacked belief. They argued that, under sceptical pressure, our beliefs turn out to be groundless and that we have no more reason to believe than to disbelieve. As a result, they supposed, our beliefs would vanish. We should, of course, lose all knowledge; but that would be merely a trivial consequence of our general loss of belief. The ancient sceptics do not claim to *know* that the water in the kettle will boil – but nor do they *believe* that it will boil. Rather, they neither believe nor disbelieve that the water will boil: if you ask them 'Will it boil?' they shrug their shoulders – and if you ask them 'Will it freeze?' they make the same gesture of indifference.

Not all modern sceptics, however, are happy to leave belief intact: scepticism, after all, implies doubt, and doubting something appears to be incompatible with believing it and not just with knowing it. But modern sceptics who talk about doubt typically intend a somewhat special notion – something which they will call 'philosophical' doubt or, following Descartes, 'hyperbolical' doubt. Such doubt is supposed to be as it were insulated from the affairs of life and cut off from action.

The first three of Descartes' *Principles of Philosophy* are these:

That in order to investigate the truth of things it is necessary once in one's life to put all things in doubt insofar as that is possible.

That it is useful too to regard as false those things which one can doubt.

That we should certainly not use this doubt for the conduct of our actions.

Applying the first principle, the Cartesian sceptic will doubt that he is buying a cup of coffee and doubts that twice ten is twenty; applying the second principle, he will actually regard those things as false. But the third principle warns us that his doubt is philosophical: he will not conduct his actions by it; that is to say, even while 'doubting', he will persist in, and act upon, his ordinary beliefs that the stuff in the cup is coffee and that two ten-pence pieces make up twenty pence.

'Philosophical' doubt is thus essentially idle: it cannot, by definition, have any bearing on action. It is easy to think that it is also a sham. Wittgenstein asks, of the belief that tables remain where they are even when no-one can see them:

If anyone doubted that, how would his doubt show itself in practice? Couldn't we let him quietly doubt, since it makes no difference at all? (*On Certainty* §120)

If 'philosophical' doubt does not affect action, then how is it doubt at all? What in the world are we to understand by a doubt which is compatible with ordinary belief and which has no bearing upon action?

However that may be, the ancient sceptics had no interest in philosophical doubt. The doubt they expected to induce was ordinary, non-philosophical doubt; it excluded beliefs, and it was therefore a practical doubt. Indeed, it was precisely by reference to the practical corollaries of their doubt that they used to recommend their philosophy: scepticism, they claimed, by relieving us of our ordinary beliefs, would remove the worry from our lives and ensure our happiness.

That claim may seem extravagant: we shall return to it at the end of the book. It may even be thought that the notion of a life without *belief* – unlike the notion of a life without *knowledge* – is barely coherent. Hume, who understood ancient scepticism better than many later sceptics, put the point forcefully. The radical sceptic, he says,

must acknowledge, if he will acknowledge anything, that all human life must perish, were his principles universally and steadily to prevail. All discourse, all action would immediately cease; and men remain in a total lethargy, till the necessities of nature, unsatisfied, put an end to their miserable existence. It is true, so fatal an event is very little to be dreaded. Nature is always too strong for principle. (*Enquiry concerning Human Understanding* XII ii)

Hume's judgement had been anticipated by the ancient critics of scepticism, and the sceptics had themselves constructed a subtle reply. Modern sceptics have no need for subtle replies; for they can correctly observe that Hume's judgement does not touch their insulated doubts. The irrelevance of Hume's remark to modern doubters is a symptom of the main philosophical difference between ancient and modern scepticism, and a mark, we think, of the greater interest and seriousness of the ancient variety.

2 Scepticism in Ancient Philosophy

For us, as for Descartes and his contemporaries, Sextus Empiricus is the chief representative of ancient scepticism. But Sextus was the heir to a long tradition which the sceptics themselves liked to trace back to the very beginnings of Greek philosophy. The sceptical tradition, unlike its rivals, never hardened into a school. In the Golden Age of Greek thought, from about 400 BC to about 100 BC, the chief dogmatic philosophies – Platonism, Aristotelianism, Stoicism, Epicureanism – were to some extent institutionalised. They were marked by characteristic doctrines and distinctive ideologies. They enjoyed some measure of formal organisation. They functioned as educational establishments. They had official heads or 'scholarchs'. They owned property. The history of scepticism, one episode excepted, is not like that. Leading sceptics had associates and pupils, and they were aware of their predecessors. Sceptical attitudes and arguments were transmitted from one generation to the next. But by its very nature scepticism could profess no school doctrines, and its adherents did not hanker after the institutional trappings or the professional status of the dogmatic sects. Greek scepticism has a history, but it is informal and discontinuous.

The later sceptics called themselves Pyrrhonians, 'from the fact that Pyrrho appears to us to have applied himself to scepticism more thoroughly and more conspicuously than his predecessors' (Sextus, *Outlines of Pyrrhonism* I 7). Pyrrho of Elis is for us a shadowy figure. He lived from about 360 BC to about 270 BC. He gained some celebrity in his lifetime, for his fellow citizens honoured him with a statue. He participated, along with other philosophers, in Alexander the Great's expedition through Asia and India. But he left no writings, and what we know of his views derives from later sources, some of whom are openly hostile or satirical in tone, while others anachronistically dress him in the clothes of later scepticism.

There is one early and friendly witness. Timon of Phlius was a contemporary and an associate of Pyrrho, and a report of one of his writings contains a valuable outline of Pyrrho's philosophical position:

Pyrrho's pupil, Timon, says that anyone who is going to lead a happy life must take account of the following three things: first, what objects are like by nature; secondly, what our attitude to them should be; finally, what will result for those who take this attitude. Now he says that Pyrrho shows that objects are equally indifferent and unfathomable and undeterminable because neither our senses nor our judgements are true or false; so for that reason we should not trust in them but should be without judgement and without inclination and unmoved, saying about each thing that it no more is than is not or both is and is not or neither is nor is not. And Timon says that for those who take this attitude the result will be first non-assertion, then tranquillity . . . (Aristocles, in Eusebius, *Preparation for the Gospel* XIV xviii 2–4)

The report comes from Aristocles of Messene, who was active during the first half of the second century AD. (He was the teacher of Alexander of Aphrodisias, the greatest Aristotelian scholar of antiquity.) Aristocles wrote a work *On Philosophy* in ten books, fragments of which have been preserved by Eusebius, the third-century Bishop of Caesarea. Aristocles was no friend of Pyrrhonism: the long excerpt on scepticism is sneeringly dismissive, and it is plain that Aristocles did not always trouble to understand the views he was so quick to dismiss. Nonetheless, he purports to be drawing on the writings of Timon, and Timon's words are worth attending to.

If we believe Timon, then we must suppose that Pyrrho embraced an extreme scepticism and purported to live by it. He rejected all assertion and belief, and he lived a tranquil life as a result. Various anecdotal reports add colour to Timon's outline sketch. When Pyrrho went out his friends would accompany him and pull him from the path of oncoming traffic; he was so impervious to the conventions of life that he did not mind washing pigs; he was so indifferent to pain that he could tolerate the hackings of the surgeons. But such stories – like so much in ancient and modern biography – are no more than engaging fictions: they stand to history as caricature stands to portraiture.

We cannot safely go beyond Timon's evidence. It is, however, given some indirect confirmation by a passage in Aristotle's *Metaphysics*. In Book Gamma Aristotle argues against various people who denied, or purported to deny, or were thought to have denied, such basic principles as the Law of Non-Contradiction and the Law of the Excluded Middle. In the course of this argument Aristotle declares that

you may well be surprised that people puzzle over whether sizes and colours are the way they appear to those who are far away or to those who are near, or whether they are the way they appear to those who are healthy or to those who are sick, or whether heavy things are those which appear so to the weak or those which appear so to the strong, or whether truths are what appear true to those asleep or what appear true to those awake. Of course, it is plain that they do not actually *believe* what they say – at any rate no one who dreams that he is in Athens when in fact he is in Africa sets out for the Odeon. (1010b4–11)

The position which Aristotle is attacking is plainly one of extreme scepticism. Aristotle does not name his opponents. It is unlikely, for chronological reasons, that he has Pyrrho in mind, but his discussion is enough to show that an extreme form of scepticism had been aired in the second half of the fourth century.

If the content of Pyrrho's philosophy is only sketchily known to us, we can say still less about the circumstances and influences which moved him along the sceptical road. The biographical tradition connects Pyrrho's thought with the Indian ascetics (or 'naked sophists' as the Greeks called them) whom Pyrrho allegedly met during his travels with Alexander. The story must be treated with care, but there are certain surprising similarities between some of the things which Timon says about Pyrrho and certain views and practices of contemporary Indian ascetics. It is by no means impossible that Pyrrhonism has an Indian godfather. But its natural parents were surely Greek, as Sextus indicates by his reference to Pyrrho's 'predecessors'.

Sceptical pronouncements can be found among the surviving fragments of the earliest Greek thinkers. Thus Xenophanes of Colophon, who lived from about 580 to about 470 BC asserted that

> No man has seen nor will anyone ever know the clear truth
> about the gods and the other matters of which I speak.
> For even should he happen to say something which is the case,
> nevertheless he himself will not know it: for all there is only belief.
>
> (frag. 34)

A century later, Democritus, the proponent of atomism and the leading scientific theorist of the generation before Plato, confessed that 'in reality we know nothing – for truth is in the depths' (frag. 117). Several other fragments, most of them preserved by Sextus, convey a similar message. It is not clear that Democritus was himself an adherent of scepticism; but he certainly developed sceptical arguments in some detail and at some length.

Other fifth-century figures made comparable remarks, many of which were quoted by later sceptics eager to discover a pedigree for their mode of philosophising. It is difficult to make any confident statements about the views of those early philosophers, for little of their writings has survived. A few sceptical observations do not constitute a sceptical philosophy, and it would be rash to assume that the first period of Western philosophy produced any systematically sceptical body of thought. Nonetheless, it is evident that Pyrrho did not create his scepticism *ex nihilo*: he had Greek as well as Indian material to work with. The extreme scepticism mentioned in Aristotle's *Metaphysics* is also alluded to in Plato's *Theaetetus*. Some later sceptics did not scruple to enrol Plato himself among their intellectual forebears, and they also claimed that Socrates, Plato's master, had been a sceptic. Socrates, so far as we can tell, was of a sceptical disposition: at all events, he was always ready to show how vain are our pretensions to knowledge, and he claimed that his own superior wisdom consisted precisely in the fact that he knew that he knew nothing. But Socrates' sceptical attitude is a far cry from Pyrrho's sceptical philosophy.

Those who made Plato a sceptic relied on five arguments which are conveniently summarised in an anonymous *Introduction to Plato's Philosophy* which dates from the sixth century AD:

In his discussion of things, they say, he uses certain adverbs indicating ambivalence and doubt – e.g. 'probably' and 'perhaps' and 'maybe'; and that is a mark not of one who knows but of one who fails to apprehend any precise knowledge ... They argue secondly that inasmuch as he tries to establish contrary views about the same things he clearly extols inapprehensibility – e.g. he tries to establish contraries when discussing friendship in the *Lysis*, temperance in the *Charmides*, piety in the *Euthyphro* ... Thirdly, they say that he thinks that there is no such thing as knowledge, as is clear from the fact that he refutes every account of knowledge in the *Theaetetus* ... Their fourth argument is this: if Plato thinks that knowledge is two-fold, one sort coming through perception and the other through thought, and if he says that each sort falls down, it is clear that he extols inapprehensibility ... This is their fifth argument: they say that he himself says in his dialogue 'I know nothing and I teach nothing: all that I do is raise problems'. (pp. 205–6 Hermann)

The anonymous author of the *Introduction* rightly rejects all those arguments. The arguments are not merely captious; for there are passages in Plato – and not only in the early 'aporetic' dialogues – which reveal a certain sceptical disposition. But Sextus, who discusses the question at some length (*Outlines of Pyrrhonism* I 221–5), comes to the correct conclusion: 'even if Plato evinces doubt on some matters, he is not a sceptic; for in some places he appears either as making assertions about the existence of unclear objects or as giving preference to what is unclear in respect of conviction' (§225).

However that may be, it was Plato's school which produced the second sceptic of note after Pyrrho. Arcesilaus of Pitane (315–240 BC) became head of the Academy and converted the school to scepticism. The New Academy, as it was later called, claimed as a matter of course that it was returning to the true spirit of Platonism after the dogmatic slumbers of the preceding century; and for a further two hundred years the Academy remained sceptical, providing in its two leading figures – Arcesilaus and Carneades (214/13–129/8) – thinkers of remarkable power and subtlety.

To outside observers there was little difference between the sceptical Academics and the Pyrrhonists. It is plain, too, that Arcesilaus and his followers, who were surely influenced by Pyrrho, influenced in their turn the later Pyrrhonists. But the Pyrrhonists insisted that their views differed substantially from those of the Academics, so that 'the difference between the Academics and the Pyrrhonists' became a standard topic for scholarly debate. Whatever the truth of the matter, the history of Academic scepticism is a subject on its own.

According to Cicero, Arcesilaus 'held that everything lay hidden and that for that reason no-one should assert or affirm or give assent to anything' (*Academics* I 45). But Cicero is either mistaken or careless. Arcesilaus and his followers were not positive sceptics, asserting that nothing should be asserted. Rather, they were essentially critics. Their style of philosophising was *ad hominem*. Typically, they would take hold of one of the doctrines of a dogmatic philosopher (the Stoics were their usual target) and attempt to reduce it to absurdity. 'If you Stoics are right', they would argue, 'and such-and-such is the case, then we cannot know the truth about so-and-so. You Stoics are committed by your own principles to scepticism.'

For Pyrrho scepticism had been a way of life. In the arguments between the Academics and their opponents scepticism became a part of professional philosophy. And at the same time epistemological issues came to be seen as the fundamental questions of philosophy. The philosophers of the Hellenistic schools had claimed to know many things – as, of course, had all their predecessors. The Academics attempted to show that their claims were all groundless. But they did not do so by arguing in favour of some alternative view; rather, they questioned the credentials of any dogmatic view whatever. 'Why do you believe that?' became the leading question in philosophical discussion. 'You can have no reason to believe that' became the sceptical refrain. Arcesilaus was the Descartes of his generation: both thinkers made their contemporaries treat epistemology as the primary part of philosophy.

The practical scepticism of Pyrrho and the professional scepticism of Arcesilaus were fused in the later tradition, and the fusion was begun by the third major figure in the sceptical tradition. Aenesidemus was recognised as one of the heroes of Pyrrhonism, and the Ten Modes of Scepticism, with which this book is primarily concerned and which formed the centrepiece of ancient scepticism, in all probability originated with him. Yet wretchedly little is known about him: he probably flourished in the early decades of the first century BC – at any rate he is said to have been a member of the Academy at the end of its sceptical period, when he claimed to find his contemporary Academics too dogmatic, and determined to promote a more radical form of scepticism.

Later authors refer to various of Aenesidemus' works, but none has survived for us to read. Some of the references are puzzling. (Aenesidemus had an interest in the views of the Presocratic thinker Heraclitus – but quite what form that interest took is a major problem.) Most of the references are brief and tell us little. We do, however, possess a short summary of the whole of one of Aenesidemus' works. The Byzantine patriarch Photius, active in the ninth century AD, was a learned man and an energetic scholar. His *Bibliothēkē* (or *Library*) contains summaries of nearly three hundred books, both pagan and Christian. One of those works, surprisingly enough, was Aenesidemus' *Pyrrhonian Arguments* (cod. 212). From it we can learn that Aenesidemus retained all the philosophical interests of the Academic sceptics and attacked their traditional targets, while at the same time claiming that the Academics were no longer genuinely sceptical and stressing that his own scepticism, or Pyrrhonism as he chose to call it, marked a return to the tradition which the Academy had recently betrayed.

Aenesidemus saw himself as a revolutionary, and some later authors were prepared to picture him in that light. But he appears to have made little splash in his lifetime. At any rate, Cicero, writing in 55 BC, felt able to assert that Pyrrhonism, as a philosophy, was extinct, and Seneca, writing a century later, repeated the assertion. Pyrrhonism never rivalled the major philosophical schools in popularity. Nonetheless, the reports of its death were greatly exaggerated. From the two centuries which separate Aenesidemus from the last great sceptic, Sextus Empiricus, we hear of a dozen or so Pyrrhonists; and there is some evidence that Pyrrhonism grew and developed in those years.

A notable fact about Aenesidemus' successors is that many of them were doctors. Medicine and philosophy had long been closely allied in Greece, and physicians had always shown a professional interest in philosophical questions. In the Hellenistic period this interest was maintained. One school of medical thought, which traced its origins to the celebrated doctor Herophilus in the early third century BC, held that theory and reasoning should have no part in medical science – the art of medicine ought to rest upon experience and observation alone. The empiricist doctors, as members of that school were called, had close connexions with the Pyrrhonist tradition in philosophy. Cassius, who was described by Celsus as the greatest doctor of his age, was a Pyrrhonist; Menodotus, the leading doctor of the next generation, wrote philosophical works of a sceptical nature; Sextus Empiricus himself, as his surname indicates, was generally held to have been an empiricist.

Scepticism was not merely a hobby with these doctors: it had a profound effect upon their medical thought and practice. Thus the empiricists rejected any appeal to causal explanations within medical science, for reasons wholly abstract and philosophical in nature. Again, they rejected the practice of anatomy, and in particular of vivisection, on grounds which were in part at least Pyrrhonian. The subtle interconnexions between theory and practice, between philosophical scepticism and medical activity, are an intriguing topic which scholars have not yet investigated with any thoroughness. It is clear that the empiricist doctors were not extreme sceptics – they did not follow Aenesidemus in rejecting all beliefs and all assertions. But their scepticism was certainly founded upon philosophical argument and determined a philosophical attitude. At the same time it had an unambiguous and far-reaching effect on their professional behaviour.

Thus we come to Sextus Empiricus, doctor and sceptic. Of Sextus' life virtually nothing is known. It seems most probable that he flourished in the middle of the second century AD, and he may have spent some time in Alexandria in Egypt. Beyond that we can say nothing. But if his life is obscure, his works are not. Not all that he wrote has survived, but we still possess the *Outlines of Pyrrhonism*, a general introduction to Pyrrhonism in three books, and a further group of eleven books known collectively as *Against the Mathematicians*. Those two works constitute our chief source for ancient Greek scepticism – and also, incidentally, for many other aspects of Hellenistic philosophy.

The *Outlines of Pyrrhonism* (which we shall refer to as *PH*, from the initial letters of its Greek title) contains in its first book a positive account of what Pyrrhonism is, how it is practised, how its goal is achieved, and how it differs from certain other philosophies which have a sceptical aspect. Half of the book is occupied by Sextus' treatment of the Ten Modes of scepticism. The second and third books are wholly negative and critical in approach. They discuss in turn the three traditional parts of philosophy – logic (which is construed broadly to include epistemology), 'physics' (which in effect comprises metaphysics and philosophy of science), and ethics. Sextus considers the various views of his dogmatic opponents, and marshals against them a massive array of argumentation. The arguments, which vary from the subtle to the crass, have been repeated and refined by modern sceptics, who have provided remarkably few additions to Sextus' forces.

Against the Mathematicians (henceforth *M*) is made up of two distinct works ('Mathematician' here translates the Greek word *mathematikos*. A better translation might be 'professor' – since Sextus is against scientists and philosophers of every description, and not merely against what we think of as the mathematical sciences.) Books VII–XI contain sceptical attacks upon the three parts of philosophy. These books are essentially large-scale versions of *PH* II–III. They cover the same ground and reproduce many of the same arguments; but they do not merely expand the treatment in *PH* – they contain many arguments not found in *PH*, and often order the material differently. Books I–VI, which are probably the latest of Sextus' extant writings, are a series of connected essays on various particular sciences: they produce sceptical arguments against linguistics, rhetoric, arithmetic, geometry, astrology, and musical theory. On the whole their tone is more measured than that of *PH* or *M* VII–XI, and many of their arguments have a force independent of Sextus' general position of extreme scepticism.

In Sextus' writings we see Greek scepticism fully formed. Scepticism is conceived of as 'a philosophy', as something which offers a 'way of life', and as a serious rival to the dogmatic philosophies of the Epicureans, the Stoics, the Peripatetics and the Academics. Sextus is insistent that the Pyrrhonist philosophy is a practical thing. We may live as Pyrrhonists – Pyrrhonism is not a mere academic exercise. What is more, the way of life produces happiness. For scepticism, in Sextus' view, leads to a tranquillity of spirit, and in such tranquillity human well-being is to be found. Pyrrhonism is also and essentially a philosophical position. Its philosophy is entirely negative, but it is nonetheless seriously philosophical. The various opinions and attitudes which other thinkers have advocated are considered at length and in detail. Sextus' attention to them is learned and he does not dismiss them lightly. Pyrrhonism is, or at least professes to be, a *philosophy* of life.

Greek scepticism did not die with Sextus. We know the names of one or two later Pyrrhonists, and scepticism is occasionally attended to by the dogmatic philosophers. In the fourth century a Christian bishop and a pagan emperor saw fit to warn against the perils of Pyrrhonism. St Gregory of Nazianzus complains that

ever since the Sextuses and the Pyrrhos and the practice of arguing to opposites have, like a vile and malignant disease, infected the churches, babbling has been regarded as culture and – as the Book of Acts says of the Athenians – we spend our whole time in speaking or listening to some novelty or other. (*Speech* XXI 12)

Julian, the apostate emperor who vainly hoped to recall the world to paganism, agreed with his Christian opponent:

Writings engender a certain disposition in the soul: they slowly awaken the desires and then suddenly light a terrible flame which we should, I think, avoid and flee from. Do not give entry to an Epicurean or a Pyrrhonian work – indeed the gods have properly destroyed them, so that most of those books are not to be found. (*Letter* 89B)

These two passages perhaps provide evidence of a resurgence of interest in scepticism in the fourth century AD.

If there was a revival, it was short-lived. Sextus' works were indeed sometimes read in later antiquity (and we have already alluded to Photius' knowledge of Aenesidemus); but they were not widely known. Scepticism, and the issues which it raised, lost their earlier prominence. It was not until some fourteen hundred years after Sextus' death that his writings and his thought again occupied the centre of the philosophical stage.

3 The Ten Modes

Sextus, *PH* I 35–9:

35 In order for us to get a more accurate impression of these
oppositions, I shall append the modes through which suspension
of judgement is inferred. But I make no affirmation either about
their number or about their power – they may be unsound, and
there may be more than those I shall describe.

36 The older sceptics have normally passed on modes, ten in
number, through which suspension of judgement is thought to
be inferred. (They use 'arguments' and 'schemata' as synonyms
for 'modes'.) They are: first, the mode depending on the variations among animals; second, that depending on the differences
among humans; third, that depending on the differing constitutions of the sense-organs; fourth, that depending on circumstances; fifth, that depending on positions and intervals and

37 places; sixth, that depending on admixtures; seventh, that
depending on the quantities and preparations of existing things;
eighth, that deriving from relativity; ninth, that depending on
frequent or rare encounters; tenth, that depending on lifestyles
and customs and laws and belief in myths and dogmatic sup-

38 positions. (We use this order conventionally.)

Superordinate to these are three modes: that deriving from the
subject judging; that deriving from the object judged; that
combined from both. For under the mode deriving from the
subject judging are ranged the first four, since what judges is
either an animal or a human or a sense, and* is in some circumstance. The seventh and the tenth are referred to the mode
deriving from the object judged. The fifth, sixth, eighth and
ninth are referred to the mode combined from both.

39 These three are in turn referred to the relativity mode. So we
have as most generic relativity, as specific the three, as subordinate the ten. In this account of their number we are merely

saying what is plausible. As to their power, we make the
following remarks.

Diogenes IX 78–9:

78   What the statements of the Pyrrhonists are, then, is a kind of
record* of what appears or is in any way thought of, a record in
which everything is set alongside everything else and is found in
the comparison to contain a great deal of anomaly* and disturbance, as Aenesidemus says in his outline introduction to Pyrrhonism. To arrive at the oppositions inherent in inquiries they would
first demonstrate the modes in which things convince us, and then
use the same modes to destroy our conviction about them. For
they say that things are convincing when there is accord in
perceiving them, or when they never – or at any rate rarely –
change, or they are familiar or determined by law or pleasing or
79   unsurprising.* So they used to display* cases of equal plausibility
from among things contrary to those which convince us.

The puzzles they produced arising from the discordances* in
what appears or is thought of were organised in ten modes in
respect of which objects appear in various ways. These are the
ten modes he* sets out.

Philo 169–70:

169   Anyone priding himself on his deliberations or on an adequate
capacity to choose and avoid things should be reminded of the
following considerations. If it were always the case that the same
unvarying appearances were produced from the same things,
then no doubt we should of necessity admire as unerring and
incorruptible those two standards, perception and thought,
which are established in us by nature, and we should not be in
two minds and suspend judgement on anything, but rather
should credit things as soon as they appear, and so choose some
things and conversely reject others.

170   But since we find that we are actually affected* differently by
them, there is nothing firm we can say about anything; for what
appears is not stationary, but undergoes changes of many kinds
and many forms. For where the appearance is not fixed, the
judgement on it cannot be fixed either. The reasons for this are
many.

The Ten Modes of scepticism were a central and striking part of the Pyrrhonist philosophy. They were, in all probability, first formulated by Aenesidemus in the first century BC. Many later authors discussed them, either approvingly or critically, and they became a recognised topic in philosophical education. In the fourth century AD, Hermogenes, who was to rise to a position of some eminence at the court of the Emperor Constantine, received in his youth a thorough grounding in philosophy. In addition to his study of Plato and Aristotle, Stoicism and Epicureanism, 'he followed out the modes of Pyrrho and the flourishing controversy which they were arousing in all quarters – treating them, however, not as a matter of great moment but rather as a sort of *hors d'oeuvre* to the rest of philosophy' (Himerius, *Speech* xiv 24).

We have used the word 'mode' to translate the Greek term *tropos*. Other translators prefer to transliterate, and speak of the Ten Tropes. According to Sextus (§36), the Pyrrhonists also employed the word *logos*, presumably in its sense of 'argument', to designate the modes. Sextus also says (if the text is right) that the word *tupos* was used: *tupos* will mean either 'outline' or, better, 'pattern' or 'schema', in the sense of 'argument-pattern'. The title of a work by Plutarch indicates (but again the text is uncertain) that a further term was introduced, namely *topos*. *Topos* means literally 'place'; but it also has a logical sense – the sense it bears for example in Aristotle's *Topics* – in which it means something like 'general principle of argument'.

This variety of names has no particular significance. The standard term for a mode is *tropos*. In ordinary Greek *tropos* is fairly colourless, meaning simply 'way' or 'manner'. The *tropoi* of Pyrrhonism may thus be ways or manners of introducing suspension of judgement. But *tropos* also had a technical sense. In Stoic logical theory, 'a *tropos* is a sort of pattern of argument, e.g. "If *A* then *B*; but *A*; therefore *B*" ' (Diogenes Laertius VII 76). Now the sceptical modes are – in a somewhat relaxed sense – patterns or schemata of argument, and it is possible that the Pyrrhonists intended their use of the term *tropos* to be understood in its technical logical sense.

Whether the word *tropos* means, technically, 'argument pattern' or, non-technically, 'way', cannot be determined on the evidence we possess. The issue is unimportant, for the modes are in fact patterns or schemata which constitute ways of inducing scepticism.

The Pyrrhonists produced several sets of modes. In addition to the Ten Modes with which we are concerned there are sets of Five Modes, of Two Modes, and of Eight Modes. The Eight Modes, which Sextus ascribes to Aenesidemus, have a special object: they are the modes of 'aetiology' – lines of thought by way of which the Pyrrhonist can cast doubt upon any aetiology or causal explanation which a dogmatist might propound (*PH* I 180–5). The Eight Modes (which we translate in Appendix B) are subtle and interesting, but they play relatively little part in the surviving sceptical texts.

The Five Modes are reported both by Sextus (*PH* I 164–9) and by Diogenes Laertius (IX 88–9), who names their author as Agrippa. (Nothing else is known of this Agrippa, who must have lived at some time in the period between Aenesidemus and Sextus.) The Five Modes are critical in purpose and wholly general in scope. They are abstract argument patterns by the application of which, individually or collectively, the Pyrrhonist purports to render dubious any statement whatsoever. The Five Modes are used by Sextus, with or without explicit notice, throughout his critical works, in *PH* II–III and in *M*. The Five Modes are also introduced more than once in Sextus' account of the Ten Modes: we shall discuss them when they turn up in our text and we translate Sextus' version in Appendix C, but we shall not offer any general treatment of the Five Modes of Agrippa.

The Two Modes are of uncertain origin. They are mentioned only by Sextus (*PH* I 78–9 – translated in Appendix D). They appear to represent an attempt to 'reduce' the Five Modes to the smallest possible set.

According to Sextus, the function of the Ten Modes of Suspension of Judgement is to facilitate the production of 'oppositions' (*antitheseis*), and hence to bring on 'suspension of judgement' (*epochē*). In effect they make it easier for the sceptic to assemble his material by providing a systematic framework within which he can arrange his various particular arguments.

The 'oppositions' are oppositions of 'appearances'. There is an opposition of appearances when something appears so-and-so and also such-and-such, 'so-and-so' and 'such-and-such' picking out opposite or incompatible properties. Such an opposition is expressed by, for example, the sentence:

> The bathwater appears warm – and it also appears cold

(it feels cold, let us suppose, to my elbow, but it plainly seems warm to the baby). In general, oppositions will be expressible by way of sentences of the form:

> x appears F and x appears F^*

(where 'F' and 'F^*' pick out incompatible properties).

When the Pyrrhonists talk of appearances or of how things appear they are not indulging in technical philosophical jargon. The word *phainesthai*, which we translate as 'appear', is a common Greek term. ('Appearance' translates *phantasia*, the cognate noun. The terms *to phainomenon* and *ta phainomena*, which other translators sometimes transliterate or else render as 'impressions' or 'appearances', are literally 'what appears' or 'what is apparent'.) There is no suggestion that 'appearances' are somehow entities distinct from the objects which purportedly produce them. The Pyrrhonists are not assuming that when we attend to 'the appearances' we are attending to a peculiar sort of entity, a mental image or a sense-datum, say. On the contrary, to attend to the appearances is simply to attend to the way things appear – it is to notice that honey appears sweet, oil viscous, butter rancid.

Appearing is not something which only perceptible objects can do: music may sound, and hence appear, loud; sandpaper may feel, and hence appear, rough; but equally an argument may appear valid, a statement may appear true, an action may appear unwarranted – and arguments, statements and actions are not perceptible items. To say how things appear is to say how they impress us or how they strike us, whether or not it is *via* our perceptual apparatus that the impression is made. In this sense we regularly contrast how things appear or seem with how they really are. This contrast lies at the heart of Pyrrhonism and its Ten Modes. The honey tastes, and so *appears*, sweet; but is it *really* sweet? The argument strikes us as sound, and hence *appears* sound; but is it *in fact* sound? Sextus uses a variety of phrases to connote the contrast with appearances; he talks about how things 'purely' or 'absolutely' are, about how they are 'in their natures' or 'in themselves', often simply about how they 'are'. Some of these phrases raise special questions, which we shall discuss as the occasion arises. Here it is enough to make the general point that appearance contrasts with reality. The Pyrrhonist is going to suggest that we are limited to appearances: we can indeed say how things appear, we can never say how they really are.

A final point about appearing should be made. In English we sometimes use the phrase 'That appears so-and-so' to indicate a guarded belief: I may say 'The claret appears corked' or 'The defendant appears guilty' in order to evince a belief, tentative or guarded, that the claret is corked or the defendant guilty. The Greek verb *phainesthai* is also used in the same way to express tentative belief. But that use of 'appear' and of *phainesthai* must be sharply distinguished from the use we have previously described. The Pyrrhonist, when he talks about appearances, is saying nothing at all about his beliefs, tentative or firm: he intends to register how things strike him, not how much confidence he is putting in the way they strike him. Philosophers have spoken of a 'phenomenological' and a 'judgemental' use of the word 'appear': in the phenomenological sense, the verb expresses the ways things impress us, while in the judgemental sense, it expresses our beliefs. Throughout the Ten Modes the word 'appear' must be taken in its phenomenological sense.

Appearances vary. The variations depend upon the subject to whom the thing appears, the background against which it appears, the circumstances in which it appears, and so on: in general, how a thing appears depends on the context or situation. Thus wine, for example, appears sweet or sour depending on whether you have been eating nuts or dates (see *PH* I 110). It is these variations which generate the sceptic's 'oppositions', and the Ten Modes are differentiated one from another by the different contexts or situations to which they appeal. 'Oppositions' can thus be expressed schematically by means of pairs of sentences of the form:

(1) x appears F in situation S
(2) x appears F^* in situation S^*.

(Here 'F' and 'F^*' again designate incompatible properties, while 'S' and 'S^*' designate different situations. Note that we use '*in* situation ...' as shorthand for 'depending on situation ...'.) The particular modes are then distinguished by the different ways in which they specify the schematic formula 'in situation S'. Oppositions falling under the First Mode, which turns upon the differences among animals, have the form:

(1.1) x appears F to animals of kind K
(2.1) x appears F^* to animals of kind K^*.

Again, oppositions falling under the Seventh Mode, the mode of quantities, have the form:

(1.7) x appears F in quantity Q
(2.7) x appears F^* in quantity Q^*.

And similarly for the other eight modes of the set.

The Pyrrhonist holds that 'we arrive at suspension of judgement because of the equipollence (*isostheneia*) of the opposed objects and arguments' (*PH* I 8), where 'by equipollence we mean an equality with regard to credibility and incredibility' (*PH* I 10). In other words, we cannot prefer *S* to *S** and so decide that *x* is really *F* rather than *F**; for *S* and *S** are equally matched, the appearances they generate equally plausible. Consequently, we shall arrive at 'suspension of judgement', or 'a standstill of the intellect as a result of which we neither deny nor affirm anything' (*PH* I 10).

Schematically, then, the modes work like this. There are oppositions:

(1)   *x* appears *F* in *S*
(2)   *x* appears *F** in *S**

but the appearances are equipollent, i.e.

(3)   we cannot prefer *S* to *S** or *vice versa*;

Hence we arrive at suspension of judgement, i.e.

(4)   we can neither affirm nor deny that *x* is really *F* or really *F**.

Sextus implies (§39) that there may be more than the Ten Modes that he enumerates, and the set of ten does not appear to have been constructed along any general principles or in such a way as to guarantee its exhaustiveness – may there not be other varieties of 'situations' over and above those specified in the Ten Modes, giving rise to other varieties of opposition? No ancient source mentions any additional modes. Sextus' observation may be no more than a piece of characteristically sceptical caution: for all he knows, further modes may at some time come to light. But it should be said that the individuation of the modes is in places somewhat arbitrary: as we shall see, it is easy to increase their number beyond the statutory ten.

Sextus does attempt to make a structured system out of the modes when, in §§38–9, he sketches a 'tree' of genus, species and subspecies.

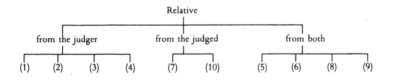

There is no trace of this 'tree' in any other source, and it is not a very vigorous growth in Sextus himself. In fact the structure which Sextus erects is both artificial and puzzling – artificial in that it distinguishes the species by forced means, puzzling in that relativity appears twice in it, once as the highest genus and once as a subspecies. We shall have more to say on this in our comments on the Eighth Mode. Here it is enough to remark that the 'tree', whatever its merits, seems to have had no effect upon Sextus' presentation of his material.

Sextus ascribes the Ten Modes to Aenesidemus (*M* VII 345), and we learn from another source that they appeared in Aenesidemus' *Outline* (i.e. in an *Outline of Pyrrhonism*). We do not possess Aenesidemus' account of the Ten Modes – and, it might be added, the Ten Modes are not mentioned in Photius' summary of Aenesidemus' *Pyrrhonian Arguments*. Instead we have three accounts from later authors. The longest and most detailed of the three is that given by Sextus in Book I of his *Outlines of Pyrrhonism*. A second account appears in Diogenes Laertius' *Lives of the Philosophers* where it forms part of the biography of Pyrrho (IX 79–88). Diogenes, who wrote after Sextus, is an obscure figure but an important source for our knowledge of Greek philosophy. His work is a compilation (unkind critics would say a farrago) put together from the works of earlier writers, almost all of which are now lost. Diogenes' account of the Ten Modes, like much else in the *Lives*, is highly compressed, sometimes to the point of unintelligibility. Diogenes had no philosophical pretensions himself, and he was certainly not a Pyrrhonist: he was more interested in chatty biographical anecdotes than in philosophical ideas. For all that, his account of the Ten Modes, which draws on an unknown source who is certainly distinct from Sextus, preserves a certain quantity of interesting material.

The third account of the Ten Modes is the earliest. It is preserved in a curious context. Philo of Alexandria was a Jewish philosopher and scholar whose career spanned the years 20 BC to AD 45. One of his major works was a vast commentary on the books of the Pentateuch. At the end of an essay *On Drunkenness* which formed part of that commentary (the drunkenness is that of Noah at Genesis IX 21), Philo produces what is in effect a partial account of the Ten Modes. Philo, like Sextus, writes as a philosopher and not as a historian of philosophy or a biographer; and as a philosopher he had some sympathy for scepticism. But he was not a Pyrrhonist, and his essay does not purport to give an accurate account of the Ten Modes. (In fact Philo does not mention Pyrrhonism and he does not call the modes by that name: it is the content of the passage which shows beyond any doubt that Philo is making use of an account of the Ten Modes of the Pyrrhonists.) Nonetheless, Philo's text, quite apart from its intrinsic interest, has some significance for the student of Pyrrhonism.

We might refer in passing to a curious mediaeval compilation, put out under the title of a commentary on Aristotle's *Metaphysics* and ascribed to 'Herennius', which contains as the third of its disparate chapters an interesting discussion of scepticism. The chapter includes an account of the Ten Modes which is for the most part so very close in wording to Philo's that one of the texts must have been copied directly from the other. Scholars have generally supposed that the mediaeval compiler, or some intermediate source, copied from Philo. But it has recently been suggested that matters stand the other way about and that Philo copied from the text which the compiler has preserved. If that suggestion were correct, it would be a discovery of considerable importance to the history of ancient scepticism; for the compiler's chapter contains a number of fascinating items quite apart from its account of the modes. If it were indeed Philo's source, then it would be the earliest surviving version of the Ten Modes. But it is so similar in content to Philo's text that we cannot consider it as a separate and fourth account.

In addition to these three accounts we possess a brief outline of the modes by Aristocles of Messene. In the course of his criticism of Pyrrhonism, Aristocles writes thus:

When Aenesidemus in his *Outline* goes through the nine [?] modes – that is the number of ways in which he tried to show that objects are unclear – shall we say that he describes them with knowledge or from ignorance? He says that animals differ, and that we ourselves do, and also states and ways of life and customs and laws; and he says that our senses are weak and that many external factors – distances, sizes, movements – distort knowledge; and that so too does the fact that the young and the old, sleepers and wakers, the healthy and the sick, are not in similar conditions; and that we grasp nothing simple and unmixed – for everything is confused and relative. (Eusebius, *Preparation for the Gospel* XIV xviii 11–12)

(The manuscripts of Eusebius refer to 'the *nine* modes'. Some scholars have based elaborate theories about the history of the modes on that fact, supposing that an original Nine Modes of Aenesidemus were later increased to ten. We are inclined to be sceptical of such theories, which have little or nothing to support them apart from the word 'nine' in this text. We suspect that Aristocles himself originally wrote of 'the *ten* modes', and that either Eusebius misread Aristocles' text – or perhaps used a corrupt copy – or else the error was introduced by the scribes who copied Eusebius' text.)

Other ancient treatments of the Ten Modes are known. Sextus himself probably gave a second account, in addition to the one preserved in *PH*. At *M* VII 345 he refers back to an earlier discussion of the modes. It is often supposed that Sextus means to refer to the discussion in *PH* I; but recent research has made it likely that the reference is rather to an introductory book which originally prefaced *M* VII–XI. (Just as *M* VII–XI are parallel in content to *PH* II–III, so the lost book will have been parallel to *PH* I.)

Plutarch, *c.* 50–120 AD, wrote a work entitled *On the Ten Places of Pyrrho.* The work is lost: all we know is its title, which is preserved, as entry 158, in the ancient list of Plutarch's writings known as the Lamprias catalogue.

Favorinus of Arles, an industrious polymath (and 'a eunuch who had not been castrated but was born without testicles'), also wrote at length on the topic. His contemporary, the second-century antiquarian Aulus Gellius, reports as follows:

> The Pyrrhonists deny that any signs or pure properties of anything can be known or apprehended, and they try to teach and exhibit the fact in many ways [*multis modis* – perhaps *modis* is here being used to mean '*mode*']. On this subject Favorinus too has written ten books of great subtlety and acumen which he entitled *Pyrrhonian Modes.* (Aulus Gellius, *Attic Nights* XI v 4–5)

Favorinus' book too is lost, and the loss is to be lamented. Favorinus himself apparently subscribed to the views of the Academic sceptics, and his version of the modes will perhaps have been as detailed and as sympathetic as that of Sextus. In fact, all we know of his work is the brief notice in Diogenes, IX 87.

We thus learn of nine ancient accounts of the Ten Modes. First, there is Aenesidemus' own account in his lost *Outline.* Next, chronologically, there is the extant account in Philo's work *On Drunkenness.* Then the lost accounts by Plutarch and by Favorinus. Then Aristocles' brief summary – if indeed that paragraph should be dignified with the title of 'account'. After that, the two discussions by Sextus, one extant in *PH* I and the other lost. And then the version in Diogenes Laertius. The ninth account is the one in Diogenes' unknown source. Much of the material of the modes can be found, as we shall see, in works much earlier than Aenesidemus. Some scholars have suggested that the modes themselves originated not with Aenesidemus but with some earlier sceptic – perhaps with Pyrrho himself. But there is no good evidence for that suggestion, and we believe that the Ten Modes were first assembled by Aenesidemus in the first century BC.

The nine accounts span three centuries. We should not suppose that the modes continued unchanged throughout that period. Indeed, the three accounts we possess differ from one another in various particulars, and we know that some at least of the lost accounts were different yet again. Three types of difference can be noticed. First, the illustrations included under each mode differ from author to author: there are overlaps and there is much common material, but each of the extant accounts has illustrations peculiar to itself. It is clear that the examples were accumulated over the centuries, and that different authors used different illustrative material, as their information or their tastes dictated. Secondly, the argumentative structure within the modes differs from one source to another. Most importantly, Sextus has incorporated ideas from the Five Modes of Agrippa into his presentation of the Ten Modes, thereby changing their character in a significant fashion. Some of those differences are of philosophical importance: they will be discussed in our commentary.

Thirdly, the order in which the modes were arranged was not fixed. Sextus says that his order is 'conventional' (§38). The orders in Sextus, Diogenes and Philo are all different. Aristocles' note perhaps implies a fourth order. Diogenes (IX 87) says that

Favorinus makes the Ninth the Eighth, while Sextus and Aenesidemus make it the Tenth. Sextus calls the Tenth the Eighth, and Favorinus calls it the Ninth.

The passage is puzzling, since what Diogenes says about Sextus does not agree with what we find in *PH*. It is possible that Diogenes is simply muddled, or that his text is corrupt (numerals in Greek manuscripts are easily corrupted). But it is also possible that Diogenes is correctly reporting a part of Sextus' ordering of the modes in the lost part of *M*.

The information we have on the order of the modes can be set out in a table, thus:

	PH	DL	Philo	Arist.	Aen.	Fav.	M
Animals	1	1	1	1			
Humans	2	2	2	2			
Senses	3	3					
Circumstances	4	4	3	6			
Positions	5	7	4	4			
Mixtures	6	6	7				
Quantities	7	8	5	5			
Relativity	8	10	6	7			
Rarity	9	9			10	8	10
Persuasions	10	5	8	3		9	8

4 Humans and Other Animals

Sextus, *PH* I 40–79:

40 First, we said, is the argument according to which animals, depending on the differences among them, are not impressed by the same appearances from the same things. This we deduce both from the differences in the ways they are produced and from the variation in the compositions of their bodies.

41 In the case of the ways they are produced, this is because some animals are produced without copulation and some as a result of intercourse. Of those produced without copulation, some are produced from fire, like the little creatures that appear in ovens, some from stagnant water, like mosquitoes, some from wine turning sour, like gnats, some from earth,* some are produced from slime, like frogs, some from mud, like maggots, some from donkeys,* like dung-beetles, some from green vegetables, like caterpillars, some from fruit, like the gall-insects that come from wild figs, some from rotting animals, like bees that come

42 from bulls and wasps that come from horses. Of animals produced as a result of intercourse, some are bred from the same species, like the majority, some from different species, like mules. Again, in general some animals are produced viviparously, like humans, some oviparously, like birds, and some carniparously, like bears.

43 It is likely, then, that the dissimilarities and differences in ways of being produced should lead to large differences in the ways they are affected, giving rise to imbalance, disharmony and conflict.

44 But it is the differences among the most important parts of the body, especially those which are naturally fitted for deciding and perceiving, that can produce the greatest conflict of appearances. For instance, people with jaundice say that what appears white to us is yellow, and people with a blood-suffusion in the eye say that

it is blood-red. Since, then, the eyes of some animals are yellow, of others blood-shot or white or some other colour, it is likely, I think, that their grasp of colours is different.

45   Further, when we have stared for a long time at the sun and have then bent over a book, we think that the letters are golden and moving round. Since, then, some animals have a natural brilliance in their eyes and give off a fine mobile light from them so that they can see even in the dark, we shall rightly think that the external objects do not impress us and them similarly.

46   Further, magicians, by smearing lamp-wicks with bronze-rust or cuttlefish-ink, make the by-standers appear bronze-coloured or black, all through a slight sprinkling of the mixture. It is surely far more reasonable, given that animals' eyes contain mixtures of different humours, that they should also get different appearances from existing objects.

47   When we press the eye from the side, the forms and shapes and sizes of the objects we see appear elongated and narrow. It is likely, then, that those animals (such as goats, cats and the like) which have slanting and elongated pupils, should sense existing objects differently and not in the same way as animals with round pupils suppose them to be.

48   Mirrors, depending on their differing constructions, sometimes show external objects as minute (e.g. concave mirrors), sometimes as elongated and narrow (convex mirrors); and some of them show the head of the person reflected at the bottom and
49   their feet at the top. Since, then, some of the vessels of sight protrude and project beyond the body because of their convexity, while others are more concave and others are set level, it is likely that the appearances are altered by this too, and that dogs, fish, lions, humans and locusts do not see the same things as equal in size or similar in shape; rather, what they see depends on the kind of imprinting produced in each case by the eye which receives what is apparent.

50   The same argument holds for the other senses too. How could it be said that touch produces similar effects in animals with shells, animals with fleshy exteriors, animals with prickles, and animals with feathers or scales? How can there be a similar grasp of sound in animals with a very narrow auditory channel and those with a very broad one? or in animals with hairy ears and those with ears that are bare? Indeed, we too are affected different-

ly by sound when we stop up our ears and when we use them in the ordinary way.

51 Smell too will differ depending on the variation among animals. For we too are affected in one way when we have a chill and there is an excess of phlegm in us and in another when the region of the head collects an excess of blood; and we reject what to others seems fragrant and think ourselves as it were battered by it. So, since some animals are naturally flabby and full of phlegm while others are extremely rich in blood, and in others yellow or black bile is dominant and excessive, it is reasonable that for this reason too what they smell should appear different to each of them.

52 Similarly with objects of taste, since the tongues of some animals are rough and dry while those of others are very moist. For we too, when in fevers our tongues are drier than usual, think that what we are offered is earthy and unpalatable or bitter – and we are also affected in one way or another depending on the different dominance in us of the so-called humours. Since, then, animals have organs of taste that differ and in which different humours are excessive, they will receive different appearances of
53 existing objects with regard to taste too. For just as the same nourishment when dispersed becomes in one place veins, in another arteries, in another bone, in another sinew and so on, displaying different powers depending on the differences among the parts receiving it; and just as the same undifferentiated water when dispersed in trees becomes in one place bark, in another a branch, in another fruit and hence figs, pomegranates and so on;
54 and just as one and the same breath blown by a musician into a flute becomes in one place a high note and in another a low note, and the same pressure of the hand on a lyre produces in one place a low sound and in another a high one: in the same way it is reasonable that external existing objects should be observed as different depending on the different constitutions of the animals that receive the appearances.

55 One can learn this more vividly from the things which animals choose and avoid. For instance, perfume appears very pleasant to humans, but intolerable to dung-beetles and bees. Olive oil benefits humans but when sprayed over wasps and bees it destroys them. Sea-water is unpleasant to humans when they drink it, and poisonous, but is very pleasant and drinkable to
56 fish. Pigs find it more pleasant to wash in the most foul-smelling

mud than in clear, pure water. Among animals some feed on grass, some on shrubs, some in forests,* some on seeds, some on flesh, some on milk. Some enjoy their food rotten and others fresh, some enjoy it raw and others prepared by cooking. And in general what is pleasant to some is to others unpleasant and to be
57 avoided or even* fatal. For instance, hemlock fattens quails and henbane fattens pigs, which, indeed, enjoy eating salamanders, as deer enjoy eating venomous creatures and swallows enjoy eating blister-beetles. Ants and mosquitoes if swallowed by humans cause displeasure and gripings; but if she-bears feel weak in some way they lick these up and so recover their strength.
58 Vipers are numbed by the mere touch of a branch of oak, as are bats by the touch of a plane-leaf. Elephants avoid rams, lions avoid cocks, sea-beasts avoid the crackling of beans as they are pounded, tigers avoid the noise of drums.

More cases than these can be given; but let us not be thought to waste time unnecessarily – if the same things are unpleasant to some and pleasant to others, and if the pleasant and unpleasant lie in appearances, then appearances produced in animals from existing objects are different.

59 But if the same objects appear dissimilar depending on the variations among animals, then we shall be able to say what the existing object is like as observed by us, but as to what it is like in its nature we shall suspend judgement. For we shall not be able ourselves to decide between our own appearances and those of the other animals, being ourselves a part of the dispute and for that reason more in need of someone to decide than ourselves able to judge.
60 And besides, neither without proof nor with a proof will we be able to prefer our own appearances to those produced in the irrational animals. For quite apart from the fact that there is no doubt no such thing as proof, as we shall suggest [*PH* II 134–92], the so-called proof will itself be either apparent to us or not apparent. If it is not apparent, then we shall not bring it forward with confidence. But if it is apparent to us, then since what is being investigated is what is apparent to animals, and the proof is apparent to us, and we are animals, then the proof itself will be under investigation to see whether it is true as well as apparent.
61 But it is absurd to try to establish the matter under investigation by means of the matter under investigation, since the

same thing will be both credible and not credible (credible insofar as it aims to prove, not credible insofar as it is proved) which is impossible. We shall not, therefore, have a proof by means of which to prefer our own appearances to those produced in the so-called irrational animals. If, therefore, appearances become different depending on the variations among animals, and it is impossible to decide between them, it is necessary to suspend judgement about external existing objects.

62   But for good measure we do actually compare the so-called irrational animals with humans in respect of appearances. For after the effective arguments we do not mind joking at the expense of the deluded and self-satisfied dogmatists. Now we sceptics are accustomed straightforwardly to compare the
63 irrational animals *en masse* with humans, but since the dogmatists with their ingenious explanations say that the comparison is unequal, we will (purely for good measure and carrying the joke further) rest the argument on one animal – for example the dog, if you like, which is thought to be the lowest animal of all. We shall find even so that the animals which the argument concerns do not fall short of us as regards the credibility of what is apparent to them.
64   That this animal excels us in its perception the dogmatists agree. By means of its sense of smell it grasps more than we do, tracking down by its means wild beasts it cannot see – and with its eyes it sees them more quickly than we do; and with its sense of hearing it perceives acutely.
65   Let us come to reasoning. Of this, one kind is internal and the other expressed. So let us first look at the internal kind. This (according to the dogmatists who are our chief opponents here, namely the Stoics) seems to be anchored on the following capacities: choice of what is appropriate [*oikeios*] and avoidance of what is alien; acquaintance with the kinds of expertise contributing towards this; a grasp of the virtues relevant to one's appropriate nature . . .* the affects.
66   Now the dog (on which we thought we would rest our argument for the sake of an example) does choose the appropriate and avoid the harmful – he pursues food and retreats from a raised whip. Further, he has an expertise that provides what is appropriate – hunting.
67   Nor is he outside the scope of virtue. At least, if justice is a

matter of distributing to each according to his value, the dog, which fawns on and guards his friends [*oikeioi*] and benefactors but frightens off enemies and offenders, will not be outside the
68 scope of justice. But if he has this, then since the virtues follow from one another, he has the other virtues too – which the wise men deny that most *humans* have. He is courageous, as we see when he frightens off enemies, and intelligent, as Homer witnessed when he portrayed Odysseus as unknown by all the people in his household [*oikeioi*] and recognised only by Argus [Homer, *Odyssey* XVII 300] – the dog was not deceived by the alteration to the man's body and did not abandon his 'apprehensive appearance' which he appears to have kept better than the humans.

69   According to Chrysippus (who is particularly hostile* to the irrational animals) the dog even shares in their celebrated Logic. For instance (the above author says) he lights upon the fifth unprovable with several disjuncts whenever he comes to a crossroads and, having tracked down the two roads along which the wild animal did not go, starts off at once along the third *without* tracking down it. For (says our early author) he is implicitly reasoning as follows: 'The animal went either this way or this or this; but neither this way nor this: therefore this way.'

70   Further, he can both grasp and relieve his own affects. When a thorn has got stuck in him he hastens to remove it by rubbing his paw along the ground and by using his teeth. And if he has a wound anywhere, then, since dirty wounds heal with difficulty while clean ones are easily cured, he gently wipes away the pus that gathers.

71   Further, he keeps to Hippocratic methods extremely well. Since the way to cure a foot is to rest it, if he ever gets a wound in his foot he lifts it up and keeps it as free from pressure as possible. And when he is disturbed by inappropriate [*anoikeios*] humours, he eats grass, with the aid of which he vomits up what was inappropriate and gets well again.

72   If, then, it has appeared that the animal on which we have rested our argument for the sake of an example chooses what is appropriate and avoids what is disturbing, has expertise to provide what is appropriate, can grasp and relieve his own affects, and is not outside the scope of virtue, then, since in these lies the perfection of internal reasoning, the dog will be, in this

respect,* perfect. This is, I think, the reason why some philosophers have glorified themselves with the name of this animal.

73   As for expressed reasoning, first of all, it is not necessary to
investigate that. For some of the dogmatists themselves have
deprecated it as working against the acquisition of virtue, which
is why during their time of learning they practised silence. And
again, let us suppose a person is dumb – no-one will say that he is
irrational.

But to pass over these issues: first, we see the animals that we
are discussing, such as jays and some others, uttering sounds that
are actually human.

74   But to leave that aside too: even if we do not understand the
sounds of the so-called irrational animals, it is not at all unlikely
that they do converse and we do not understand them. For when
we are listening to the sounds made by foreigners we do not
understand them but think that *they* are undifferentiated.

75   And we hear dogs producing one sound when frightening
people off, another when howling, another when they are beaten
and a different one when fawning. Generally, if someone were to
study this matter, he would find that there is much variation of
sound (in the case of this animal and of others) in different
circumstances; so for this reason it could fairly be said that the
so-called irrational animals share in expressed reasoning too.

76   But if they fall short of humans neither in the accuracy of their
senses nor in internal reasoning nor (saying this for good
measure) in expressed reasoning, they will be no less credible in
respect of the appearances than we are.

77   It is of course possible to rest the case on any one of the
irrational animals and show* the same thing. For instance, who
would deny that birds stand out in cleverness and have the use of
expressed reasoning? They have knowledge not only of the
present but also of the future, and they make this clear to those
able to understand, giving various signs and foretelling things by
their sounds.

78   I have made this comparison, as I indicated before, for good
measure, having before* shown adequately, I think, that we are
not able to prefer our own appearances to those produced in the
irrational animals.

So, if the irrational animals are not less credible than we are when
it comes to judging appearances, and if different appearances

are produced depending on the variations among animals, then I shall be able to say how each existing object appears to me, but for the above reasons I shall be forced to suspend judgement on how it is by nature.

79   Such is the first mode of suspension of judgement.

Diogenes IX 79–80:

First is the mode depending on the differences among animals with regard to pleasure and pain and harm and advantage. Through this it is inferred that different appearances are produced by the same things, and that suspension of judgement follows conflict of this kind. Some animals are produced without copulation, like fire-creatures, the Arabian phoenix and worms;
80   others after intercourse, like humans and the rest. And some have one kind of constitution, others another. Hence they differ in their perception too – hawks, for example, have very keen sight and dogs very keen smell. It is reasonable, therefore, that the sense-appearances presented to animals with different kinds of eyes should themselves be different. Vine-shoots are edible by goats but bitter to humans, hemlock nourishes quails but is fatal to humans, and manure is edible by pigs but not by horses.

Philo 171–5:

171   First of all, there are countless differences among animals, not just in one respect but in nearly all – differences in their production and constitution, in their diet and way of life, in what they choose and avoid, in the activities and motions of their senses, in the peculiarities of the countless ways in which they are affected both in body and in soul.

172   Quite apart from the judging subjects, look at some of the objects of judgement, such as the chameleon and the octopus. The chameleon, so they say, changes its colour and assimilates itself to the ground over which it usually crawls; the octopus assimilates itself to the rocks in the sea around which it clings. Perhaps nature, in order to preserve them, has given them this ability to turn into many colours as a talisman or antidote against capture.

173   Have you never seen a dove's neck changing in the rays of the sun into a thousand different shades of colour? Is it not magenta

and deep blue, then fiery and glowing like embers, and again
yellow and reddish, and all other kinds of colours, whose very
names it is not easy to keep in mind?
174   And indeed they say that among the Geloan Scythians there is
found a most amazing animal. It is rare, but it does exist, and
they call it the reindeer. In size it is no smaller than an ox, and it is
very like a deer in the shape of its head. The story goes that it
regularly changes the colour of its coat to match the landscape
and the trees and in general whatever its background may be,
with the result that, owing to the similarity of colour, it escapes
the notice of anyone looking for it, and is hard to hunt down for
this reason rather than because of any bodily strength.
175   These facts and others like them are clear warrants that things
are inapprehensible.

The First Mode collects conflicts of appearances between different
animal kinds. Thus, as we have already remarked, it produces pairs of
propositions of the form:

(1.1) x appears F to animals of kind K
(2.1) x appears F^* to animals of kind K^*

but the appearances are by design conflicting, and

(3.1)   we cannot prefer K to K^* or *vice versa*;

Hence

(4)   we suspend judgement as to whether x is really F or F^*.

In principle, the kinds K and K^* are any pair of animal species; in
practice – and for obvious reasons – the sceptics usually contrast
humankind to some other animal kind.

We shall have to ask later on how exactly the sceptical conclusion,
(4), is related to the three premisses. First, though, let us look at the
conflict of appearances itself. How does the sceptic commend (1.1) and
(2.1) to us? Sextus says (§40) that we 'deduce' that things appear
differently to different animals. The inference is based on three further
types of difference: different animal species differ in their modes of
reproduction, in their physical constitution, and in their appetitive
behaviour.

In Sextus it is clear that each of these three differences is thought to
supply evidence for differences in appearance. Diogenes uses the same

material as Sextus, but he appears to construct the argument in a slightly different way. He treats differences in modes of reproduction as evidence for differences in physical constitution; and he then takes differences in constitution and differences in appetitive behaviour as two independent reasons for supposing there to be differences in appearances. Diogenes' version of the argument is in one respect superior to Sextus', for it is hard to see why differences in modes of reproduction should in themselves provide any reason for suspecting differences in appearances. But Diogenes' account is, as usual, highly compressed: he may be preserving a genuine Pyrrhonian alternative to Sextus' argument, but it is more likely that, in compressing his source, he has produced a better argument simply by chance.

Thus the Pyrrhonists pointed to observable differences among the animal species, and they inferred that it is 'likely' (to use Sextus' term) that things appear differently to different animal species. Sextus does not seem to regard his inferences as problematic, or his conclusion as controversial. And indeed he was not the first Greek to have remarked that things appear different to different species. In Plato's *Theaetetus*, Socrates puts the question: 'Would you insist that every colour appears to a dog – or to any other animal – in just the same way as it does to you?' Theaetetus replies: 'Of course not' (154A).

Not all thinkers have shared this confidence in our ability to know what the experiences of other animals are like. In an essay entitled 'What is it like to be a bat?' Thomas Nagel says:

We describe bat sonar as a form of three-dimensional forward perception; we believe that bats feel some versions of pain, fear, hunger, and lust, and that they have other, more familiar types of perception besides sonar. But we believe that these experiences also have in each case a specific subjective character, which it is beyond our ability to conceive. And if there is conscious life elsewhere in the universe, it is likely that some of it will not be describable even in the most general experiential terms available to us . . . If anyone is inclined to deny that we can believe in the existence of facts like this whose exact nature we cannot possibly conceive, he should reflect that in contemplating bats we are in much the same position that intelligent bats or Martians would occupy if they tried to form a conception of what it was like to be us. The structure of their own minds might make it impossible for them to succeed. (*Mortal Questions*, pp. 169–70)

If Nagel is right, the experience of bats and other animals is beyond our conception. We cannot say how things appear to animals of kind K, unless K is *homo sapiens*.

Now it is a striking feature of Sextus' account of the First Mode that he never does try to say *how* things appear to animals other than humans. He never gives a single illustrative example of conflicting appearances of the form (1.1) and (2.1). Instead of saying, for example, that grass appears green to humans but grey to cows, he would say that grass appears green to humans but, in all likelihood, different to cows. This fact has two consequences. First, it means that Sextus need not be put out by the sort of arguments which Nagel advances, arguments towards which he would indeed find himself well disposed. For his appeal to animal experiences does not suppose that we humans can know what it is like to be non-human. Secondly, it means that Sextus never presents a single actual example of the First Mode. He cannot produce an actual conflict of appearances, he can only produce arguments to show that there probably *are* conflicts of appearances (although we can know at most one side of the conflict). We shall say more about this second point in connexion with the Ninth Mode.

Of Sextus' first argument, which infers differences in appearance from differences in mode of reproduction, little need be said. As it stands, it seems to us to have not the slightest force. But it is worth making a historical point about the examples which Sextus and Diogenes bring forward under this head – mosquitoes and gnats, maggots and wasps, mules and bears. These biological 'facts' are not the product of the sceptics' own scientific researches. On the contrary, they come from books. In general, the items of information and misinformation with which each of the Ten Modes is illustrated are all pillaged from the writings of the dogmatists. Some of them are relatively recent – there is a reference to the Emperor Tiberius in *PH* I 84 which cannot have been added to the sceptic's treasury of useful facts until the middle of the first century AD. Some of them are very old: there are items which we can trace back some six hundred years from Sextus' time to the Presocratics, and Sextus refers to Homer more readily than to Tiberius. In the case before us, some of the examples of spontaneous generation which Sextus lists in §41 can be found in Aristotle's *History of Animals*. Aristotle is no doubt the ultimate source of some of Sextus' information. But we need not suppose that Sextus himself had hunted through the works of the ancient zoologists. It is more likely that some earlier sceptic had done so, and that the information filtered through to Sextus at second or third hand. In some cases – not, of course, in all – we shall say a little about the history of the Pyrrhonian examples. The history has an interest in its own right. In addition, there is some general philosophical significance, as we shall shortly see, in the fact that the Pyrrhonians rely for their information on the dogmatists.

Sextus' second argument calls on differences in physical constitution, and in particular in the constitution of the sense-organs. Here the sceptic seems to be on firmer ground. For surely it is plausible to hold that differences in the structure of the sense-organs in different animals will lead to differences in the way things appear to them? We now believe, for example, that cattle see the world in black and white – that grass appears different to them from the way it appears to us – because we have discovered that the eyes of cattle lack the rods and cones in virtue of which humans are capable of perceiving colours. Difference in eye-structure implies difference in appearances.

Sextus does not, and probably could not, appeal to recondite scientific information of this sort. Rather, he appeals to examples within our ordinary human experience to show how physical differences do give rise to differences in the way things appear to us, and then he argues by analogy that the manifest differences between species probably give rise to species-wide differences in the way things appear.

The actual arguments which Sextus produces are usually flawed. It is hard to see, for example, what the purpose of §§53–4 can be: Sextus refers to three striking cases of the way in which a uniform substance – food, water, breath – may become different in different circumstances. These are hardly examples of cases where *appearances* conflict, and if they are meant not as examples but merely as analogies, it is not clear what force they have. The examples recur in the Third Mode (§95) where they are equally out of place. Again, consider Sextus' appeal to jaundice (§44). When humans have jaundice and their eyes are temporarily yellowish in colour, they tend to see things as yellow. By analogy, animals which have permanently yellowish eyes may be supposed to take a permanently jaundiced view of the world. There are two noteworthy things about that argument. First, it is very crude from a scientific point of view – we do not generally think that the colour of an animal's eye-tissue determines the colour things appear to it. (How could Sextus account for the fact that blue-eyed humans do not see things consistently differently from brown-eyed humans?) Secondly, the argument contains a false premiss: things do *not* appear yellow to sufferers from jaundice. The claim that they do has had an extraordinarily long life among philosophers and scientists, who have copied it from book to book for two thousand years. Yet it is – or so the books now tell us – entirely without foundation.

Nonetheless, even if Sextus' arguments are in fact fragile, there is nothing wrong in principle with the style of argument he adopts. If, for example, we learn to associate some aberrancy in human colour vision with a certain defect in the eyes, and if we find a similar defect in the eyes of some animal species, then it is plausible to suppose that the visual appearances of that species are similar to those of aberrant humans and different from those of normal humans.

Sextus' third argument rests upon differences in appetitive behaviour – in the things animals pursue and avoid. It is assumed, plausibly but without argument, that animals would not pursue anything unless it appeared pleasant or beneficial to them, and that they would not avoid anything unless it appeared unpleasant or harmful. Although Sextus mentions harm and benefit explicitly (e.g. in §55) he sums up his argument in §58 in terms of pleasure and pain. But we should not suppose that he is 'reducing' the notion of benefit to that of pleasure and the notion of harm to that of pain; rather, §58 is an innocent simplification.

Some animals pursue things which others avoid. Hence 'the same things are unpleasant to some and pleasant to others'. But since 'the pleasant and unpleasant lie in appearances', we may infer that objects appear differently to different animals (§58). In what sense do 'the pleasant and unpleasant lie in appearances'? Sextus might mean, simply, that pleasure and pain *are* appearances. Since the same things are pleasant to some animals and unpleasant to others, that very fact is itself an instance of the general claim that appearances differ from animal to animal. In later modes we shall find Sextus treating pleasure and pain as appearances in this way. Alternatively, Sextus might mean that pleasure and pain are *caused* by appearances. The pleasure or pain which an animal feels in an object is determined or caused by the way the object appears to it. Thus if one animal feels pain and another pleasure in the same object, it is plausible to infer that the object appears differently to the different animals, in the one case presenting a pleasure-causing appearance, in the other a pain-causing appearance.

We cannot be sure which of these two things Sextus meant, and since essentially the same argument recurs, in a slightly more tractable form, in connexion with the Second Mode, we shall reserve further consideration until then.

Many of the examples with which the diversity of appetitive behaviour is illustrated can be traced back to earlier dogmatic literature. The bears who find a tonic in ants (§57), for example, are found again in Plutarch's essay *On the Intelligence of Animals*, 974 B–C, where they partner the dog who turns up in Sextus in §71; and without doubt the material is much older than that. The effect of olive-oil on wasps and bees (§55) is noted by Plato in the *Protagoras* (334B). The effect of hemlock on quails (§57), which is mentioned also by Diogenes, was a commonplace. It appears in Galen, Sextus' contemporary (*On Temperaments* I 684K). It is reported by Lucretius (*On the Nature of Things* V 899–900) and – in a slightly confused form – in the pseudo-Aristotelian treatise *On Plants* (820b3–6) which is probably roughtly contemporary with Lucretius. Again, when Sextus says (§55) that sea-water is poisonous to men but pleasant to fish, he is paraphrasing a remark of Heraclitus – 'Sea-water is most pure and most foul: for fish it is drinkable and salutary, for humans undrinkable and fatal' (frag. 61). Sextus' next example, on the pleasures of pigs, also derives ultimately from Heraclitus: 'Pigs take pleasure in mud rather than in pure water' (frag. 13).

Sextus requires a little work from his readers. The information that vipers are paralysed by oak-twigs, or that some animals are herbivores and others carnivores, does not at first blush seem to have much to do with the conflict of appearances: where is the conflict, and what are the appearances? We seem merely to have a difference, not a conflict, and a reaction, not an appearance. In fact, we must reflect briefly on the data of which Sextus reminds us. Vipers are numbed by oak-twigs, other animals are not. Hence, we are meant to reason, vipers will shun oak-twigs, other animals will not. So oak-twigs will be unpleasant to vipers, to other animals not. So oak-twigs will appear differently to vipers and to other animals. And since the difference in appearance underlies a contrast in reaction, the difference itself is likely to be a conflict. Similar reflections are required for most of Sextus' other concise illustrations.

Even after such reflection, many – indeed most – of Sextus' examples may well fail to convince us and even strike us as silly; for the alleged facts on which they rest are in many cases highly dubious. It is natural to wonder whether Sextus himself really believed in the information he recorded. At least one ancient critic thought that this was a decisive question. Aristocles of Messene, having briefly outlined Aenesidemus' account of the Ten Modes (in a passage quoted earlier in Chapter 3), continues as follows:

When he puts forward clever arguments of this sort, we should like to ask him whether he *knows* that things are as he says or rather speaks from *ignorance*. For if he does not know, why should we believe him? And if he does know, then he is perfectly silly – for he asserts that everything is unclear and at the same time says that he knows all this. (Eusebius, *Preparation for the Gospel* XIV xviii 12)

Since Sextus is a sceptic, he cannot properly claim that his examples are true. But if the premises of his arguments are not true, why in the world should we accept his sceptical conclusions?

That objection sounds plausible at first hearing. But in fact it betrays a fatal misconception of the nature of sceptical argumentation. 'The sceptic', Sextus says at the end of the *Outlines*, 'being a philanthropic sort, wants to cure by argument, to the best of his ability, the conceit and rashness of the dogmatists' (*PH* III 280). He presents himself as a doctor (or better, as a psychiatrist) whose task it is to cure the intellectual diseases – the rash beliefs and the conceited opinions – of his fellows. Just as a doctor need not take his own drugs, so a sceptic need not believe his own premises.

In Chapter 2 we remarked that the arguments of the Academic sceptics were essentially *ad hominem*: they took as their premises propositions which were accepted not by themselves but by their opponents. Sextus' arguments are similarly *ad hominem*. The propositions about animals on which his First Mode depends are propositions which have commended themselves to his non-sceptical opponents or patients: that is why the Pyrrhonists cull their examples from the work of the dogmatists. Sextus himself, being already a sceptic, does not and cannot believe in the truth of the propositions he advances. But that is no objection to his procedure: it is the non-sceptic who needs argumentative treatment, and the non-sceptic to whom the premises must commend themselves.

Aristocles supposes that if *the Pyrrhonist* does not believe the premises of his arguments, then those arguments are without force. But in fact the Pyrrhonist only requires that *his opponents* believe the premises. Moreover, even if we ourselves, as representative non-sceptics, remain unmoved by some of Sextus' arguments, that is no matter. For it should not be expected that the same drugs will be effective on all patients. Those of us who are not cured by the remedies which Sextus offers under the First Mode may be affected by other remedies which are yet to be discovered – or else by some or all of the later modes.

Suppose, finally, that *none* of the arguments in the modes cures us. The Pyrrhonist says to us: 'You hold that *P* and *Q* – and look how that leads you into scepticism.' Each time, rejecting the Pyrrhonist's premises, we reply: 'No, your argument has no hold over us; for we do *not* believe that *P* or that *Q* – any more than you do yourself.' In that case we shall indeed be unaffected by the Pyrrhonian arguments. But equally we shall not be in need of them; for if we do really reject *all* of the Pyrrhonist's premisses, then, the Pyrrhonist will argue, we are already Pyrrhonists ourselves.

Philo's treatment of the First Mode is odd. He begins, like Sextus, by noting that animal species differ in their modes of reproduction, in their physical constitution, in their ways of nourishing and maintaining themselves, in their appetitive behaviour, in the workings of their sense-organs, in their mental and physical peculiarities. But he makes no use at all of that material. Instead he switches to an argument based upon the differences among animals as *objects* of perception. He does not explain how this argument is supposed to lead to scepticism. Presumably he thinks that the differences among animals make the ways they appear to us somehow problematic, so that our judgements about them must be problematic and thus we must end in suspension of judgement about the way animals really are.

Philo has not changed the argument inadvertently. He explicitly marks the change: 'Quite apart from the judging subjects, look at some of the objects of judgement . . .' (§172). And his particular examples, too, are quite different from those we find in Sextus and Diogenes. (Even so, the examples are all traditional. The octopus, the chameleon and the reindeer have a particularly interesting history: they are found in the *Marvellous Stories* of Antigonus of Carystus (§25), in the pseudo-Aristotelian treatise *On Marvellous Things Heard* (832b6–17), and in a fragment of Theophrastus' essay on *Animals that Change their Colour* which is preserved by Photius (*Bibliothēkē* cod. 278). In this particular case the wording in all these texts is so similar that we can confidently assert that Philo, or rather Philo's sceptical source, was using material which had been taken almost *verbatim* from a Peripatetic handbook.)

Why does Philo give us this unorthodox account of the First Mode? It is worth noting that he is writing on Jewish themes, and that elsewhere too he drops material alien to that tradition. Philo holds that man has dominion over the other animals because he is their divinely ordained superior. This view comes out in his comments on certain verses in Genesis (see *On the Creation of the World* 64–8, 72ff, 83ff), and it is the main theme of his treatise *On Animals*, which concludes that 'to elevate animals to the level of the human race and to grant equality to unequals is the height of injustice' (§100). In its standard form, the First Mode purports to elevate animals to the human level: for that reason Philo would have found it inadequate or even offensive, and he may therefore have looked for an alternative way to present the mode.

Philo's treatise *On Animals* bears on the First Mode in another way too. The work, which survives only in an Armenian translation, is concerned with the question 'whether dumb animals possess reason'. Philo first presents a series of arguments to show that animals are rational, and he then attempts to refute those arguments and to establish the superiority of humans over the rest of the animal kingdom. His work draws heavily on earlier Greek philosophy, for the question which he discusses was widely debated by Hellenistic thinkers. Sextus alludes to the debate in §§62–3, and the curious coda to his treatment of the First Mode which those paragraphs introduce reflects a part of the Hellenistic discussion.

In this coda, Sextus pokes fun at the dogmatists, and in particular at the Stoics (§65). His allusions to internal and external reason (§65), to 'appropriateness' (§66), to the interdependence of the virtues (§68), and to 'apprehensive' appearances (§68) all concern characteristically Stoic doctrines. It is thus particularly pointed for him to summon Chrysippus as a witness on his behalf. Chrysippus, 'who is particularly hostile to the irrational animals' (§69), nevertheless admits – indeed argues – that dogs possess reason. The story which Sextus tells is also found in several other sources. Philo relates it as follows:

A hound was after a beast. When it came to a deep shaft which had two trails beside it – one to the right and the other to the left – having but a short distance yet to go, it deliberated which way would be worth taking. Going to the right and finding no trace, it returned and took the other. Since there was no clearly perceptible mark there either, with no further scenting it jumped into the shaft to track down hastily. This was not achieved by chance but rather by the deliberation of the mind. The logicians call this thoughtful reckoning 'the fifth complex indemonstrable syllogism'; for the beast might have escaped either to the right or to the left or else might have leaped. (*On Animals*, 45–6)

The dog is faced with three options. A quick sniff eliminates two of the options. Without further sniffing, the dog takes the third path. How is its action to be explained? Chrysippus argues that it must have engaged in some simple reasoning: it said to itself, in effect, 'Either A or B or C; but not A, and not B: therefore C.' (The five 'indemonstrables' or basic argument-forms of standard Stoic logic are listed by Sextus at *PH* II 157–8. The fifth indemonstrable has the form: 'Either A or B; but not B: therefore A.' The dog's syllogism is 'complex' inasmuch as its first premiss contains three disjuncts rather than two.)

Philo is not convinced by Chrysippus' explanation:

Even the assertion of those who think that hounds track by making use of the fifth mode of the syllogism is to be dismissed. The same could be said of those who gather clams or any other thing which moves. That they seem to follow a definite pattern is only logical speculation on the part of those who have no sense of philosophy, even in dreams. Then one has to say that all who are in search of something are making use of the fifth mode of the syllogism. (*On Animals*, 84)

Philo is too quick. He does not appreciate the force of Chrysippus' example. For Chrysippus does not imply that *any* piece of animal tracking provides evidence of reasoning. There is something special about his dog, for the dog runs confidently down the third track *without* first sniffing it out. It is the fact that the dog selects the third track without further experiment which requires explanation – and the explanation which Chrysippus offers is highly plausible.

Sextus presents the case of the rational hound as a jocular extra (see §§62, 78). But it is not merely a joke. It recalls a serious debate on the mental status of non-human animals, a debate which is still going on. And it argues against a position which may well have been thought damaging to the First Mode. For if animals really are as different from humans as the dogmatists allege, then that might provide us with some reason for preferring our own appearances to those of the other animals, and for thinking that there is a favoured kind K, namely the human kind, whose appearances are to be given precedence.

However that may be, Sextus certainly thinks that an appeal to (1.1) and (2.1) alone may not be enough to induce suspension of belief. In §59 he states the sceptical conclusion, that 'as to what ‹the existing object› is like in its nature we shall suspend judgement', but he immediately proceeds to give reasons for that conclusion over and above the simple recitation of conflicting appearances. Before looking at those reasons we must say a little about the sceptical conclusion itself.

Philo is deviant in his statement of the conclusion. He says that the mode indicates that things are 'inapprehensible'. The term he uses is a technical one, deriving from the sceptical Academy's attacks on the Stoics, who thought that things could be 'apprehended' or grasped or known for certain. The Pyrrhonists, as Sextus is careful to explain, do not assert that things are inapprehensible. They are not 'negative dogmatists': if they do not assert that things are apprehensible, they do not assert that they are inapprehensible either. More importantly, the Pyrrhonists are not primarily interested in apprehension or knowledge. Philo's conclusion would leave it open for us to say that we might have tentative or plausible beliefs about the way things are. The true Pyrrhonist will have no truck with that – he wants us to end up entirely free from belief.

Either Philo is following an Academic (rather than a Pyrrhonian) source, or he is consciously adapting a Pyrrhonian source to the less extreme conclusion, or he is simply speaking loosely. However that may be, Diogenes and Sextus both speak of suspension of judgement, of *epochē*. Their conclusion from the First Mode is an entire absence of assent or belief.

But it is important to see in what sense suspension of judgement is the 'conclusion' of the modes. We have presented the First Mode as a schematic argument in which proposition (4) – 'we suspend judgement . . .' – appears as the conclusion. But it is clear that proposition (4) does not strictly *follow* from the premises of the argument. Nor can the Pyrrhonists have thought that it did: although Sextus sometimes says that suspension of judgement is 'inferred', he does not mean that we infer that people do in fact suspend judgement – he is well aware that, despite the manifold oppositions of appearances, many people persist in making judgements.

Then how does proposition (4) relate to the premises of the mode? Occasionally the Pyrrhonists will say 'You *ought* to suspend judgement' (e.g. *PH* I 34; Diogenes IX 81). The 'ought' here presumably refers to rationality: given the premises, then any rational person will suspend judgement – given the premises, then surely (4) *ought* to be the case. But such 'oughts' are not very common in our texts, and in any case a consistent Pyrrhonist would have to be careful about employing the notion of rationality.

Usually the Pyrrhonists will say 'We *shall* suspend judgement' or 'Suspension of judgement *is introduced*' or 'We are *compelled* to suspend judgement.' They hold that suspension of judgement is 'an affect that comes about in the inquirer after the investigation' (*PH* I 7): it is something that *happens* to us, not a thing that we are *obliged* or can *choose* rationally to adopt. The relation between the premises of the modes and suspension of judgement is therefore this: once we recognise the premises, we shall in fact suspend judgement; suspension follows on, or is inferred from, the premises in the sense that it is the actual – perhaps even the inevitable – result of our recognising the force of the premises.

The medical metaphor is again apposite. We suffer from the disease of dogmatism, believing, say, that grass is green. The Pyrrhonist applies his drugs. He reminds us that though grass may appear green to us, it probably does not do so to other animals. He adds that we have no reason to prefer what appears to us to what appears to cats or dogs. As a result we find ourselves suspending judgement: is grass really green?

Perhaps, perhaps not. Our unbelief is not something which we have inferred from a set of premises, and we have not inferred that we ought not to believe any more. Rather, we find that we do not believe any more.

The medical metaphor by which arguments are likened to drugs and philosophy becomes a form of therapy is not peculiar to the Pyrrhonists: other philosophers, both ancient and modern, have made use of it. But the Greek sceptics took the metaphor more seriously than any other school has done, and it gave their mode of philosophising a special character. In the rest of this book we shall continue to speak of sceptical *arguments*, and we shall frequently ask questions of the form 'Why, given these premises, *should* we suspend judgement?' Such questions are surely legitimate and appropriate; but they are so only from the point of view of the critic of scepticism. The Pyrrhonists themselves take a different view. They do not concern themselves with the *soundness* of their arguments but with their *efficacy*. A 'good' argument, for the Pyrrhonists, is an argument which works – an argument which is efficacious in producing suspension of judgement.

The mere citation of conflicting appearances may not suffice to induce scepticism. Sextus plainly feels that we may respond to it not by scepticism but by an affirmation that the conflict is decidable – we *can* prefer one set of appearances, perhaps human appearances, to any other. Sextus counters this response with two highly abstract arguments, the burden of which is to convince us of the undecidability of the conflict. The arguments draw on the Five Modes of Agrippa (translated in Appendix C), and they were presumably not originally part of the presentation of the First Mode. Sextus – or some intermediary source – has supplemented the Ten Modes of Aenesidemus with material taken from the Five Modes of Agrippa.

The first of Sextus' arguments is brief: if we give preference to our own kind, we are judging our own case and thus we are not impartial judges. (For similar allegations of *parti pris* see *PH* II 35–6, *M* VII 318, 351.) The legal principle to which Sextus appeals is doubtless a good one in its legal context: we should not, in the law-courts, be judges of our own cases. But Sextus' application of it outside the legal context is dubious. Judges are not, after all, invariably corrupt, and in the cases Sextus imagines we are not allocating rewards and punishments but attempting to discover the truth. Even if we have an initial prejudice in favour of human appearances, there is no reason to think that our prejudice will always overcome our desire for the truth.

And in fact we do have what we consider to be objective ways of discriminating among appearances. There are relatively simple tests for colour-blindness in humans. Take two discs of the same size, one green and the other red. Mark the green one on its back with a *G*, the red one with an *R*. Those of us who are not red-green blind will be able to distinguish the one from the other, saying with confidence 'That is the one marked *G*' or 'That is the one marked *R*'; those who are colour-blind will not. We thereby reveal a discriminatory capacity which connects closely with the way the discs appear to us, and we are entitled to say that the way the discs appear to us is preferable to the way they appear to the colour-blind.

Similar discrimination tests may be performed across species. Typically we shall prefer our own appearances to those of other animal species; but in some cases – notably those concerned with sound and smell – we shall prefer the dog's nose or the lynx's ears to our own organs. Now insofar as we do this, we are relying in effect on various theories about the world which we suppose to be impartial between us and the other animals. Scepticism might then set in at a deeper level: how, after all, do we know that our theories are not just another set of human appearances, as anthropocentric as our perceivings? We have theories about discriminatory powers but cats, let us say, do not: perhaps this is merely another difference in the way the world appears, another case in which we must – but cannot – justify our preference for ourselves over the other animals? Sextus does not explicitly consider that line of attack, but his second argument in effect raises similar issues.

The second argument occupies §§60–1. It is presented in the form of a dilemma. If we hold that the way the world appears to humans is the way it really is, then we do so either without proof or with proof. But neither alternative is defensible.

What is wrong with believing something without proof? In a sense, nothing – unselfconscious belief is something with which the sceptic has no particular quarrel so long as it does not make us ill with anxiety and so in need of the sceptical medicine. But of course once we have read the First Mode we can hardly carry on with unselfconscious belief. For the belief has been questioned, a view incompatible with it has been advanced, and it will no longer do simply to assert it: as well assert its opposite if neither has any justification.

Beliefs once questioned stand in need, both objectively and subjectively, of justification. Does such justification have to amount to *proof*? In the present argument, Sextus implies that the only mode of justification is proof. Later on he will, more plausibly, allow the possibility of other modes of justification. But the omission is not fatal here, since the arguments which Sextus is about to produce against proof will apply equally to any proposed method of justification.

Why, then, should we not support our preference for human appearances by producing a proof? Sextus first claims that there is no such thing as proof anyway. Here he anticipates his arguments in *PH* II 134–92, and his mere assertion will carry no weight. His argument must therefore rest upon his second claim.

The claim introduces a second dilemma: if there were a proof, it would either not be apparent to us or else be apparent to us. But neither alternative is satisfactory. 'If it is not apparent, then we shall not bring it forward with confidence' (§60). By 'it is not apparent' Sextus probably means 'it does not strike us as a proof'. And surely if what is offered us as a proof does not strike us as a proof, then it has no power to persuade us of the preferability of human appearances.

Suppose, then, that the proof is apparent to us, i.e. that what is offered as a proof does strike us as a proof. What is wrong with that? Sextus suggests that we can only accept such a proof on pain of circular reasoning. We are trying to decide whether what appears to be the case to us really is the case. If we rely upon what appears to us to be a proof, then we are presupposing, in that case at least, what we have to prove: we are trying to prove the preferability of our appearances by insisting on the preferability of one of our appearances. (Perhaps, as we suggested in connexion with Sextus' first argument, our theories are ineradicably anthropocentric.)

Sextus is supposing that the dogmatists are trying to prove:

(5) If x appears F to animals of kind K, then x is F provided that kind K is human kind.

He alleges that if they attempt to prove (5) by way of a proof which is apparent to them, then they are presupposing that

(6) If x appears probative to humans, then x is probative.

And his argument in effect urges that the dogmatists are not entitled to (6) unless they have already secured (5).

Sextus' argument has – or so we have found – some persuasive force. But it is plain that any competent dogmatist can resist it. For no dogmatist of any sense wishes to support (5) – we do not (and should not and need not) always and in all circumstances prefer our own appearances. Rather than (5), a dogmatist will support a plethora of particular cases, one of which might be:

(7) If *x* appears green to humans, then *x* is green.

There is no circularity in supporting (7) by appeal to something which presupposes (6). Of course, a dogmatist must still show reason for relying on (6). And it is here that the arguments against proof in *PH* II come into their own. As far as the First Mode is concerned, however, we may say that Sextus has left a loophole for the dogmatist in his second argument.

Sextus' supporting arguments apart, how good is the First Mode? When Sextus' work was rediscovered in the Renaissance, the comparison between animals and humans was shocking – the First Mode jolted even if it did not convince. We are today less likely to be upset by the thought that the appearances of non-human animals are comparable to our own, and the mode has less power to amaze. But the power of the argument – even a sceptical argument – is not to be measured by its capacity to shock.

The First Mode is at any rate immune to two sorts of objection commonly raised against modern arguments of a similar type. First, Sextus does not rely upon specialised scientific beliefs in order to overthrow ordinary beliefs. Thus it cannot be objected to him that he uses sophisticated beliefs to unseat beliefs which are more deeply entrenched and which are the ultimate support of those sophisticated beliefs themselves. Secondly, Sextus' procedure is not self-refuting. Although he attempts to undermine common sense from within common sense, he does not use common-sense beliefs in order to infer a conclusion which implies the falsity of those common-sense beliefs. For, as we have already remarked, Sextus does not, strictly speaking, *infer* any conclusion at all.

Yet the First Mode is not beyond criticism. We may recognise oppositions of the form (1.1) and (2.1) without finding ourselves in a state of suspension of judgement. One possible reaction to such oppositions is 'relativism', a topic which we shall discuss at some length in a later chapter. And despite Sextus' arguments, the possibility of dogmatism is still open. We may persevere in holding that grass really is green, that *x* really is *F*, maintaining that we have, in some cases at least, sufficient reason to prefer *K* to *K**. If that is our attitude to the First Mode, well and good; but there remain, as the Pyrrhonist will remind us, nine more modes and nine more sceptical drugs.

5 Human Variations

Sextus, *PH* I 79–90:

The second, we said, was the mode deriving from the differences among humans. For even were one to concede, by way of hypothesis, that humans are more credible than the irrational animals, we shall still find suspension of judgement brought in by way of our *own* differences.

There are two things from which humans are said to be composed, soul and body, and in both of these we differ from one another. For example, in body we differ in our shapes and 80 our individual peculiarities. There is a difference in shape between the body of a Scythian and an Indian's body, and what produces the variation, so they say, is the different dominance of the humours. Depending on the different dominance of the humours, the appearances too become different, as we established in the first argument. Further, in virtue of these humours there are many differences in our choice and avoidance of external things; for Indians enjoy different things from us, and enjoying different things is an indication of getting varying appearances from existing objects.

81 In our individual peculiarities we differ in such a way that some people digest beef more easily than rock-fish, and get diarrhoea from weak Lesbian wine. There was (so they say) an old woman in Attica who consumed thirty drams of hemlock without harm. And Lysis actually took four drams of opium 82 without distress. Demophon, Alexander's waiter, used to shiver when he was in the sun or the baths, and felt warm in the shade. When Athenagoras of Argos was stung by scorpions or poisonous spiders he was not hurt. The Psyllaeans, as they are called, 83 are not harmed when bitten by snakes or asps, and the Tentyritae (in Egypt) are not harmed by crocodiles. Further, the Ethiopians who live by the river Astapus on the other side of Meroe eat

scorpions and snakes and the like without harm. When Rufinus –
the one from Chalcis – drank hellebore he neither vomited nor
suffered any other purgative effects, but consumed and digested
84 it as though he were used to it. If Chrysermus the Herophilean
doctor ever consumed pepper he suffered a heart attack. If
Soterichus the surgeon ever smelt sheathfish cooking he was
seized by diarrhoea. Andron of Argos was so free from thirst that
he travelled through waterless Libya without seeking drink. The
Emperor Tiberius could see in the dark. Aristotle describes a
Thasian who thought that the image of a man was continually
going in front of him.

85 So, since there is such variation among humans in body (to be
satisfied with a few examples out of the many which the dogmatists provide*), it is likely that humans differ from one
another in their souls too; for, as the science of physiognomy
shows, the body is a kind of replica of the soul.

The chief indication of the great, indeed infinite, differences
among the ways humans think is the dispute in the dogmatists'
statements about various matters and in particular about what
86 one should choose and what reject. The poets too have got it
right about these matters. Pindar says:

> One is gladdened by the honours and garlands
>   of his storm-footed horses,
> another by life in gilded palaces;
> another rejoices as he crosses the swell of the sea
> in a swift ship.

> [frag. 221 Snell]

And Homer says:

> Different men rejoice in different deeds.

> [*Odyssey* XIV 228]

Tragedy too is full of such things:

> If nature had made the same thing fine and wise for all alike,
> there would be no disputatious strife among human kind.

> [Euripides, *Phoenissae* 499–500]

And again:

> Strange that the same thing should please some mortals
> but by others be hated.

> [anon., frag. 462 Nauck]

87   Since, therefore, choice and avoidance are located in pleasure and displeasure, and pleasure and displeasure lie in perception and appearance, then when some choose and others avoid the same things, it is logical for us to deduce that they are not similarly affected by the same things, since otherwise they would have chosen and rejected the same things in similar ways. But if the same things affect humans differently depending on the differences among them, then it is likely that suspension of judgement will be introduced in this way too, since we are no doubt able to say how each existing thing appears, with reference to each difference, but are not able to declare what it is in its nature.

88   For we shall credit either all humans or some. But if all, we shall be attempting the impossible, and accepting opposed views. And if some, let them say whom we should assent to. The Platonist will say, 'To Plato', the Epicurean, 'To Epicurus', and the others analogously, and so by their undecidable dissensions they will bring us round again to suspension of judgement.

89   Anyone who says that we should assent to the majority view is being puerile. Nobody can canvass all mankind and work out what is the preference of the majority. It is possible that among some nations of which we have no knowledge what is rare with us is true of the majority and what is true of most of us is there rare – for example, that most people when bitten by poisonous spiders do not suffer though some occasionally do suffer, and analogously with the other individual peculiarities mentioned above. So suspension of judgement is necessarily introduced by way of the differences among humans too.

90   When the self-satisfied dogmatists say that they themselves should be preferred to other humans in judging things, we know that their claim is absurd. For they are themselves a part of the dispute, and if it is by preferring themselves that they judge what is apparent, then by entrusting the judging to themselves they are taking for granted the matter being investigated before even beginning the judging.

Diogenes IX 80–1:

Second is the mode depending on the natures and customs and constitutions* of humans. For instance, Demophon, Alexander's waiter, used to feel warm in the shade and shiver in the sun.

81 Andron of Argos, according to Aristotle, used to travel through
waterless Libya without drinking. One person devotes himself
to medicine, another to farming, another to trade. The same
things harm some and benefit others. Hence judgement should
be suspended.

Philo 176–7:

Next there are the diversities of every kind that are found not
176 just among animals in general but among humans themselves. It
is not only that they judge the same things differently on
different occasions – different people judge them in different
ways, receiving pleasure and displeasure in opposite ways from
the same objects.* What some find displeasing, others enjoy; and
on the other hand, what some accept and are drawn to as
attractive and appropriate, others spurn utterly as alien and
hostile.
177   For instance, I have often been in the theatre and watched the
effect of one and the same melody produced by the performers
on stage, or by the musicians. Some of the audience are so carried
away that they are excited and join in and involuntarily shout
their appreciation. Some are so unmoved that as far as this goes
you would think them no different from the lifeless seats they are
sitting on. Others again are so alienated that they actually get up
and leave the show and even block their ears* with both hands
lest any echo of the music should linger there and produce
displeasure in their fastidious and easily annoyed souls.

The Second Mode follows naturally upon the First. Just as there are
differences among species of animals, so there are differences within
species; and the latter, like the former, will occasion differences in
appearances. Thus even if we were to allow, for the sake of argument,
that one species, mankind, were epistemologically pre-eminent, we
should still not be free from dispute and anomaly.
   The Second Mode has the general form:

   (1.2) x appears F to H
   (2.2) x appears F^* to H^*

but

   (3.2) we cannot prefer H to H^* or *vice versa*

so that

(4) we suspend judgement as to whether *x* is really *F* or *F**.

In the concrete instances of the mode, '*H*' and '*H**' will be replaced sometimes by terms for kinds or groups ('Indians', 'Scythians'), sometimes by names for individuals ('Demophon', 'Soterichus').

The differences which underlie the Second Mode are differently characterised in our three sources. Philo refers to differences in judgements and in pleasures and displeasures. This appears to correspond to one part of Sextus' more elaborate account, where differences in choice and avoidance (or, equivalently, in pleasure and displeasure) are called the chief indication of differences in intellect or judgement. Diogenes does not refer explicitly to pleasure and displeasure; but the Greek text at this point is badly corrupt, and it is quite uncertain how Diogenes described the mode.

Sextus begins by distinguishing the two components of humans, body and soul. Bodily or physical differences themselves fall into two groups: there are differences of 'shape' and differences of 'individual peculiarities'. Sextus wastes little time on shape. He says that differences of shape depend, according to the dogmatists, on differences in the mixture of the 'humours'. (Many ancient doctors embraced the theory of the four 'humours' or juices – blood, phlegm, bile, black bile – which were supposed to govern the body and determine its characteristics. The theory is long discredited, and indeed not all Greek doctors accepted it. But Sextus' argument does not rely essentially on the theory: we can replace reference to the humours by reference to whatever physiological theory now holds sway without altering the structure of the argument.) Differences of humoral constitution give rise in turn to differences in the ways things appear – as Sextus has already noted in the First Mode (§52). The argument requires no further comment. But observe that here, as in the First Mode, Sextus does not put us in a position to produce any actual cases of conflicting appearances. If we observe, say, that the noses of Indians are characteristically different in shape from those of Scythians, we may perhaps infer that things smell differently to the two nations; but we are not in a position to say *how* they smell to either, and we cannot present any concrete instances of (1.2) and (2.2).

The second sort of bodily difference does introduce a new element into the discussion. The term we translate by 'individual peculiarity' is a technical term of Greek philosophical medicine: *idiosunkrasia* (the English 'idiosyncrasy'). All individuals have their own 'individual peculiarities', which are constituted or determined by their particular humoral constitutions. On this view, Plato's material constitution was different from Aristotle's, and from everyone else's. Thus if bodily differences of 'shape' were intended as differences among groups of humans, bodily differences of 'individual peculiarity' are certainly differences among individuals. In §§81–4 Sextus offers illustrative anecdotes which are meant to persuade us that there are in fact such 'individual peculiarities'. The peculiarities are, by hypothesis, grounded upon the peculiarities of individual humoural constitutions; and, as we already know, humoural differences give rise to differences in the ways that things appear.

After bodily differences Sextus turns to psychological differences. He shows their existence in two ways. First, he refers to 'the science of physiognomy', i.e. to the alleged science of determining psychological traits from physiological characteristics. In antiquity this 'science' was well established. Several manuals of *Physiognomics* have come down to us – one is transmitted under the name of Aristotle, although it is certainly not by him. Most of the surviving examples, which are depressingly silly, involve comparisons between human and other animals. Aristotle himself, for example, mentions (though he does not endorse) the physiognomical argument that, since lions, which are brave, have large feet, humans who have large feet are likely to possess the psychological characteristic of bravery (*Prior Analytics* 70b6–32). But if this is foolish, it is no more foolish than the nineteenth-century 'science' of phrenology, which tried to determine people's mental capacities by the bumps on their skulls. Nor is a science of physiognomy silly in principle; for there surely are, at least in some cases, external physical signs of internal psychological traits. Physiognomy, Sextus says, shows that the body is a 'replica' of the soul: since there are bodily differences among people, there are also psychological differences.

The 'chief indication' that humans differ from one another psychologically is given not by the science of physiognomy but by ordinary observations about what humans pursue and avoid. Different people like and dislike different things, and hence have different psychological characteristics. This is another point already familiar from the First Mode. There, as we noted (above, p. 43), Sextus' remarks are ambiguous or indeterminate. Here, in §87, he makes much more explicit the nature of the connexion between choice on the one hand and appearances on the other. Choice, he says, depends on pleasure, pleasure on appearance; and so differences in choice will indicate differences in appearance.

The first quotation from the poet Pindar shows what Sextus intends. Suppose I choose to breed race-horses; then winning horse-races (or at least the hope of doing so) must please me in some way. So choice depends on pleasure. And if winning the Derby pleases me, then there must be some way in which it appears to me which explains why it pleases me; it must have some characteristic which is a pleasure-giving characteristic. So pleasure depends on appearance. In general, if it is the case that x chooses y, then y must please x; and if y pleases x, then there must be some special way in which y appears to x, i.e. y must appear F to x, where 'F' denotes a pleasure-giving characteristic.

We might question the last step in that argument. Why should success with horses not appear in exactly the same way to Socrates and to Alcibiades, and yet please the latter while leaving the former cold? Why should any difference in appearance underlie the difference in taste? Perhaps differences in taste are simply differences in taste.

However, the objection is not fatal. Sextus could reply that the Pyrrhonist is not committed to the argument in §87, for it is the dogmatists (some or all of them) who advance it, and insofar as it is *their* argument it is effective against *them*. After all, the sceptic sees nothing wrong with *ad hominem* reasoning – he uses it all the time. Alternatively, Sextus could advance the line of thought we suggested earlier in the discussion of the First Mode. That is to say, he could treat the pleasantness or unpleasantness of a thing as itself an appearance. On this view, if success in the Derby pleases me but not you, then that is itself a difference in appearance, and the Pyrrhonist does not need to appeal to any further differences in appearance underlying that difference in taste.

As usual, Sextus' illustrations of the differences among humans are more numerous and varied than those in Diogenes or in Philo. Philo indeed restricts himself to a single example, the differing reactions of members of an audience to the music they hear. He elaborates the example in some detail, and says explicitly that he has 'often been present and watched' such a thing happening. The example does not recur anywhere else, and it is tempting to suppose that Philo has indeed, as he claims, introduced it from his own experience. But elsewhere in Philo's writings we find similar claims to personal experience which are demonstrably derived from other sources. It is prudent to treat 'I have seen it myself' as a literary device.

Again, many of Sextus' examples are highly dubious, and many need considerable reworking if they are to exhibit the form of the conflicting-appearances argument which this mode puts forward. The

Pyrrhonists lift information from other sources and do not always bother to adapt it to their own particular needs. They lift the information quite openly. Thus Sextus casually remarks that he will be satisfied with a few of the many things said by the dogmatists (§85). The remark follows an explicit allusion to Aristotle: the man who always saw someone walking in front of him is described, and his complaint explained, in Aristotle's *Meteorology* 373a35–b10. (Oddly enough, our text of Aristotle makes no mention of the man's nationality, while Sextus says that he came from Thasos. Is our text of Aristotle's *Meteorology* corrupt? Did Sextus (or an intermediate source) embroider the story? Did Aristotle tell the story again, with more detail, in a work now lost?) An earlier example in the same paragraph is also drawn from Aristotle. Sextus gives no authority for his story of Andron of Argos, but Diogenes explicitly ascribes it to Aristotle. We happen to know the story from another source too: Apollonius, who perhaps wrote in the second century BC, records it in his collection of *Marvellous Stories*, adding that it was told by Aristotle in his work *On Drunkenness*.

It is perhaps surprising that Sextus does not adduce the most celebrated of all oppositions of this second type. The example derives from the fifth-century sophist Protagoras. It is reported by Plato in his *Theaetetus*:

SOCRATES: Sometimes when the wind blows, doesn't one of us shiver and the other not? or one of us slightly and the other violently?
THEAETETUS: Yes indeed.
SOCRATES: So shall we say that the breeze is then itself cold or not cold? or shall we follow Protagoras in holding that it is cold for the one who shivers, not cold for the one who does not? (*Theaetetus* 152B)

The same wind appears cold to Socrates and warm to Theaetetus: that is a clear instance of the opposition (1.2) and (2.2). The Pyrrhonist has his sceptical answer ready for Socrates' question: 'Shall we say that the breeze is in itself cold or not cold?' 'No, we shall affirm neither that it is cold nor that it is not cold.' (Protagoras gives a different, relativist, answer: we shall return in a later chapter to the relativist response to conflicts of appearances.)

It is also surprising that Sextus *argues* for the existence of differences among humans. In the First Mode some argument was indeed called for, since it is not immediately evident that things appear in different ways to different kinds of animals. But it is a commonplace that there are oppositions falling under the Second Mode, and Sextus' arguments to that effect may seem superfluous.

However that may be, Sextus emphasises not the establishment of oppositions but rather the proof that the existence of such oppositions has sceptical implications. We could well allow that there are oppositions but question their sceptical significance. Philo does not answer that question for us, taking it as obvious both that and how the oppositions lead to suspension of judgement. Diogenes asserts that 'hence judgement should be suspended', but he does not explain or justify the assertion. Again Sextus is more satisfactory.

In the First Mode Sextus deployed arguments from the Modes of Agrippa. In the Second Mode his argument does not invoke Agrippa: it may have been invented by Sextus himself, or it may possibly go back to Aenesidemus. The argument takes the form of a dilemma. Suppose that x appears F_1 to y_1, F_2 to y_2, ..., F_n to y_n. Then if we are to determine how x really is, we must credit either *all* the ys, or only some of them. But we can do neither; hence we cannot determine how x really is.

This seems to be a false dilemma, for Sextus has overlooked one option. The object may be the way it appears to all observers or the way it appears to some – or it may appear to *no* observers the way it really is. Why does Sextus ignore the third option? Perhaps he is assuming that we can only determine that x really is F_i if x appears F_i to some observer or other: we cannot decide that an object has a certain property if it never appears to anyone to have it. But that assumption is questionable. We might grant Sextus that our only access to the real properties of things is by way of appearances. But the concession can be taken in at least three distinct senses. (a) 'We can only determine that x really is F_i on the basis of the various ways in which things (u, v, ... , as well as x) appear.' (b) 'We can only determine that x really is F_i on the basis of the various ways in which x itself appears.' (c) 'We can only determine that x really is F_i if at least in some cases x appears F_i.' We might perhaps concede (a); but Sextus in fact assumes (c) – and there is no reason to grant that assumption. Insofar as the assumption is open to doubt, Sextus' argument in §§87–90 is weakened. But Sextus would not have been greatly troubled: in the Third Mode, as we shall see, he has an effective rejoinder to the doubt.

What of the options which Sextus does offer us? We cannot credit *all* the ys, for 'we shall be attempting the impossible and accepting opposed views'. Since the Fs are incompatible, we cannot hold that x is all the Fs at once. We might wonder if it is even worth mentioning this horn of the dilemma. Surely no dogmatist would have dared to accept it? In fact, it was chosen, for some cases at least, by the Epicureans.

They explain that, since all things are mixed and mingled together, and different things are naturally adapted to different people, everyone does not touch or grasp the same quality nor do external objects affect everyone with all their parts in the same way; rather, each of us makes contact only with those parts for which his senses are proportioned. (Plutarch, *Against Colotes* 1109D)

The wind is composed of innumerable 'parts', some of which are hot and some cold. The hot parts affect Theaetetus but not Socrates; with the cold parts it is the other way round. (The different ways in which they are affected are explained by the fact that the sense-organs of the two men are differently constituted.) Thus, according to the Epicureans, the wind really is both hot and cold, and, in general, x may be both F_1 and F_2 and . . . and F_n. In making this supposition we are not 'attempting the impossible'.

Sextus might reply that the Epicureans are not truly choosing the first horn of his dilemma; for, strictly speaking, they hold not that the wind *itself* is both hot and cold, but that *parts* of the wind are hot and *parts* cold. He might go further, and urge that this Epicurean 'solution' does not really address itself to the problem of the Second Mode at all. For in the case the Epicureans envisage, it is not that some one thing, the wind, appears both hot and cold, but rather that parts of the wind appear hot and parts appear cold. And he might finally add that the Epicurean 'solution' cannot be applied in genuine oppositions, when, for example, the *same* parts of the wind appear both hot and cold. (The Epicureans could of course reply that genuine oppositions of that kind never arise; but it is not clear what grounds they would have for doing so.)

Let us turn finally to the other horn of Sextus' dilemma: why can we not say that x really is the way it appears to *some* observers? Sextus distinguishes two cases: we may attempt to give preference to some named observer or group of observers (Plato, Epicurus), or we may vote for the majority view. The first case is rejected in §88 and §90, the second in §89. (The structure of Sextus' argument is disjointed: §90 might better follow directly upon §88. It seems likely that Sextus is drawing upon two different sources here, and has knitted them together inelegantly.)

If we trust some named observer, then whom? According to Sextus, y_1 will say, 'y_1', y_2 will say 'y_2', and so on. (It is worth noting that he names two philosophers, and is surely thinking of philosophical disputes over the nature of reality. But the oppositions by which the Second Mode is illustrated are not philosophical but everyday.) In §88 Sextus merely states that the dispute between y_1 and y_2, Plato and Epicurus, is undecidable. In §90 he offers two reasons for this. First, the disputants are themselves a party to the dispute, and hence they may not act as judges in their own case. Secondly, any attempt to settle the dispute must beg the question. We have met these same two arguments in connexion with the First Mode: no more need be said of them here.

The suggestion that we should vote with the majority is rejected in §89. Sextus does not say that majority opinion is no guide to truth. Had he done so, he might have called Plato as a witness on his behalf:

My friend, you are trying to refute me in the way orators think they do in the law-courts. For there the one party thinks it refutes the other when it produces numerous reputable witnesses to what it says and its opponents produce just one or none at all. But that sort of refutation is of no value with regard to the truth; for in some cases you might actually be beaten down by a number of fair-seeming false witnesses. (*Gorgias* 471E)

Plato's opinion may seem implausibly severe. Aristotle, for one, rejected it: he held that beliefs shared by a majority of people were 'reputable' (*endoxos*), and that if a belief is reputable then it has some claim to be thought true. The general question is this: Is the fact that x appears F to most people any evidence that it really is F? To which the general answer is doubtless a highly qualified Yes. In some particular cases the affirmative answer may perhaps need no qualification. Thus some modern philosophers have held that objects really have just those 'secondary' qualities (colours, tastes, odours, etc.) that they appear to have to most observers, i.e. to normal observers in normal conditions. Tomatoes, for example, *are* red inasmuch as they appear red under normal lighting conditions to observers who enjoy normal eyesight.

In the Second Mode Sextus does not question the credentials of the majority or consider the view that normal appearances are a guarantee of truth. In a later mode he does take up this point, and we shall consider it further there. Here in §89 he simply denies that we can ever determine what the majority view is. For we cannot 'canvass all mankind'.

The point may seem curiously naive. No doubt we cannot literally canvass all mankind, but why do we need to? We can be sure that the summer sky appears blue to most people without conducting a referendum on the subject. For we know, by virtue of a vast mass of indirect evidence, that most people's eyes work in similar ways, and we can discover easily enough, by taking a representative sample, that most people see the summer sky as blue. Sextus, however, was writing seventeen hundred years ago, when the notions of statistical sampling and of probability had not been elaborated. Moreover, in his time the known world was recognised to be only a small part of the actual world.

The force of the latter point may be brought out by a remark in a treatise of Philodemus, an Epicurean philosopher of the first century BC. He reports certain objectors to inductive generalisations as claiming, 'we shall not argue that, since men here are mortal, so too are men in Libya; still less that since animals here are mortal, so too are animals in Britain – if there are any' (*On Signs* V). Perhaps there are animals in Britain. But we know nothing about them, and it would be rash to infer their characteristics from the characteristics of those animals we are familiar with. 'All swans are white', said Aristotle. 'That is an unwarrantable generalisation', the objectors would have replied; 'for there may, for all we know, be swans in Australia, say, which are not white but black.' And the objectors would have been right.

Sextus' observation that there may be nations, of which he knows nothing, among which the bite of spiders causes no pain is thus not a desperate attempt to defend scepticism against the evident facts. On the contrary, it is a reasonable reflexion on the state of contemporary knowledge. Anybody in Sextus' time who ventured the opinion that a majority of mankind were subject to such-and-such experiences would have been making an unwarrantably rash judgement.

6   The Senses

91   Nonetheless, so as to arrive at suspension of judgement even when resting the argument on a single person, such as the Wise Man they dream up, we bring out the mode which is third in order. This, we said, is the one deriving from the differences among the senses. Now, that the senses disagree with one another, is clear.

92   For instance, paintings seem to sight to have recesses and projections, but not to touch. And honey appears pleasant to the tongue (for some people) but unpleasant to the eyes; it is impossible, therefore, to say whether it is purely pleasant or unpleasant. Similarly with perfume; it gratifies the sense of smell, but dis-
93   pleases the sense of taste. Again, since spurge-juice is painful to the eyes but painless to the rest of the body, we will not be able to say whether, as far as its own nature goes, it is purely painless to bodies or painful. Rain-water is beneficial to the eyes, but is rough on the windpipe and lungs – so too is olive oil, though it comforts the skin. The sea-ray when applied to the extremities paralyses them, but can be put on the rest of the body harmlessly.

Hence we will not be able to say what each of these things is like in its nature, though it is possible to say what they appear to be like on any given occasion.

94   More cases than these can be given; but so as not to waste time, given the purpose of our treatise,* we should say this. Each of the objects of perception that appear to us seems to impress us in a variety of ways – for example an apple is smooth, fragrant, sweet and yellow. It is unclear, then, whether in reality it has these qualities alone,* or has only one quality but appears different depending on the different constitution of the sense-organs, or actually has more qualities than those which are apparent, some of them not making an impression on us.

95   That it has only one quality can be argued from what we said before [I 53–4] about the nourishment dispersed in our bodies and the water dispersed in trees and the breath in flutes and pipes and similar instruments;* for the apple can be undifferentiated but observed as different depending on the differences among the sense-organs by which it is grasped.

96   That the apple may have more qualities than those apparent to us we deduce as follows. Let us conceive of someone who from birth has touch, smell and taste, but hears and sees nothing. He will suppose that there is absolutely nothing visible or audible, and that there exist only those three kinds of quality which he is

97   able to grasp. So it is possible that we too, having only the five senses, grasp from among the qualities in the apple* only those we are capable of grasping, although other qualities can exist, impressing other sense-organs in which we have no share, so that we do not grasp the objects perceptible by them.*

98   But nature, someone will say, has made the senses commensurable with their objects. What nature? – given that there is so much undecidable dispute among the dogmatists about its very existence. For if someone decides this question (namely, whether there is such a thing as nature), then if he is a layman he will not be credible according to them, while if he is a philosopher he will be part of the dispute and under judgement himself rather than a judge.

99   But if it is possible* that just those qualities exist in the apple which we think we grasp, or that there are more than them, or again that there are not even those that impress us, then it will be unclear to us what the apple is like.

The same argument applies to the other objects of perception too.

However, if the senses do not apprehend external objects, the intellect is not able to apprehend them either (since its guides fail it); so by means of this argument too suspension of judgement about external existing objects will seem to be inferred.

Diogenes IX 81:

Third is the mode depending on the differences among the channels of perception. An apple, for instance, is experienced as yellow to sight, sweet to taste, and fragrant to smell. The same shape is observed as different depending on the differences in the mirrors. So it follows that what appears is no more such-and-such than so-and-so.

The First Mode dealt with differences among animal species, the Second with differences within the human species: the Third Mode now turns to differences within one human individual. For humans perceive things by way of five senses, and the different senses may produce 'oppositions' of the sort the Pyrrhonist loves. Thus the Third Mode follows intelligibly on the Second and the First. Strangely enough, it is omitted in Philo's account. Philo's remarks at the beginning of §178 would, as a matter of fact, serve well to introduce the Third Mode, but instead he goes on to what in Sextus is the Fourth Mode.

Sextus introduces the mode with a reference to the 'Wise Man' who appeared in the Second Mode in §88. But the mode has no special reference to the ideal wise man or 'Sage' of the dogmatic philosophers: it raises problems about the perceptions of ordinary people. Diogenes introduces the mode by talking about 'channels of perception'. The term 'channels' was widely used in ancient scientific – and especially medical – literature on perception; but there are no further traces in Diogenes' account (or in Sextus) of any scientific theorising underlying the mode. The term 'channels' should not mislead us into thinking that the mode presupposes some particular scientific theory of perception.

Sextus begins, in §§91–3, by producing standard conflicts of appearances, in this case of the form:

(1.3) x appears F to sense s
(2.3) x appears F^* to sense s^*

but

(3.3) we cannot prefer s to s^* or *vice versa*;

thus

(4) we shall suspend judgement as to whether x is really F or F^*.

Diogenes presumably means to exemplify the same conflict of appearances. He concludes with the reflection that 'what appears is no more such-and-such than so-and-so'. Here he is using one of the orthodox Pyrrhonist phrases to express suspension of judgement. Sextus tells us, at *PH* I 191, that Pyrrhonists regularly use the phrase 'no more such-and-such than so-and-so', and that when they do so they do not mean to express the belief that something actually *is* no more F

than $F*$ but rather to indicate that they do not know whether to assent to 'x is F' or to 'x is $F*$'. The 'no more' phrase may appear to commit the Pyrrhonist to a belief about how things are (and in ordinary usage that is just what the phrase would do); but the Pyrrhonist makes it plain that in Pyrrhonian usage the phrase is simply one among several ways of indicating that he suspends judgement.

Sextus' illustrations of conflict are unsatisfactory. They are taken, as usual, from the dogmatic handbooks. Thus, for example, Sextus' spurge and his perfume can be found also in Pliny's *Natural History* (XXV 7 and XIII 3). His sting-ray is described in numerous passages from scientific and quasi-scientific works – a cento of texts is put together by the third-century AD antiquarian Athenaeus in his *Deipnosophists* (314AE). (The most celebrated philosophical location is in Plato's *Meno*, 80A, where Socrates is compared to the sting-ray for the numbing effect of his arguments.) But whatever their provenance, many of the examples are weak. Honey appears pleasant to the tongue, unpleasant to the eyes (§92): but honey does not *look* unpleasant – or at least, we do not think that it does. Sextus means in fact that honey is unpleasant when it is smeared on or dripped into the eyes. No doubt that is true, but it does not set up any conflict of *appearances*. Sextus, in several of these examples, confuses the way something *affects* us with the way it *appears* to us.

The most interesting of Sextus' examples is the one about paintings: 'paintings seem to sight to have recesses and projections, but not to touch' (§92). Elsewhere, Sextus talks about 'recesses and projections' in connexion with the imprint left by a seal on a piece of wax (e.g. *PH* II 70). It is natural to suppose that he has the same thing in mind here. In that case we should have to change the text, making it say that paintings *look* smooth but *feel* rough. But in fact ancient painters did not use thick impasto, so that their paintings would both look and feel smooth. Sextus must have something else in mind.

At *PH* I 120 he refers to paintings seen from different angles and thereby looking different. It is probable that he has the same sort of phenomenon in mind here in §92. Some paintings, when looked at from certain angles, give a three-dimensional effect: the painting feels flat, but it looks three-dimensional – it appears to the sight to have 'recesses and projections'. (We might think of the painted ceilings in some Baroque churches which look three-dimensional from some positions but not from others.) If that is the right interpretation of Sextus, then the conflict which he invokes was noticed by Plato. At

Republic 602C–603B Plato refers to the three-dimensional effect which scene-painting has on us. He says that the eyes here give us information which is contradicted by 'the better part of the soul'. On the basis of the objective procedures of 'measuring, counting, and weighing', the better part of the soul determines that the sight is misleading us. Plato does not speak of a conflict between the sense of sight and the sense of touch, but rather of a conflict between sight and reason; but in fact he has in mind cases where sight and touch give conflicting information.

In his *Essay towards a New Theory of Vision* of 1709 Berkeley develops a series of arguments to show that sight and touch apparently conflict. But he concludes neither (with Plato) that touch must prevail over sight, nor, conversely, that sight must prevail over touch, nor yet (with Sextus) that we cannot tell which of the two senses is in the right. Rather, he argues that 'the objects of sight and touch are two distinct things' (§49): we may *say* 'It looks round and it feels round' or 'It looks flat and it feels rough', but in the first case the word 'round' is not being used in the same sense on each occasion, and in the second case there is no conflict between flat-looking and rough-feeling.

Berkeley thus in effect denies that there *can* be conflicts of the sort which illustrate the Third Mode. For the Third Mode presupposes that there are what philosophers since Aristotle have called 'common sensibles' – qualities apprehensible by more than one sense – and Berkeley denies this presupposition. The normal list of 'common sensibles' includes shape, size, motion, and number as well as roughness and smoothness. And the doctrine of common sensibles holds that, say, the shape of an object – its roundness or squareness – is perceptible alike by sight and by touch: we can both see and feel that saucers are round or that tiles are square. Berkeley, on the other hand, maintains that the squareness we see is something quite distinct from the squareness we feel. The two qualities are as different as felt roughness is from seen blueness. If as a matter of fact all, or most, things which are square-looking are also square-feeling, then that is an interesting fact about the regularity of the world for which we must give thanks to God.

Plainly, the Third Mode depends on rejecting Berkeley's view. For if there are no common sensibles, then there are no conflicts of the sort the mode collects.

Supposing that Berkeley is wrong and that there are conflicts of the sort Sextus describes, how should they be resolved, if they can be resolved at all? Plato's view seems plausible. Surely we do prefer touch to sight when the two conflict, and surely we are right to do so. For the sight and feel of the scene-painting are not insulated from the rest of our experience. We can – to take only the most obvious point – walk around the painting and see the things behind it. If we still maintain, following our eyes, that the canvas is three-dimensional, then we shall have to suppose radical error in much of the rest of our experience. Sextus misleads us to the extent that he pretends that we ought to consider the two conflicting appearances in isolation from the rest of our experience: once we reflect on the general context within which his conflicts take place, we shall readily opt for touch and Plato's 'better part of the soul'.

We cannot leave the point, however, without mentioning some evidence which appears to tell against Plato. Psychologists who have investigated the interplay between vision and touch have come to the unPlatonic conclusion that when touch reports and sight reports conflict, it is sight which dominates: we learn to reinterpret our sensations of touch in such a way as to make them consistent with vision. In cases of everyday adult conflict, touch may dominate; but our way of regarding the world is based on a learning process in which vision dominated and touch was the junior partner. (See I. Rock and C. S. Harris, 'Vision and Touch', *Scientific American*, May 1967.)

Perhaps a sceptical conclusion is, after all, appropriate.

Diogenes' first illustration of the mode does not invoke common sensibles. 'An apple, for instance, is experienced as yellow to sight, sweet to taste, and fragrant to smell.' Those appearances are surely *different*, but they can hardly be thought to *conflict*. The apple appears yellow and it appears sweet: where is the conflict? Where is the sceptical puzzle? The apple reappears in Sextus, where it illustrates what is best construed as a new argument. In §§94–9 Sextus in effect abandons the conflict of appearances and turns to a different sort of argument for suspension of judgement. Diogenes' account of the Third Mode can thus be regarded as preserving an illustration for that second sort of argument, while purporting to reproduce another conflict argument of the standard sort. Sextus, it is true, does not indicate that he is turning to a new sort of argument, but it is scarcely credible that he – or any other philosopher – should have thought that the apple argument was of the same form as the conflict of appearances arguments.

Why is the example an apple? Sextus elsewhere cites apples as examples of things which have a number of different sense-qualities (*M* VII 103). He ascribes the point to 'the Pythagoreans'. Alexander of Aphrodisias uses the apple to make the same point, and so do several of the later Greek commentators on Aristotle. More interesting from our

point of view is a passage in the late Roman writer Macrobius, where he
is discussing the importance of the mind or reason in perception and
refers briefly to certain sceptical views of the New Academy. The
passage is worth quoting at length (even if, strictly speaking, it is of
marginal relevance to the Third Mode):

When the mind rests, the sight is so incompetent that the neglect of the mind
brings it about that the oar appears bent in water or that the tower, although it is
square, is thought to be round when seen from a distance. Yet if the mind exerts
itself, it recognises angles in the tower and straightness in the oar. Moreover, it
discerns all those things which the Academics have taken as condemnations of
the senses – for the senses are to be held among the most certain of things when
the mind accompanies them, although sometimes a single sense is not enough
for it to discern the form before it. For if the form of some fruit, say an apple, is
seen from a distance, it is not absolutely an apple, for the likeness of an apple
could have been put together from some other material. Hence another sense
must be summoned – so that smell makes a judgement. But the perfume of the
apples could have been put among the heap. Hence touch must be consulted,
which can judge about mass. Yet there is a danger that touch itself may be
deceived, if the cunning artisan has chosen a material which matches the mass of
the fruit. We must, therefore, turn to taste: if that agrees with the shape, then
there is no doubt that it is an apple. Thus it is shown that the competence of the
senses depends upon the mind. (*Saturnalia* VII xiv 20–3)

Macrobius thinks that, by the judicious and mind-directed application
of all our senses, we can tell that we have an apple before us and not, say,
a wax imitation; and he holds that in this way certain Academic doubts
can be laid to rest. It is a reasonable inference that the Academics used
the example of an apple in order to induce scepticism. Whether they
used it in the way Sextus does is another matter.

The apple argument starts not from a conflict of appearances but
from a multiplicity of appearances. Thus we observe that:

(A) x appears F_1 to S_1, F_2 to S_2, ..., F_n to S_n.

Now we normally, and unsceptically, suppose that the apple is (more
or less) as it appears. That is to say, we take (A) as good evidence that:

(B) x is F_1 and F_2 and ... and F_n.

(Good evidence, but not, of course, conclusive evidence: we may have
reason to think that the apple's appearances, all or some of them, are in
this case misleading. But we normally think that we can make allow-
ances for such cases.) But why ever should we suppose that (B) is the

right inference from (A)? Sextus offers us two other hypotheses to set alongside (B).

First, he suggests that perhaps the apple has only *one* quality. Instead of (B), the truth lying behind (A) is:

(C) x is F^*

– and x's actually being F^* explains why it appears as it does to the different senses. Sextus tries to make the point clear by adducing three analogies – food, drink and breath, which, though essentially uniform, become different as they pass through our bodies or through the pipe of a flute. The analogies have been used earlier (in §§53–4), and are no more helpful than they were before.

It seems possible that Diogenes preserves the traces of a better analogy. He cites the phenomenon of reflexion in his brief account of the mode: 'The same shape is observed as different depending on the differences in the mirrors.' Now if it is construed as an illustration of the Third Mode, this example is odd and unconvincing. It might, perhaps, be supposed that Diogenes has carelessly transferred to this mode some material that was originally at home elsewhere, for Sextus introduces mirrors of different powers in his account of the First Mode (§§48–9). In general, it is clear that the ancient sceptics made play with the distorting powers of mirrors, and Diogenes may merely be reproducing, somewhat ineptly, a commonplace example. (It is worth noting that ancient scientists were equally fascinated by mirrors. The phenomena of reflexion were the objects of the science of 'catoptrics', which was itself a science subordinate to optics. Several ancient treatises on catoptrics have survived, and from them we can see that Hellenistic scientists had attempted to give a rational account of the effects of distorting mirrors which their philosophical colleagues had employed for sceptical ends.)

But there is a more interesting way of understanding Diogenes' reference to mirrors. We may suppose that he has preserved an analogy to thesis (C). A cube looks, say, elongated but straight in one mirror, squat and curvy in another, hourglass-shaped in a third, and so on. One and the same shape underlies all these different (and in this case conflicting) appearances. For the cube is in reality *cubic* – and that is precisely why it appears differently in different mirrors. Perhaps, then, our senses are like mirrors, each with its own distorting powers. The apple, like the cube, has in reality some unique quality. It appears different to the different senses, just as the cube looks different in the different mirrors.

However that may be, there is, Sextus suggests, yet another way of looking at (A). Perhaps the apple has in fact a large number of qualities, many of which are quite beyond our apprehension. Perhaps, in other words, we should entertain not (B) or (C) but rather:

(D) x is F_1 and F_2 and ... and F_n and F_{n+1} and ... and F_k.

That possibility was later taken up by John Locke, who indeed thought that it was pretty certainly correct:

What other simple *Ideas* 'tis possible the Creatures in other parts of the Universe may have, by the Assistance of Senses and Faculties more or perfecter, than we have, or different from ours, 'tis not for us to determine. But to say, or think there are no such, because we conceive nothing of them, is no better an argument, than if a blind Man should be positive in it, that there was no such thing as Sight and Colours, because he had no manner of *Idea*, of any such thing, nor could by any means frame to himself any Notions about Seeing. The Ignorance, and Darkness that is in us, no more hinders, nor confines the Knowledge, that is in others, than the blindness of a Mole is an Argument against the quick-sightedness of an Eagle. He that will consider the Infinite Power, Wisdom, and Goodness of the Creator of all Things, will find Reason to think, it was not all laid out upon so inconsiderable, mean, and impotent a Creature, as he will find Man to be; who in all probability, is one of the lowest of all intellectual Beings. (*Essay concerning Human Understanding* IV iii 23)

We can say how things appear to us, but we cannot say how they really are; for, as possibility (D) indicates, reality may well project innumerable appearances of which we can know nothing.

Sextus considers a response to his argument which purportedly enables us to decide in favour of (B) and against its rivals, (C) and (D). 'Nature, someone will say, has made the senses commensurable with their objects' (§98). This is a dark saying, capable of more than one elucidation. We suppose that the point of it is that the senses have been made by a benevolent nature to correspond to the objects of sensation. There are just five senses, and similarly there are just five classes of sensible quality. There are no types of sensible quality which escape our faculties (as thesis (D) supposes), and our senses do not misleadingly multiply the types of sensible quality (as thesis (C) imagines). Nature has proportioned our senses to herself.

Sextus' reply to this response is surprising. He asks scornfully 'What nature?': there is so much dispute among the dogmatists about nature itself that the claim that 'nature . . . has made the senses commensurable with their objects' has no coherent sense. That is surprising because, as far as we know, there was relatively *little* dispute among the dogmatists about the notion of nature. It is notable that Sextus himself, in his wide-ranging discussions of 'physics' in *PH* III and *M* IX–X, does not cast any doubt on the concept of nature: he attacks such fundamental scientific concepts as time, space, motion, causation, but he never attacks what was, for the Greek thinkers, the central notion of natural science, that of nature itself.

Perhaps Sextus is alluding to disagreements which we can no longer discover. We can, however, make a few relevant remarks. First, we may suppose that the dogmatists who introduced the notion of commensurability were Stoics and perhaps also Peripatetics. A passage in Aristotle's treatise *On the Soul* 424b20–425a13, argues that there cannot be more than five senses on the grounds that there are only five types of thing in the physical environment to which animals could be sensitive. This is not exactly the same as the notion which Sextus refers to, but it is closely related to it. As for the Stoics, consider the following remarks by Epictetus:

'If god had made colours but had not made a power of seeing them, what good would it have been?' 'None at all.' 'Conversely, if he had made a power but had not made things of such a sort as to impress the power of sight, what good would *that* have been?' 'None at all.' 'And if he had made both these things but had not made light?' 'That too would have been no good.' 'Then who has fitted this to that and that to this? Who has fitted the sword to the scabbard and the scabbard to the sword?' (*Discourses* I vi 3–6)

That may express the very thesis of commensurability which Sextus has in mind.

Secondly, we suspect that the dispute about nature to which Sextus refers was a dispute over teleology: the Peripatetics and the Stoics believed that nature had goals and ends, and that any scientist must offer teleological explanations – explanations in terms of ends – of the natural phenomena he studies. The Epicureans vehemently rejected teleology and made do with purely mechanistic explanations of natural phenomena. The dispute between teleologists and non-teleologists might reasonably be represented as a dispute over 'nature', and it is certainly a dispute which is relevant to Sextus' concerns in these sections.

However that may be, the mere existence of a dispute about nature does not suffice to rule out the suggestion that our senses are commensurate with their objects. And the suggestion may seem not implausible, provided that we free it from any naive personification of Mother Nature. Is it not reasonable to think that our senses are naturally matched to their objects? We have survived for millennia as functioning animals in a complex environment, and we could scarcely have done so if our senses gave us radically misleading or incomplete information about the outside world. Thus we might give to the suggestion which Sextus scouts an appealingly evolutionary aspect.

The suggestion in fact contains two somewhat different points. First, it supposes that we should not have survived had our senses presented us with grossly *misleading* information about the external world; secondly, it supposes that we should not have survived had our senses provided us with radically *incomplete* information about the external world. The second point would rule out thesis (D), the first point thesis (C).

Now the second point is not particularly plausible. It is by no means clear that we require 'complete' information about the world in order to survive. (Indeed, it is not clear that the notion of 'complete' information is intelligible.) Locke, for one, did not think so:

God has no doubt made us so, as is best for us in our present Condition. He hath fitted us for the Neighbourhood of the Bodies, that surround us, and we have to do with: And though we cannot by the Faculties we have, attain to a perfect Knowledge of Things; yet they will serve us well enough for those ends above-mentioned, which are our great Concernment. (*Essay* II xxiii 13)

God – or Nature, or evolution – may fit us to our environment without giving us a complete grasp of it: we know, in Locke's view, all we need to know, and all we need to know is far less than all there is to know.

The first point, that we should not have survived had our senses given us radically misleading information, seems stronger. We do suppose that things really are, for the most part, the way they appear to us. If that supposition were generally mistaken we should not have survived to question it. But is that really so? We are assuming that there must be a close connexion between truth or reality on the one hand and survival value or utility on the other. But why assume this? Why assume that we could not have survived had we been in receipt of misinformation about the world? Have we any reason at all to think that information is more, rather than less, useful than misinformation? If we could discern information from misinformation and then test each for its utility, we might have some reason to prefer one to the other. But, the Pyrrhonist will urge, we cannot appeal to utility in order to discern the one from the other: that gets matters upside down.

Sextus' apple argument is intriguing. One point at least is uncontestable: the observations recorded in (A) do not by themselves determine which, if any, of (B), (C) and (D) is the correct account of reality. The way the apple appears does not determine the way it really is. We might, however, still feel that we have some reason, over and above (A), for preferring one account or other of the apple's real nature. Sextus has not done enough to show that this feeling is unjustified. He has, it is true, mentioned one reason for preferring thesis (B), and he has given a reason for rejecting it. But his reason for rejecting the suggestion is weak – even if the reason for preferring (B) in the end does not stand up to scrutiny.

It may be that §99 is designed to destroy any hope of preferring one account of the apple over the others. Sextus says that 'if the senses do not apprehend external objects, the intellect is not able to apprehend them either (since its guides fail it)'. The point is this. As far as the evidence of the senses goes, we can proceed up to (A) and no further. The senses give us the appearances, but they cannot give us anything more. Thus if we are to proceed any further, it must be by way of the mind or intellect (for the senses and the mind together constitute the sum of our cognitive equipment). But the mind can only go where the senses lead it, for they are its guides. Hence the mind cannot proceed beyond (A) either.

The idea that the senses are the mind's guides occurs elsewhere in Sextus. It is a part of the empiricism which is an almost universal feature of Greek philosophy: dogmatists of every persuasion held that all our concepts, and all our knowledge of the external world, derive ultimately from sense-perception. The mind, whatever its combinatorial and inferential powers, can contribute no new material itself: it depends for its contents on the senses. We shall return to this important issue in our discussion of the Sixth Mode, where it arises again in a more elaborate form. For the present we simply observe that Sextus' brief assertion in §99 will carry little weight with any sophisticated dogmatist; for only an empiricism of an extraordinarily narrow kind could lead us to suppose that we can proceed no further in the explanation of appearances than merely recording their occurrence.

7 Circumstances

Sextus, *PH* I 100–17:

100   In order to end up with suspension of judgement even if we rest
the argument on any single sense or actually leave the senses
aside, we also adopt the fourth mode of suspension. This is the
mode that gets its name from circumstances, where by 'circumstances' we mean conditions. It is observed, we say, in natural or
unnatural states, in waking or sleeping, depending on age, on
moving or being at rest, on hating or loving, on being in need or
sated, on being drunk or sober, on anterior conditions, on being
confident or fearful, on being in distress or in a state of
enjoyment.

101   For example, objects impress us as dissimilar depending on
our being in a natural or an unnatural state, since people who are
delirious or divinely possessed think that they hear spirits, while
we do not; and similarly they often say that they grasp an
exhalation of storax or frankincense or the like, and many other
things, while we do not perceive them. The same water seems to
be boiling when poured on to inflamed places, but to us to be
lukewarm. The same cloak appears orange to people with a
blood-suffusion in the eye, but not to me; and the same honey
appears sweet to me, but bitter to people with jaundice.

102   If anyone says that it is the mixing of certain humours that
produces inappropriate appearances from existing objects in
people who are in an unnatural state, we should tell him that,
since healthy people too have mixed humours, it is possible that
these humours are making the external existing objects appear
different to the healthy, while they are by nature the way they

103 appear to people in so-called unnatural states. For to grant one lot
of humours, but not the other, the power of changing external
objects has an air of fiction. For, just as healthy people are in a
state natural for the healthy, but unnatural for the sick, so the sick

are in a state unnatural for the healthy but natural for the sick, so that they too are in a state which is, relatively, natural, and they too should be credited.

104 Different appearances come about depending on sleeping or waking. When we are awake, we view things differently from the way we do when asleep, and when asleep differently from the way we do when awake; so the existence or non-existence of the objects* becomes not absolute but relative – relative to being asleep or awake. It is likely, then, that when asleep we will see things which are unreal in waking life, not unreal once and for all. For they exist in sleep, just as the contents of waking life exist even though they do not exist in sleep.

105 Appearances differ depending on age. The same air seems cold to old men but mild to the young, the same colour appears faint to the elderly but intense to the young, and similarly the same sound seems to the former dim but to the latter clearly audible.

106 Those who differ in age are also affected dissimilarly depending on their choices and avoidances. Children, for example, are serious about balls and hoops, while the young choose other things, and old men yet others. From this is inferred that different appearances come about from the same existing objects depending on differences in age.

107 Objects appear dissimilar depending on moving or being at rest. Things which we see as still when we are stationary seem to us to move when we sail past them.

108 Depending on loving or hating: some people have an excessive revulsion against pork, while others consume it with great pleasure. Hence Menander said:

> How foul he appears even in his looks
> since he has become like this! What an animal!
> Doing no wrong actually makes us beautiful.
>
> [frag. 790 Koerte]

And many men who have ugly girl-friends think them most attractive.

109 Depending on being hungry or sated: the same food seems most pleasant to people who are hungry, but unpleasant to the sated.

Depending on being drunk or sober: things which we think shameful when sober do not appear shameful to us when we are drunk.

110   Depending on anterior conditions: the same wine appears sour to people who have just eaten dates or figs, but it seems to be sweet to people who have consumed nuts or chickpeas. And the bath-house vestibule warms people entering from outside, but chills people leaving if they wait around in it.

111   Depending on being afraid or confident: the same object seems fearful and dreadful to the coward, but not at all to someone bolder.

Depending on being in distress or in a state of enjoyment: the same objects are annoying to people in distress and pleasant to people who are enjoying themselves.

112   Since, therefore, there is so much anomaly depending on conditions, and since at different times people come to be in different conditions,* it is no doubt easy to say what each existing object appears to be like to each person, but not to say what it *is* like, since the anomalies are in fact undecidable.

For anyone who decides on them is either in some of the above conditions or in absolutely no condition at all. But to say that he is in no condition whatsoever (for example, neither healthy nor sick, neither moving nor at rest, of no particular age, and free from the other conditions) is perfectly silly. But if he is in some condition as he judges the appearances, he will be a part of the

113   dispute. And again he will not be an unbiassed judge of external existing objects because he will have been contaminated by the conditions he is in. So a waking person cannot compare the appearances of sleepers with those of people awake, or a healthy person those of the sick with those of the healthy; for we assent to what is present and affects us in the present rather than to what is not present.

114   And there is another reason why the anomalies among such appearances are undecidable. For anyone who prefers one appearance to another and one circumstance to another does so either without making a judgement and without proof, or making a judgement and offering a proof. But he can do so neither without these (for he will not be credible) nor with them.

For if he *judges* the appearances, he will certainly judge them by

115   means of a standard. Now he will say of this standard either that it is true or that it is false. If false, he will not be credible. But if he says it is true, then he will say that the standard is true either without proof or with proof. But if without proof, he will not be

credible. If with proof, he will certainly need the proof to be true; otherwise he will not be credible.

116 Then will he say that the proof he adopts to warrant the standard is true after judging it or without judging it? If he has not judged it, he will not be credible. But if he has judged it, clearly he will say that he has judged it by means of a standard – but we shall make investigations for a proof of that standard, and then for a standard for that proof. For a proof always requires a standard in order to be confirmed, and a standard always requires a proof in order to be shown to be true. A proof cannot be sound if there is no true standard there already, nor can a standard be true if a proof has not been already warranted.

117 And in this way both standards and proofs fall into the reciprocal mode in which both of them are found not to be credible: each of them waits for credit from the other* and so each is as lacking credibility as the other.

If, then, one cannot prefer one appearance to another either without a proof and a standard or with them, the different appearances that come about depending on different conditions will be undecidable. So suspension of judgement about the nature of external existing objects is introduced by way of this mode too.

Diogenes IX 82:

82 *Fourth* is the mode depending on conditions and common variations*: for example, health and disease, sleeping and waking, joy and sorrow, youth and old age, confidence and fear, need and repletion, hate and love, heating and chilling. Depending on breathing, depending on having one's channels blocked. So things experienced appear different depending on their kind of condition. For not even mad people are in a state which is contrary to nature – why them rather than us? For even we see the sun as stationary. When Theon of Tithorea, the Stoic, went to bed he used to walk about in his sleep. (And Pericles' slave on the roof-top.)

Philo 178–80:

178 But why mention facts like these? Each single one of us on his own, paradoxical as it is, undergoes thousands of shifts and changes in both body and soul, now choosing and now rejecting

things which themselves change not at all but retain the same natural constitution.

179   People do not usually have the same experiences when healthy and ill, when waking and sleeping, when young and old. Someone standing still gets appearances different from those of someone in motion, and the same goes for people who are confident or fearful, sad or joyful, loving or on the contrary hating.

180   But what need is there for long and wearisome speeches on the subject? In a word, every motion of body and soul, whether natural or unnatural*, becomes a cause of that unstable movement of apparent things which produces in us conflicting and discordant dreams.

Sextus introduces the Fourth Mode as the one depending on 'circumstances'. The Greek word he uses (*peristaseis*) normally refers to external circumstances, but he at once says that he means the word in the sense of 'conditions' (*diatheseis*), which are states of the observer rather than circumstances in which he observes. It is not clear why Sextus chooses the misleading word 'circumstances'.

Philo speaks neither of circumstances nor of conditions; instead, he refer to the fact that each of us 'undergoes thousands of shifts and changes in both body and soul'. Diogenes refers to 'conditions and common variations'. The word we translate as 'variation' (*parallagē*) sometimes means simply 'difference', but here it is better taken in the sense of 'change', so that Diogenes bases the mode on the 'conditions and common changes' which people experience.

Thus there seems to be a difference between Sextus on the one hand and Philo and Diogenes on the other. For Sextus, the oppositions that fall under the Fourth Mode should have the form:

(a) x appears F to people in condition C
      x appears F^* to people in condition C^*.

For Philo and Diogenes the oppositions take the form:

(b) x appears F to y when y is in condition C
      x appears F^* to y when y is in condition C^*.

Given (b), the oppositions are within the experience of a single individual, like the oppositions of the Third Mode. Given (a), the oppositions divide one observer from another, like the oppositions of the Second Mode.

Sextus' illustrations of the mode tend to support the suggestion that he has (a) in mind. All the same, the suggestion may well be wrong. For in §100 Sextus implies that the Fourth Mode stands to the Third as the Third does to the Second. The Second Mode collects oppositions *between* observers *within* one species; the Third Mode collects oppositions *between* senses *within* one individual; the Fourth, therefore, should collect oppositions *between* conditions *within* one sense: in different conditions the same thing appears different to the same sense of the same observer. And that is (b). (In §112 the text we translate refers unambiguously to *changes* in an individual's conditions. But one group of manuscripts presents a different reading which equally unambiguously refers to differences *between* individuals.) Thus despite the apparent difference between Sextus and the other two authors, it seems possible that our three sources intend to give us a uniform account of the Fourth Mode, one in which oppositions take the form (b).

The structure of the Fourth Mode is of the familiar pattern:

(1.4) x appears F to y when y is in condition C

(2.4) x appears F^* to y when y is in condition C^*

but

(3.4) we cannot prefer C to C^* or *vice versa*.

so that

(4) we suspend judgement as to whether x really is F or F^*.

The mode collects oppositions depending on 'conditions'. But what exactly is a 'condition'?

Sextus gives ten examples of types of condition, nine of the examples consisting of contrary pairs (awake/asleep, drunk/sober, etc.). Philo produces seven such pairs of conditions, six of them identical with six of Sextus' examples. Philo's seventh example, also found in Diogenes, is the pair healthy/sick. Sextus' first example is the pair natural/unnatural, which appears in neither of the other two sources. But Sextus' discussion in §§101–2 shows either that healthy/sick is thought of as a special case of natural/unnatural or even that Sextus' natural/unnatural is merely healthy/sick under a different name. (It is not quite clear whether *all* the examples in §§101–3 would have been classified by Sextus as diseases.) In either case, Sextus has not omitted the pair healthy/sick.

Sextus' fourth pair, found in Philo but not Diogenes, is moving/at rest. This shows how broadly we must take the notion of a condition. Conditions are not limited to dispositions (although the word *diathesis* is often translated as 'disposition'). Rather, a condition is any state *of the subject* (this distinguishes the Fourth Mode from its successors) which is *variable* (this distinguishes the Fourth Mode from the Second).

Sextus' list contains one odd item. His eighth condition is 'anterior condition', *prodiathesis*. It is clear from §110 what this means: wine may appear acid to me if I have just been eating Brie, mellow if I have just been eating filberts. Preconditions, however, do not come in pairs, like the other conditions, nor are they, properly speaking, *conditions* of the subject. Perhaps they were interpolated into the list (by Sextus himself?) because there was no better place for them in the modes.

The last two items in Diogenes' list, 'breathing' and 'having one's channels blocked', are also puzzling. Perhaps the reference is to the way things taste and smell differently to people with colds and catarrh? (Greek doctors talk frequently of something they call 'catarrh', though it is certainly not catarrh in our sense.) But all conjectures here are imponderable, and the text in any case is probably corrupt. Here, as often in Diogenes, we must (with a certain appropriateness) suspend judgement.

The same applies to two of Diogenes' illustrations. 'Theon the Stoic' is otherwise unknown. Diogenes is presumably referring to some anecdote about him, but it is not even certain what he is supposed to be doing: is he sleep-walking, or dreaming that he is walking, or falling asleep while walking? (The Greek leaves these options open in a way that no English translation can.) It is equally uncertain how Theon's story was thought to illustrate the Fourth Mode. And, once again, Diogenes' Greek text may be corrupt.

As for Diogenes' cryptic allusion to Pericles' slave on the roof-top, here we do have other sources of information:

Pericles, the leader of the Athenians, had a favourite slave. When he was engaged in building the temple on the Acropolis he crawled along the roof-top and fell off. He is said to have been cured by a herb which was revealed to Pericles by Athena in a dream – hence it came to be called parthenium and is assigned to that goddess. This is the slave whose image in cast bronze is the celebrated Tripe-roaster. (Pliny, *Natural History* XXII xx 44; cf. Plutarch, *Pericles* 13)

The story is charming, and you can still see on the Acropolis the pedestal of the statue which the grateful Pericles dedicated to Athena goddess of Health. But it is hard to imagine how the story provided material for the Fourth Mode.

The illustrations collected for this mode are, as usual, taken from earlier sources. It is tempting to suppose that they were originally assembled for a different purpose and only subsequently used for sceptical ends: many of them appear elsewhere in Sextus, at *PH* I 218–9 and at *M* VII 61–4, where he is discussing the fifth-century thinker Protagoras. Protagoras, he reports, says that

> men grasp different things at different times, depending on their different conditions. Someone who is in a natural condition apprehends those things existing in matter which are capable of appearing to those in a natural condition, and similarly for someone in an unnatural condition. And the same argument applies to ages, to sleeping or waking, and to each kind of condition. (*PH* I 218–19).

Sextus is at pains to point out how Protagoreanism differs from Pyrrhonism. (His account of the difference is odd and unconvincing.) Nonetheless, the Protagorean material is the same as the material of the Fourth Mode, and we suspect that it was first collected by Protagoras and his followers.

In a celebrated passage in the *First Meditation* Descartes draws sceptical conclusions from the contrast between sleeping and waking.

> Here I must remember that I am a man and hence have the habit of sleeping and of imagining in my dreams the same things – or sometimes less realistic things – that madmen do when they are awake. How often have I dreamed in the night that I was here, dressed, in front of the fire, although I was in fact lying undressed in bed? . . . When I reflect on these thoughts, I see so clearly that there are no conclusive signs or certain marks by which one can distinguish sharply between waking and sleeping that I am absolutely astonished.

Descartes wonders if he is awake or asleep. It *appears* to him that he is sitting in front of the fire; but is that a dream-appearance or a waking vision? Descartes' puzzle is ancient. Epictetus, in a short essay against scepticism, picks it out for particular scorn:

> 'Do you apprehend that you are awake?' 'No', he says; 'for I don't do so when in dreams it appears to me that I am awake.' 'Then does this appearance differ from that in no way at all?' 'In no way.' Do I go on talking to him? What fire or what steel do I apply to him to make him realise that he has become a corpse? (*Discourses* I v 6–7)

Aristotle mentions the puzzle (*Metaphysics* 1011a7), and it is rehearsed by Plato:

> SOCRATES: Do you recall the following sort of dispute, which arises especially about sleeping and waking?

THEAETETUS: What do you mean?

SOCRATES: One of the kind I think you've often heard people arguing about: what evidence could we produce if someone were to ask us now whether we were asleep and dreaming everything that we have in mind, or awake and talking to each other in waking life?

THEAETETUS: Indeed, Socrates, it is difficult to see what evidence one should point to; everything corresponds, just like counterparts. The discussion we have just had could actually have been one we seemed in our sleep to be having with each other; and when in a dream we seem to be describing dreams, the likeness between them is extraordinary.

SOCRATES: So you see that it's not difficult to start a dispute, since there is even dispute over whether we are awake or asleep.

(*Theaetetus*, 158 B–C)

Socrates goes on to remark that 'the same argument applies to illness and to madness' (158D).

Plato's discussion of sleeping and dreaming takes place in a Protagorean context, and it is clear that these Protagorean musings are at the origins of the tradition on which Sextus is drawing. But Sextus' puzzle and Plato's puzzle are distinct. Plato, like Descartes, wonders how we can tell whether we are asleep or awake, or how we can distinguish between sleeping appearances and waking appearances. (Descartes seems to imply that *if* he could tell whether or not he was awake, *then* he could judge whether or not he was really sitting in front of the fire.) Sextus, on the other hand, tacitly assumes that we can distinguish between sleeping appearances and waking appearances, and he argues that even if we know that we are awake, we cannot tell whether or not we are really sitting in front of the fire. For why should we prefer waking appearances to sleeping appearances?

Sextus' puzzle is referred to by Aristotle (*Metaphysics* 1010b 8–11: above, p. 12), who implicitly distinguishes it from Plato's puzzle. The two puzzles are set side by side by Galen:

Some people say that it is unclear whether we are awake or asleep, and whether we are mad or sane. And if it should be conceded that *this* is clear, they say it is unclear which of the two groups is closer to the truth – the wakers or the sleepers? The sane or the mad?' (*Commentary on Hippocrates' On Diet in Acute Diseases* XV 449K)

Some people, according to Galen, pose Plato's puzzle; if that puzzle is solved they proceed to pose Sextus' puzzle.

The main difficulty in the Fourth Mode comes at step (3). Why can we not prefer *C* to *C**, at least in some cases? We get no answer from

Diogenes or Philo, who just set out the illustrative material and assume that suspension of judgement follows uncontroversially once we pay attention to the oppositions. Sextus, however, offers two arguments to show that the disagreements between different conditions are undecidable.

The first argument (§§112–13) is clear in outline, though puzzling in detail. If you are to judge between C and C*, you must yourself be at the time either in *some* or in *no* condition. Obviously, you cannot be in no condition. That is, you yourself must be in C or in C* (or perhaps in some other condition from the same range): you must be awake or asleep (or half-asleep); you must be young or old (or middle-aged), since you must be of *some* age. Conditions come in sets (characteristically in pairs), and everyone must be in *some* condition from each set, and in *no more than one* condition from each set. However, if, being in condition C, you yet claim to judge between C and C*, you are *parti pris*. For you are a judge in your own case; and that is improper.

We have already come across the impropriety of judging your own case. But here Sextus adds a new point: '‹you are› not an unbiassed judge of external existing objects because ‹you› will have been contaminated by the conditions ‹you› are in'. In other words, you are not merely *parti pris*, in the sense that to you, who are in C, x appears F; you are actually *biassed*, in the sense that condition C 'contaminates' your judgement and makes you favour x's appearing F. 'So a waking person cannot compare the appearances of sleepers with those of people awake . . . for we assent to what is present and affects us in the present . . . ' Our bias is shown by the way we actually assent to things: when in C we assent to the appearances that C currently produces, rather than to appearances produced at other times and places by C*. So 'we cannot compare' the appearances. (To say we 'cannot' is to say that we are not in a position to: we do, of course, have the *capacity* to make a comparison.)

Surely Sextus is wrong. Maybe the sick, for example, are *parti pris* when it comes to judging between F and F*; but that is no reason for us to think that they are always biassed. It is just not true that we always 'assent to what is present'. If I have a cold, and know that I do, then I prefer the judgement of other wine-tasters to my own; and in general we recognise the 'conditions' we are in, admit that they affect the way things appear to us, and defer to the judgement of those in other, 'natural' conditions. Of course we may not be *justified* in so doing; but Sextus is not directly concerned with justification, and his claim that we always prefer present appearances is refuted by the simple fact that we can and do prefer C* to C while ourselves being in C.

Does Sextus' argument perhaps work for certain special conditions? In particular, does it work for sleepers and wakers? Unlike the sick and the healthy, or the old and the young, sleepers and wakers do not in general defer to one another's judgements. So here, perhaps, we do find that those in condition C always prefer C to C^*.

It is surely true – bizarre possibilities apart – that the waking prefer their own appearances to those of dreamers. If the lawn looks long and shaggy to me in the daytime but I then dream that it is short and neat, I put this down to wish-fulfilment: I do not seriously wonder if perhaps the grass does not really need mowing. But our preference, even if it is always in favour of the waking, need not be put down to bias; for we do have excellent reasons to prefer waking appearances to appearances in dreams, reasons based on comparative coherence and so on.

Do dreamers conversely always prefer their own appearances to those of the waking? Some philosophers would claim that the question is misguided; for those who are dreaming are asleep, and if you are genuinely asleep then you cannot be thinking of or judging anything; so in particular you cannot judge your dreams against waking visions. But it is hard to support this claim by convincing argument: common sense allows that sometimes we make judgements in our sleep – what else, after all, is the familiar experience of saying to yourself, during a nightmare, 'Don't worry, it's only a dream'? But if sleepers can judge at all, then surely – as this same example suggests – they may sometimes judge that their dream appearances are inferior to waking experience.

Sextus' second argument fills §§114–17. It has the form of a nested sequence of dilemmas. Let us consider a concrete instance of the argument. 'Many men who have ugly girl-friends think them most attractive' (§108). Suppose, then, that Jack, while he is in love with Jill, finds her beautiful; but that when the passion passes she appears plain to him. And suppose that Jeremy, having considered these two appearances of Jack's, cynically prefers the latter: he prefers Jack sober to Jack in love.

Now according to Sextus, Jeremy prefers sober Jack's appearance *either* (1) without judging Jill to be plain, *or else* (2) after making a judgement. Alternative (1) is plainly absurd: Jeremy will, as Sextus says, not be 'credible'.

But if (2) is the case, then Jeremy must be using some standard to judge by, and he will say *either* (A) that his standard is false *or* (B) that it is true. Alternative (A) is patently absurd. (We might wonder why Jeremy must use a *standard* to judge by. But the thesis that if you judge you judge by a standard is meant by Sextus to be trivially true: a standard is simply whatever it is that you judge by, the grounds, whatever they may be, on which your judgement rests. The tautologous nature of the thesis is clear in Greek, where the word for 'standard', *kritērion*, is related to the verb 'judge', *krinein*.)

But if (B) is the case, then *either* (i) Jeremy offers no proof that his criterion is true *or* (ii) he offers a proof. Again, (i) is absurd: Jeremy will not be worthy of credit.

But if (ii) is the case, then *either* (a) Jeremy does not judge the proof *or* (b) he does. And (a) is absurd. But if (b), then *either* (I) he gives no proof of his standard of judgement, *or* (II) he gives a proof. And (I) is absurd, while (II) gives rise to a circularity of reasoning.

The structure of this argument is best shown in a diagram:

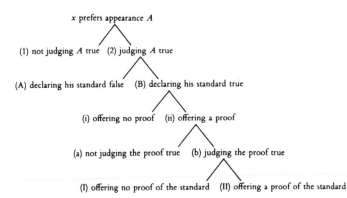

Here, each left-hand branch is absurd; that is to say, if *x* opts for any left-hand branch, his claim has no force on our credence. And the final right-hand branch is also absurd, for it involves *x* in circular reasoning.

This argument is similar, in its salient features, to many of the sceptical arguments in the later books of *PH*. It explicitly appeals to one of the Five Modes of Agrippa, and can usefully be described as Agrippan in form. It is remarkable for its complexity, for the care with which Sextus articulates it, and for the high level of abstraction at which it proceeds.

The carefulness of Sextus' exposition could, it is true, be faulted at one point. For it is not clear that the final right-hand branch, option II, involves any circular reasoning. Admittedly, option II requires us to give a proof of a standard of a proof of a standard; but the two proofs, like the two standards, are distinct from one another and do not import circularity. But if the right-hand branch in the diagram does not involve circularity, it surely falls foul of another of Agrippa's Modes; for it leads to an infinite regress.

The complexity of Sextus' argument may well appear unnecessary. Why not offer a much simpler set of considerations? They might go somewhat as follows: 'Either x gives a proof for his preference or he merely asserts it. If the latter, we are under no obligation to credit him. If the former, either he proves that the proof is sound or he does not. If the latter, we are under no obligation to credit him. If the former, he falls into circularity (or rather, into an infinite regress of proofs).'

The abstract level of the argument is also odd. The argument is not tailored to the specific features of the Fourth Mode, for it does not turn on the fact that x is attempting to prefer one *condition* to another. It is not even tailored to the general structure of the Ten Modes, for it does not turn on the fact that x is judging among *appearances*. Indeed, the argument works with equal force against any judgement whatsoever. For we may say, quite generally, that if anyone judges that p, then either he offers a proof that p or he merely asserts that p; and so on. This is indeed a striking characteristic of many of the Agrippan arguments Sextus uses: if they work at all, they work against any judgement whatsoever, not merely against the particular judgement for which they happen to be invoked.

Thus to assess the argument of §§114–17 is in effect to assess one of the most general arguments for scepticism. In a simpler form the argument was known to Aristotle (and to Plato before him), and it has survived to reappear in numerous sceptical contexts. Here we can only look very superficially at some of the issues the argument raises.

The simplest form of the Agrippan argument, expressed schematically and with full generality, looks like this. 'Suppose you assert that p_1 (whatever p_1 may be). Am I to credit you? If you *merely* assert that p_1, then I have no reason at all to credit you, for you might just as well have asserted that not-p_1. Suppose, then, that you give a reason for your assertion that p_1, and do so by asserting that p_2. Now that gives me a reason to credit you *only if* I am to credit you when you assert that p_2. If you *merely* assert that p_2, then I have no reason to credit you, and hence no reason to accept that p_1. If p_2 is in fact *the same* as p_1, then again I have no reason to credit you – you are arguing in a circle. So you must give a further reason, p_3, for your assertion that p_2. But then the same problem arises over p_3: either you merely assert it, or it is identical with p_1 or p_2, or else you give a further reason for it. Thus Agrippa offers you three options, each of which is allegedly untenable: your claim that p_1 *either* rests ultimately on a mere assertion, *or* involves circular reasoning, *or* invokes a never-ending succession of reasons.'

The third option has commended itself to few philosophers. How could we possibly express or articulate or even be aware of an infinite succession of reasons?

The second option has occasionally been accepted. For some philosophers have held that there need be nothing disreputable in a circle of reasons. If the circle is large enough, the beliefs which constitute it may indeed support one another: taken as a collection, our beliefs cohere, and a coherent collection of beliefs is all we can or should aspire to. The difficulty in this is that for every coherent collection of beliefs there can be found another coherent collection incompatible with it; and we have no way of choosing among internally coherent and mutually incompatible collections.

Most philosophers who have hoped to evade scepticism have agreed with Agrippa that both infinite regresses and circularities must be rejected; they have accepted the first of the three options, holding that some beliefs may with propriety rest on 'mere assertion'. Or rather, they have held that some beliefs have a very special status: we are justified or warranted in maintaining them even though we can cite no reasons and give no grounds for them. These are basic or fundamental beliefs. In an ancient metaphor, which has been reused by epistemologists of every age, they constitute the *foundations* of our knowledge or of the structure of our beliefs.

What sort of beliefs are basic in this way? Some philosophers have given a psychological characterisation of basic beliefs: they are things which are 'self-evident' or 'intuitively obvious' or 'immediately given'. Sometimes, but not always, they are supposed to be reports of our own mental experiences. Thus A. J. Ayer remarks that the statements of basic beliefs

characterize some present state of the speaker, or some present content of his experience. The sort of example that we are offered is 'I feel a headache' or 'this looks to me to be red' or 'this is louder than that', where 'this' and 'that' refer to sounds that I am actually hearing, or, more ambitiously, 'It seems to me that this is a table' or 'I seem to remember that such and such an event occurred.' (*The Problem of Knowledge* (1956), p. 53)

Ayer observes that such statements are held to be epistemologically fundamental; for 'I cannot be unsure whether I feel a headache, nor can I think that I feel a headache when I do not.'

Other thinkers have located basic beliefs not in our immediate experience but rather in our ultimate scientific hypotheses. In an influential chapter of the *Posterior Analytics* (I 3), Aristotle discusses the sceptical argument we are considering. He claims that there are certain 'primary' truths or 'first principles' which we must and may accept even though they themselves rest on no reasons. But they are not – or at any rate need not be – *obvious* truths. Rather, they are the truths which *explain* all other truths. When we study a science we see that some of its component propositions explain others; and we find that some special propositions are fundamentally explanatory in that they furnish, directly or indirectly, explanations for all the other propositions of the science while they are not in themselves amenable to explanation. Such propositions, in Aristotle's view, are proper objects of basic beliefs.

Yet other thinkers have looked neither to immediate experience nor to scientific explanation but rather to the practical context in which our beliefs operate and to the role they play in our private and communal lives. Wittgenstein allows that 'at the foundation of every well-founded belief lies a belief that is unfounded' (*On Certainty* §253). But he claims that 'the end is not an unfounded presupposition – it is an unfounded way of acting' (§110). For 'my *life* consists in my being content to accept many things' (§344). The basic beliefs, on this view, are those which, in one way or another, are constitutive of our way of life. They form a miscellaneous collection. Thus Wittgenstein says that

we know, with the same certainty with which we believe *any* mathematical proposition, how the letters 'A' and 'B' are pronounced, what the colour of human blood is called, that other humans have blood and call it 'blood'. (*On Certainty* §340)

The dogmatists have taken seriously the challenge thrown down by the Modes of Agrippa. Their answers to the challenge have differed greatly – a fact which the Pyrrhonists will seize upon. The positions to which we have just alluded have been described and supported with great subtlety and sophistication: it is evident that Agrippa's challenge, despite its highly abstract form, raises deep philosophical issues and is not a factitious quibble.

In §102 Sextus considers the suggestion that 'it is the mixing of certain humours that produces inappropriate appearances from existing objects in people who are in an unnatural state'. The suggestion, which we have already met in connexion with the Second Mode, amounts to this: if x appears F in C, then x is really F provided that C is a natural condition. The walls may appear pink to you if you have bloodshot eyes (cf. §44); but they really are the colour they appear to people in natural conditions.

This is an attractive suggestion, and it clearly had some currency in ancient debates over scepticism. Sextus discusses it elsewhere (*PH* I 102–3, II 54–6, *M* VII 62–3). Diogenes alludes to it in §82, Philo, probably, in §180. The suggestion has also proved popular among modern dogmatists. In an essay on 'Common Sense and Physics' Michael Dummett refers to the idea that

the use of expressions for observational qualities is properly described by saying that their application depends upon the judgements we make when the observation is conducted 'under normal conditions'. The idea is that we learn to discount judgements made under special conditions known to give rise to error: it has become a cliché, in philosophical discussions of perception, to say that an object has those observational qualities it is judged to have by normal observers under normal conditions. Thus, someone who has been handling ice will overestimate the temperature of things he touches; while anyone is liable to misjudge the colour of a surface if he sees it under, say, a sodium vapour lamp. (*Perception and Identity*, ed. G. F. Macdonald (1979), p. 24)

The idea which Dummett here describes is not exactly the same as the idea which Sextus discusses: Dummett talks of 'normal' rather than 'natural' conditions, and he is concerned with the general conditions in which observation takes place and not simply with the condition or state of the observer. But Dummett's idea is clearly a generalisation of the one Sextus knows. (Note, too, that Dummett's example of the ice-handler is a perfect illustration of the effect of what Sextus calls 'anterior condition'.)

How did the ancient sceptics react to this idea? Nothing can be extracted from the allusion in Philo. Diogenes is characteristically cryptic. He *appears* to deny that the distinction between what is natural and what is unnatural has any ground in reality. 'Not even mad people are in a state which is contrary to nature – why them rather than us?' You cannot dismiss the appearances of lunatics on the grounds that lunacy is unnatural or abnormal. For perfectly 'normal' people have lunatic impressions – we all say that the sun is stationary.

What are we to make of this? Perhaps Diogenes is denying that there is any clear boundary separating the mad from the sane (or the healthy from the ill, the young from the old). Sanity declines into madness by slow degrees, so that the neat division into two classes suggested by the notions of normality and abnormality is a fiction. If this is Diogenes' point, surely it is true: the pairs mad/sane, young/old, and the like do not divide people into classes with the precision exhibited by the division of, for example, numbers into odd/even and prime/ composite. It is not clear, however, that the point has any sceptical force. The advocate of the normal and the natural will agree that 'normal' and 'natural' are vague terms without conceding that we cannot distinguish the normal from the abnormal. Even if 'sane' and 'mad' are vague terms, we do not infer that nobody is sane and nobody mad, or that we cannot tell of anyone whether they are mad or sane. At *PH* II 54–6 Sextus offers two arguments against the suggestion that we should prefer the 'natural' appearances. First, 'if you say this without proof you will not be credited; and you will not possess a proof that is true and judged, for the reasons we have given'. This is a concise application of the Agrippan style of argument. We need not discuss it again. Secondly, Sextus remarks that even if we were to allow that natural appearances are preferable, we should not be out of the wood; 'for sight, say, even when it is in a natural state, says that the same tower is now round, now square ...'. If we prefer the natural, and so evade the Fourth Mode, there are other oppositions to encounter – and Sextus explicitly refers to 'what I have already said about the modes of suspension of judgement'.

The argument at *PH* I 102–3 is different. It falls into two parts. In §102 Sextus urges that if the constitution of someone in an *unnatural* state affects and confounds his appearances, so too may the constitution of someone in a *natural* state. The point is this: being in an unnatural state will not in itself suffice to explain why someone's appearances are of a certain sort. Rather, there must be something about that state (the particular mixture of the humours, for example) which interferes with and perverts the appearances. But if the humours of unnatural people affect their appearances, surely the humours of natural people will affect theirs. If we reject unnatural appearances, this can only be because they are confounded by unnatural humours. But once we allow that the state of people's bodies affects the way things appear to them, it is arbitrary and implausible to suppose that only unnatural states have a distorting effect.

From its opening words, we should suppose that §103 continues the argument in §102. It is preferable, however, to take the sentence 'For, just as healthy people ...' to introduce a new argument. What is 'natural' for anything, Sextus implies, depends upon what that thing is: being sick is not natural for a healthy person, or perhaps for a human; but it is natural for a sick person. Being healthy, conversely, is natural for the healthy, though unnatural for the sick.

This suggestion may well seem sophistical. On the one hand, it seems to trivialise the whole notion of what is 'natural'. For surely *every* state will turn out to be 'natural' (and also 'unnatural') since in general the state *S* will be natural for those in state *S*, and unnatural for those not in state *S*. On the other hand, the suggestion seems to be an *ignoratio elenchi*. For we are being invited by the dogmatists to prefer not what is natural *tout court*, but what is natural *to humans*. Certainly, being sick is natural to sick people; but it is unnatural to humans, and since it is *human* nature we are preferring, we shall prefer a healthy to a sick condition.

But we need not construe Sextus' argument in this way. A better interpretation can be produced if we compare a passage in the treatise *On the Best Medical School*, which our manuscripts falsely ascribe to Galen.

Natural symptoms are very similar to unnatural ones. For the same things are natural to some people and unnatural to others – e.g. an unnatural black skin is similar to a natural one; it is unnatural for us, natural for Indians. And unnatural shapes are similar to natural: different people are by nature differently jointed; a sharp nose and hollow eyes are fatal symptoms for some people, but to others these same things are natural; motion and rest if they occur voluntarily are natural, if involuntarily unnatural. (I 178K)

This text, like *PH* I 103, indicates that what is natural for a thing depends on what that thing is; but it does not suggest the trivialising view that every state is 'natural' to something or other.

How, then, can we escape the trivialisation? The ancient view was perhaps the following. To say that *S* 'is natural' is always elliptical: states are natural *for things of a determined type*. The locution we need, then, is '*S* is natural for members of class *c*.' But not any term may be substituted for '*c*' – the set of one-legged men, say, does not form a class of the appropriate sort, nor does the set of four-leaved clovers. The classes must be 'natural' classes, in other words, classes whose members occur naturally. ('Naturally' now turns up in the *definiens* as well as in the *definiendum*. But this does not produce circularity: we can perfectly well define natural *states* in terms of *classes* that occur naturally.)

How does this apply to Sextus' argument? First, the 'conditions' which the Fourth Mode discusses must all count as constituting 'natural' classes, so that in these cases Sextus may correctly speak of what is 'natural' for the old, or for the healthy, or for those asleep. (The pseudo-Galenic treatise notes that 'the denseness of old men is natural for them, unnatural for children; the looseness of children is natural for them, unnatural for old men': I 179K. Ages are thus taken to constitute natural classes.) Secondly, given the propriety of such talk of 'nature', Sextus can ask why his opponents pick on what is natural *for humans* as their yardstick of truth. No doubt some things are natural for humans, others not. But some states which are natural for humans are unnatural for, say, old men; and some states which are unnatural for humans are natural for, say, sleeping humans. Why pick on humans as the preferred class? If the opponent replies that there is a pre-established harmony between the world and *human* organs in their *humanly* natural states, Sextus will recall that he has already, in §98, scouted that suggestion.

Sextus has thus pointed to two difficulties in the dogmatists' appeal to natural or normal conditions: their appeal presupposes, arbitrarily, that only unnatural or abnormal conditions affect an observer's appearances; and they cannot give grounds for preferring one sort of nature to any other. We might add a further, related difficulty. Michael Dummett, in the paper to which we referred earlier, puts it as follows:

> Only brief reflection is required in order to reveal that the whole terminology of 'normal conditions' involves a crude oversimplification. It is a well known fact that a piece of metal, being a much better conductor, feels much colder to the touch than a piece of wood when they are both at room temperature. Are we, then, to say that a thermometer records real – i.e. observational – temperature inaccurately? If not, what are the 'normal conditions' under which we perceive the two temperatures of a piece of metal? Common experience familiarises us with the phenomenon of resolution, as when, in driving, a distant blur resolves itself into separate street lights. But what are the 'normal conditions' for viewing an object the surface of which appears to the naked eye, however close, to be uniformly coloured, but resolves into bits under magnification? What are 'normal conditions' for viewing the Milky Way? Or for viewing the sun, an oxyacetylene torch or a nuclear explosion? ('Common Sense and Physics', p. 25)

In §104 Sextus suggests that when asleep we see things which are 'unreal in waking life, not unreal once and for all'. If x appears F in C and F^* in C^*, then we should infer that x is neither F nor F^* simply but rather F-in-C and F^*-in-C^*. The existence of oppositions, in short, suggests a relativistic conclusion: things are not F in themselves, but are F in relation to C. Sextus deals explicitly with relativity in the Eighth Mode; but since relativism also rears its head outside the Eighth Mode – we have already touched on it in connexion with the First Mode – it will be useful to make a few remarks here about the relation between scepticism and relativism.

Aulus Gellius, in his brief account of scepticism, reports that the Pyrrhonists hold that

> absolutely everything that affects the human senses is relative. That means that there is nothing at all which exists in its own right or which has its own power and nature: everything is referred to something else and appears such as its

appearance is while it is appearing, i.e. such as it is made in our senses to which it has arrived and not such as it is in itself from which it has set out. (*Attic Nights* XI v 7–8)

According to Gellius, the sceptics are all relativists. The same point is made in an ancient commentary on Plato's *Theaetetus*. The commentary, part of which is preserved on papyrus, is anonymous: it probably dates from the first century BC and is the work of a Platonist philosopher. A passage from it is worth quoting at length:

> The Pyrrhonists say that everything is relative, inasmuch as nothing exists in its own right but everything relative to other things. Neither shapes nor sounds nor objects of taste or smell or touch nor any other object of perception has a character of its own. For otherwise things that are the same would not affect us differently depending on their intervals and the things observed together with them – as we are marked differently by the sea depending on the state of the air. Nor do our sense-organs possess a substance of their own; for otherwise animals would not be affected differently – as goats take pleasure in vine-shoots and pigs in mud while humans object to both. From the objects of perception they move to reason, urging that this too is relative; for different people assent in different ways, and the same people change and do not stand by it. (Col. 63)

There are many echoes of the modes in this passage. But the commentator's general argument is just this: the Pyrrhonists are relativists.

Gellius and the commentator both assimilate scepticism to relativism. The assimiliation is easy to make – indeed, in a loose sense of the term 'sceptic' everyone will agree that relativists are sceptics. Moreover, the assimilation has some grounding in the Pyrrhonist texts: Sextus occasionally makes relativistic remarks, and although he gives himself the opportunity to distinguish relativism from scepticism he does not take it. (Discussing Protagoras, Sextus says that 'he introduces relativity, and so he seems to have something in common with the Pyrrhonians' (*PH* I 217). Sextus is at pains to argue that Protagoras was *not* a Pyrrhonian; but he conspicuously fails to say that the introduction of relativity is not a sceptical move.)

Nonetheless, the assimilation is wholly mistaken. We must get the matter clear even if the Pyrrhonists themselves did not. Suppose that your coat appears white to me today, but that tomorrow I get a black eye and your coat appears orange (*PH* I 101). A *sceptic* is led to suspend judgement about the colour of the cloak. That is to say, he holds *first* that the coat really is in itself white or orange (or some other colour); and *secondly* that he cannot tell what colour it is. His scepticism consists precisely in the fact that there is something there to be known which he is not in a position to know. A *relativist* does not suspend judgement. He holds, *first*, that your coat is not in itself white or orange (or any other colour) but rather that it is white relative to those with normal eyes, orange relative to those with black eyes, and so on. And he holds *secondly* that he can tell all there is to tell about colours: he can tell that the coat is, say, orange relative to those with black eyes – and there is nothing else to tell about its colour.

Let us now generalise the point. Take any opposition of the form:

(1) x appears F in S
(2) x appears F^* in S^*.

Sceptics suppose that x really is F or F^*; but they cannot tell which. Relativists infer that x is neither F nor F^*: it is F in S and F^* in S^* – as they can easily tell.

Relativism, far from being assimilable to scepticism, is actually incompatible with it. For relativists *deny* that there is anything to be known about x which they do not know: they know that x is F in S, F^* in S^* – and there is nothing more than that to be known about x, F, and F^*. They are not sceptics, for they deny that there is anything to be sceptical about. Where the sceptic finds matters on which he must suspend judgement, they find no matter at all.

We have laboured this point partly because relativism and scepticism are persistently confused, partly because relativism often seems to us a correct alternative to scepticism. Consider an easy case. Mud appears pleasant to pigs, unpleasant to humans. The sceptic finds a puzzle here, and claims that he cannot tell whether mud is really pleasant or unpleasant. The relativist finds no puzzle: mud is pleasant for pigs, unpleasant for humans – and that is all there is to it. The relativist is surely right: scepticism about 'real' pleasantness in this case is silly.

Other cases are harder. Relativism is not *always* the right response, and in many cases it is a difficult and controversial question whether relativism is true. Nor is relativism always a *trivial* response. Take colours, for example. Many philosophers take a relativistic view of colours. But some people will resist the suggestion that rubies are not red in themselves or by nature but only red relative to normal human observers. However that may be, and whether we decide for or against relativism in any particular case, we must recognise that the relativist is the sceptic's enemy, not his ally, and that victory for relativism is defeat for scepticism.

8 Places and Positions

Sextus, *PH* I 118–23:

118   The fifth argument is the one depending on positions and intervals and places – for depending on each of these the same objects appear different.

For example, the same colonnade appears foreshortened when seen from one end, but completely symmetrical when seen from the middle. The same boat appears from a distance small and stationary, but from close at hand large and in motion. The same tower appears from a distance round, but from close at hand

119 square. These depend on intervals.

Depending on places: lamplight appears dim in sunlight but bright in the dark. The same oar appears bent in water, but straight when out of it. Eggs appear soft in the bird but hard in the air. Lyngurion appears liquid inside the lynx, but hard in the air. Coral appears soft in the sea, but hard in the air. And sound appears different when produced in a pipe, in a flute, or simply in the air.

120   Depending on positions: the same picture when laid down appears flat, but when put at a certain angle seems to have recesses and projections. Doves' necks appear different in colour depending on the different ways they turn them.

121   Since, then, all apparent things are observed in some place and from some interval and in some position, and each of these produces a great deal of variation in appearances, as we have suggested, we shall be forced to arrive at suspension of judgement by these modes too.*

For anyone wishing to give preference to some of these

122 appearances over others will be attempting the impossible. If he makes his declaration simply and without proof, he will not be credible. But if he wants to use a proof, then if he says the proof is false, he will overturn himself, and if he says the proof is true, he

will be required to give a proof of its being true, and another
proof of that, since it too has to be true, and so *ad infinitum*. But it
123 is impossible to establish infinitely many proofs. And so he will
not be able to prefer one appearance to another with a proof
either. But if no-one can decide among the above appearances
either without proof or with proof, suspension of judgement is
inferred: we are no doubt able to say what each thing appears to
be like given this position or that interval or this place, but we are
not able, for the above reasons, to declare what it is like in its
nature.

Diogenes IX 85–6:

Seventh is the mode depending on distances, kinds of position,
places and occupants of places. According to this mode, things
that seem big appear small, square things appear round, level
things appear to have projections, straight things appear bent,
pale things appear coloured. For instance, the sun, depending on
its interval from us, appears a foot across.* Mountains appear
airy* and smooth from a distance, but rugged from close at hand.
86 Again, the sun as it rises has a quite different appearance from the
sun at its zenith. The same body* has a different appearance in a
thicket and on open ground. A picture appears different depending on its kind of position, and a dove's neck depending on the
way it turns. So, since it is not possible to perceive these things
apart from places and positions*, it is not known what their
nature is.

Philo 181–3:

181   The instability of appearances depends in no small measure on
the positions, the intervals and the places in which things are
located.
182   Do we not see fish in the sea appearing larger than they are in
reality when they swim with their fins stretched out? Oars too,
however straight they are, come to look bent under water.
183 Distant objects produce false appearances and usually deceive
our minds: lifeless things are on occasion assumed to be living
and living things on the contrary to be lifeless; again, stationary
things are taken to be moving and moving things to be
stationary, approaching things to be receding and departing

things to be advancing, extremely long things to be very short and angular things to be round. And plain sight produces a thousand other distortions which no-one in his senses would endorse as being firm.

With the Fifth Mode, which depends on 'positions and intervals and places', Sextus turns from the observer to the observed. In connexion with this mode Philo remarks that 'plain sight produces a thousand other distortions' (§183), and his remark suggests an explanation of the order of the modes: even if we manage to rebut the first four modes and are able to settle on some favoured observer or sense ('plain sight', for example), there are still features of the appearances independent of the observer which will generate suspension of judgement. The very best of observers, could we find one, would still discover that his appearances gave rise to oppositions of the kind the sceptic collects.

The three elements in Sextus' version of this mode – position, interval, place – are present in Philo's version also. Diogenes adds a fourth element, 'occupants of places', but this is hardly intelligible except as a misleading gloss on the third element. Instead of 'intervals' (*diastēmata*), Diogenes has 'distances' (*apostaseis*). (Aristocles refers to 'distances' (*apostēmata*) too, so Diogenes' text is unlikely to be a mere mistake or a corruption.) The 'intervals' in question are spatial intervals between observer and observed. The variations to which the mode appeals usually turn upon the *size* of the intervals, i.e. upon 'distances'. But they do not all do so; indeed, in Sextus' first illustration of 'intervals' (§118) a colonnade is said to look different from different *angles*, not from different *distances*. (The Greek for 'colonnade' is *stoa*: no doubt the Pyrrhonists found it amusing to take the example from the meeting-place of their main dogmatist opponents, the Stoics.) Thus Diogenes' use of the word 'distance' is slightly inaccurate.

By the 'position' of an object Sextus intends its posture: the 'position' of a picture, or of a dove's neck (§120), is not a matter of *where* it is but rather of how it is posed or arranged. As an object is, say, rotated, its appearance will alter, even though it remains, in one sense, in the same position. By the 'place' of an object Sextus intends to refer to its spatial context or background. Oars appear different depending on their 'place', that is to say on their physical surroundings: if the tide ebbs and leaves the oared boat stranded, the oars will look different, even though they remain, in one sense, in the same place.

Sextus clearly and explicitly distinguishes the three elements of the mode, dealing first with intervals (§118), then with places (§119) and finally with positions (§120). Philo's discussion is equally clearly marked out, though he adopts a different order from Sextus and is not concerned to make the distinctions explicit. Diogenes lists eleven illustrations of the mode: the three elements are not separated and the ordering of the illustrations seems to be capricious.

We may ask why Sextus treats the Fifth Mode as a *single* mode. For in fact the 'oppositions' which the mode collects fall into three different groups:

> (1.5a) x appears F at interval I
> (2.5a) x appears F^* at interval I^*
> (1.5b) x appears F in background B
> (2.5b) x appears F^* in background B^*
> (1.5c) x appears F in posture P
> (2.5c) x appears F^* in posture P^*

The Tenth Mode is similar to the Fifth in containing several distinct elements; but there, as we shall see, Sextus has good reason for assembling the elements under a single mode. It is sometimes said that the Fifth Mode deals specifically with the so-called 'primary' qualities (shape, size, motion, number); and were that true it might provide a thematic unity for the mode. But it is not true. One of Diogenes' illustrations of the effects of distance concerns colour, a 'secondary' quality: from afar, mountains appear 'airy' or cloud-coloured. And the most celebrated illustration of the effects of position – the case of the dove's neck, which was first invoked by Protagoras – again introduces the 'secondary' quality of colour. We find no unity in the Fifth Mode, and it might properly be regarded as a set of three distinct modes. Perhaps Sextus has this in mind when he observes, in §39, that he does not vouch for the number of the modes (see above, p. 25).

How does the mode induce scepticism? Both Sextus and Diogenes remark that we can never observe anything *apart from* a background, a position, and an interval: we always observe objects from some interval or other, and the objects themselves are always in some posture or other and in some place or other. That is clearly true, and it is reasonable to infer that we never get any bald appearances of things. Whenever x appears F to us, it appears F at interval I, in background B, in posture P.

Of our three sources, only Sextus offers any argument for the crucial claim that we cannot decide among the different intervals, backgrounds, and postures. His argument (§§122–3) is a relatively simple application of the Modes of Agrippa. If you prefer one appearance to another, then either you offer no proof (and are not to be credited) or you offer a proof; if you offer a proof, then either you claim that it is false (and so overturn your own argument) or you claim that it is true; if you claim that it is a true proof, then either you offer no proof for that (and so are not to be credited) or you offer a proof; etc., etc. We have discussed this style of argument already in connexion with the Fourth Mode, and have nothing more to say about it here. It is disappointing in the way that Agrippan arguments often are: no points are raised, and so none are settled, which are relevant to the specific puzzles generated by this mode.

The Fifth Mode is richly illustrated, and the illustrations, as usual, are a mixed bag. Some of them, indeed, do not seem to produce any genuine conflict at all. No doubt eggs feel soft when inside the chicken, hard when laid. But where is the problem? Eggs *are* soft inside the bird, and they harden during the laying process. It is absurd to wonder whether eggs are *really* hard or soft. The same holds of coral and lyngurion. (Lyngurion is a kind of amber, so-called from the belief that it was formed from the congealed urine of the lynx.) In these cases, the alleged oppositions are not genuinely oppositions of appearances of the kind the sceptic requires. We do not mean that eggs, coral and lyngurion are bad examples because they are not really examples of *appearances* – because, say, eggs do not just *appear* hard when laid. We mean that there is no *conflict* between eggs appearing soft in the bird and hard when laid.

But not all of the examples are to be dismissed in this way. Indeed, the illustrations of the Fifth Mode include some of the most celebrated and durable examples of perceptual illusion. Plato had referred to such illusions in a passage from the *Republic* which we have already had occasion to mention (above, p. 69–70):

'The same magnitude, I suppose, appears to us not to be equal when seen from nearby and when seen from a distance?'

'Yes'.

'And the same things appear bent and straight when they are observed in water and out of it, and again concave and projecting because of the error of sight about their colours – and all this is clearly a disturbance present in our souls. And it is this affection of our nature on which scene-paintings and conjuring tricks and many other such devices rely in order to work their magic on us.' (*Republic* 602CD)

(Note, by the way, that Philo's odd suggestion that 'lifeless things are on occasion assumed to be living' and *vice versa* alludes to a passage in Plato's *Philebus*, 38CE: from afar, a statue may be mistaken for a person and *vice versa*.)

The phenomenon to which Plato refers had long been known. Ion, in Euripides' play of that name, observes that

> Things do not appear the same in form
> when they are far off and when they are seen from nearby.

(Ion 586–7)

Ion speaks metaphorically, presupposing a familiarity with literal examples of such effects.

Under the heading of distance, a common type of example involved apparent change of size. Philo and Diogenes both note this; Sextus makes the point concrete by the example of a ship which appears to get larger as it approaches port. The example itself is a commonplace (see, for instance, Cicero's *Academics* II xxv 81) and the puzzle had a long life: in the third century AD Plotinus devoted a short treatise to the problem of 'How things seen from afar appear small' (*Enneads* II 8).

The perception of magnitude or size is not as straightforward as the ancient philosophers, both sceptics and dogmatists, imply. Here is a passage from one of the least obfuscatory of modern philosophers, J. L. Austin.

> There is the difficulty that the question 'What size does it appear *to be?*', asked of a star, is a question to which no sensible man would attempt to give an answer. He might indeed say that it 'looks tiny'; but it would be absurd to take this as meaning that it looks as if it *is* tiny, that it appears to *be* tiny. In the case of an object so immensely distant as a star, there is really no such thing as 'the size that it appears to be' when one looks at it, since there is no question of making that sort of estimate of its size. (*Sense and Sensibilia* (1962), p. 93)

Austin, who here distinguishes carefully between '*x* appears *F*' and '*x* appears to be *F*', is not advocating any form of scepticism about how things *appear* to us; but reflexion upon these remarks of his will readily confirm that the appearance of size is not the simple thing it might be thought to be: before the Pyrrhonist can set up his oppositions he must inspect closely the very notion of apparent magnitude.

However that may be, the favourite ancient example of effects due to interval or distance concerns not size but shape. It is the square tower which appears round when seen from a distance. Sextus refers to the tower more than once (*PH* I 32; *M* VII 208, 414). It is found in numerous other ancient texts. It remained a favourite, turning up again in Descartes' *Meditations*.

Like many of the illustrations of this mode, the tower was discussed by the Epicureans. Indeed, much of the Fifth Mode can best be seen as a sceptical application of material originally assembled (in this case by the Epicureans) for a non-sceptical purpose. (We have seen something similar in the case of the Fourth Mode, which uses Protagorean materials.) The Epicureans had to deal with cases of this sort because of their striking views about perception. Epicurus held that our perceptions are always veridical. There is an obvious objection to this: perceptual mistakes and illusions surely do occur. Epicurus dealt with the objection by holding that when error does occur and we judge the distant tower to be round, that is because we do not stick to the appearances but impose an 'additional judgement' on them.

The Epicurean Lucretius, in his philosophical poem *On the Nature of Things*, discusses the tower as follows:

> When we see the square towers of a city from a distance,
> it often happens that they appear round
> because every angle is seen from a distance as blunt
> or rather is not seen at all – its blow perishes
> and its impact does not penetrate to our eyes
> because while the images are travelling through a quantity of air
> the air by frequent collisions causes them to grow blunt.
> Thus when every angle has eluded our perception
> it is as though we were looking at stones turned on a lathe
> – yet not like those which are nearby and really round:
> rather they seem in a sketchy way to resemble them.

> (IV 353–63)

Lucretius is plainly in difficulties. On the one hand, he seems to concede that a tower which is actually square may appear round from a distance; and he offers a scientific explanation of why this should be so: the 'images' or atomic films which the tower throws off and whose impact on our eyes causes us to see it are distorted by their passage through the intervening air, and thus cause the illusory appearance of roundness. On the other hand, it is his set Epicurean purpose to show how the senses are always veridical: appearances are not in themselves illusory or distorted – rather it is the observer's hasty judgement which introduces the error. Thus he is led in the end to suggest that the tower does not, from a distance, *really* look round; rather, it seems 'in a sketchy way' to resemble round objects, and if we attend carefully to our perceptions we shall see that in fact the tower looks square.

Lucretius is not simply saying, as some modern philosophers have said, that the square tower looks *like a square tower* or that the square tower looks just the way square towers, when seen from a distance, *do* look. For that is trivial, and it is quite compatible with holding that square towers look *round* from a distance. Rather, he is saying that the tower really does *look* square. Now this is surely just false, and the Epicureans are denying commonplace truths (as ancient critics of their theory were quick to point out).

The Epicureans presented the most systematic attempt in ancient philosophy to meet problems of this sort: they denied that we really are presented with conflicting appearances. Their attempt was a gallant failure, and the sceptics were among the critics who pointed this out. The more common dogmatic response, however, was also that of common sense and scientific theory. This response allows, with the Pyrrhonists and against the Epicureans, that we do have conflicting appearances of the form (1.5a) and (2.5a), but insists that we can discriminate between them. The tower sometimes looks round and sometimes looks square. It really is square – and we can explain how this is compatible with its sometimes producing a round appearance. The Pyrrhonist, on the other hand, maintains that we cannot decide between such conflicting appearances.

It might be thought that the Pyrrhonist has an easy victory over the Epicurean, whose attempt to 'defend' the senses may seem merely quixotic, but that the other dogmatists, allied to common sense and scientific theorising, present a more formidable front. Consider the oar which looks straight in air, bent in water. This, the most celebrated of the oppositions depending on 'place' or background, hardly seems to lead ineluctably to scepticism or suspension of judgement. Here is Austin's robust response to the sceptic's claim:

What is wrong, what is even faintly surprising, in the idea of a stick's being straight but looking bent sometimes? Does anyone suppose that if something is straight, then it jolly well has to *look* straight at all times and in all circumstances? Obviously no one seriously supposes this. So what mess are we supposed to get into here, what is the difficulty? (*Sense and Sensibilia*, p. 29)

The oar looks *straight in the air*; it looks *bent in water*; as long as we know which medium it is in, there is no problem.

Common sense, however, has its limitations. There is a story that an enemy of common-sense philosophy once showed Austin a stick half immersed in a glass of water. 'What is this?' he asked. 'A straight stick', said Austin; 'of course it *looks* bent – but that's just the way straight sticks do look when you put them in glasses of water'. The stick was then taken out of the water – and it still looked bent. Crude common sense can be mistaken, and the Pyrrhonist will fasten on this possibility of error.

But if common sense alone is not strong enough to beat the sceptic, can it not be reinforced by the powers of science? In antiquity, optical illusions like that of the oar were widely discussed not only by philosophers but also by scientists. Proclus, writing in the fifth century AD, explains that

optics and harmonics are offshoots of geometry and arithmetic. The former science uses visual lines and the angles made by them. It is divided into a part called optics proper, which accounts for the illusory appearances presented by objects seen at a distance (such as the converging of parallel lines or the round appearance of square towers), and general catoptrics, which is concerned with the various ways in which light is reflected . . . (*Commentary on Euclid* 40)

In surviving optical treatises, for example in Ptolemy's *Optics*, we find detailed scientific explanations, in terms of reflexion and refraction, of the phenomena which led the Pyrrhonist to suspend judgement.

A fragmentary papyrus text, now in the Louvre in Paris, contains tantalising references to phenomena of the sort we are considering. The text is early, for the papyrus was written in the third century BC; but its author is unknown. It begins in mid-sentence with a phrase that recalls Diogenes' 'airy' mountains:

to us airy, both colours appearing together and the air tending to predominate because of its mass. In the end, vast magnitudes gradually disappear. For islands and cities and countries cover large intervals, like all those things whose colours the air is least capable of hiding; hence they can only be seen from a considerable distance, and their bulks appear very small instead of very large. (Col. I)

Here, and in its other five columns, the text is obscure in detail. Moreover, even if its general content is plain, its general purport is not: scholars have usually regarded it as part of a treatise on optics, but its most recent editor has argued that it is in fact a chapter from a work on scepticism. This disagreement underscores the fact that ancient scientists and ancient sceptics, in their discussions of perceptual illusions, were talking about the same subject.

Nonetheless, the scientists do not refer to the Pyrrhonists' account of the phenomena, and the Pyrrhonists do not pause to consider the scientists' explanations. Both omissions are unfortunate. In the present context we must ask why the Pyrrhonists ignored the work of their scientific contemporaries and whether they could have produced an adequate reply to the putative scientific resolutions of their doubt. The scientists and the Pyrrhonists agree that, for instance,

(A) Oars appear straight in air

and

(B) Oars appear bent in water.

The sceptic denies that we can decide which of the two appearances is true. The scientist argues that a decision is possible. He produces a general theory of the refractive properties of various media in terms of which he can explain the two appearances. Given the general theory of refraction, and given a particular hypothesis about the refractive co-efficient of water, he can infer that an oar which is actually straight will appear bent when immersed. Moreover, he can infer exactly *how* bent it will look; for the coefficient of refraction will supply him with a specific conclusion to the effect that the oar will appear to be bent at an angle of $n°$ where it enters the water.

Thus science resolves the sceptical doubt. On the assumption that the oar is actually straight we can explain its bent appearance. And the availability of such an explanation is a strong argument in favour of the assumption that the oar is in reality straight. The argument is an 'argument to the best explanation'.

We know of no specific sceptical reply to any specific scientific resolution of this type. But in the Eight Modes of Aenesidemus against causal explanation the Pyrrhonists presented general recipes for the concoction of specific replies. (The Eight Modes are translated in Appendix B.) Consider here the second of the eight:

some people often give an explanation in only one mode, although there is a rich abundance enabling them to explain the subject of investigation in a variety of modes. (*PH* I 181)

There is always more than one theory to fit any given set of data; for the data, in the modern jargon, 'underdetermine' theory.

Suppose, then, that some professor of optics advances a theory T_1 to explain, *inter alia*, items (A) and (B). The Pyrrhonist will observe that there are several other theories, T_2, T_3, ..., T_n, each of which is as good as T_1, in the sense that each accounts for all the data for which T_1 accounts. The theories are different from, and indeed incompatible with, one another: some, like T_1, will assume that the oar really is straight; others that the oar really is bent. There is no ground for preferring T_1 to any other theory, since each theory is equally powerful. Since some of the theories do not assume that the oar is really straight, the availability of T_1 constitutes no argument in favour of that assumption.

In general, if we appeal to theory in order to discriminate among appearances, the Pyrrhonist will point to the underdetermination of theory by data, and infer that no appeal to theory can have any discriminatory force. This sceptical reply raises large questions in the philosophy of science which are still hotly debated. Here we shall only say that it is, at the very least, not *evident* that the ancient scientists and their optical theories had the capacity to resolve the Pyrrhonists' doubts, or to repel the sceptical conclusions which they drew from these examples.

9 Mixtures

Sextus, *PH* I 124–8:

124   Sixth is the mode depending on admixtures. According to it we infer that, since no existing object makes an impression on us by itself, but rather together with something, it is perhaps possible to say what the mixture is like which results from the external object and the factor that it is observed with, but we cannot say purely what the external existing object is like.

    That no external object makes an impression by itself but in every case together with something, and that it is observed as differing in a way dependent on this is, I think, clear.

125   For instance, the colour of our skin is seen as different in warm air and in cold, and we cannot say what our colour is like in its nature, but only what it is like as observed together with each of these. The same sound appears different together with clear air or with muggy air. Aromatic herbs are more pungent in the bath-house and in the sun than in chilly air. And a body surrounded by water is light, surrounded by air heavy.

126   But, to leave aside *external* admixtures, our eyes contain membranes and liquids inside them. Since, then, what we see is not observed without these, it will not be apprehended accurately; for it is the mixture that we grasp, and for this reason people with jaundice see everything as yellow, while people with a blood-suffusion in the eye see things as blood-red. And since the same sound appears different in open places and in narrow winding places, and different in pure and in contaminated air, it is likely that we do not have a pure grasp of sound; for our ears have winding passages and narrow channels, and are contaminated by vaporous effluvia, which are said to be carried from the

127 region of the head. Further, since there are kinds of matter in our nostrils and the regions of taste, it is together with these, not purely, that we grasp what we taste and smell.

So, because of the admixtures, our senses do not grasp what external existing objects are accurately like.

128   But our intellect will not do so either, especially since its guides, the senses, fail it. And no doubt it too produces some admixture of its own to add to what is announced by the senses; for we observe the existence of certain humours round each of the regions in which the dogmatists think that the 'ruling part' is located – in the brain or the heart or in whatever part of the animal one wants to locate it.

According to this mode too, therefore, we see that we cannot say anything about the nature of external existing objects, and are forced to suspend judgement.

Diogenes IX 84–5:

Sixth is the mode depending on mixtures and shares; it shows that nothing appears purely in itself, but together with air, with light, with moisture, with solid body, heat, cold, movement,* evaporations and other forces. For instance, purple shows a different colour in sunlight, moonlight and lamplight. Our skin-colour has a different appearance at mid-day – and so does 85 the sun.* A stone which in the air it takes two men to lift* is easily moved in water: either it is heavy and made light by the water, or it is light and weighed down by the air. So we are ignorant of things in their own nature, as we are of oil in a perfume.

Philo 189–92:

189   And why should this be surprising? Anyone who goes into things more closely and looks at them in a purer light will recognise that no one thing affects us according to its own simple nature; all of them contain the most elaborate mixtures and blends.

190   For a start, how do we grasp colours? Surely together with air and light on the outside, and also together with the moisture in the eye itself. In what way are sweet and bitter assessed? Independently of the flavours, whether natural or unnatural, in our own mouths? Hardly. Well, do the smells from burning incense present us with the natures of these substances in a simple and pure form, or rather as blends of themselves and of

the air – and sometimes of the fire which melts the substances and of the workings of our nostrils?

191   From these cases we infer that we grasp not colours, but the blend produced from the objects and light; not smells, but the mixture brought about by the effluence from the substances and the hospitable air; not flavours, but what is produced by the incoming thing tasted and the moist substance in our mouths.

192   Since things are this way, people who persist in making ready agreements or denials about any subject at all deserve to be condemned for their simple-mindedness or rashness or pretentiousness. For if the simple powers of things are inaccessible, and only mixed powers, with contributions from several factors, are open to view, and if there is no way in which we can see the invisible powers or perceive through the blends the particular character of each of the contributions, what remains but the necessity to suspend judgement?*

The Sixth Mode deals with 'admixtures' (Sextus) or 'mixtures and shares' (Diogenes). It depends on the fact that everything contains 'the most elaborate mixtures and blends' (Philo). All appearances come to us in a mixed or contaminated form, and this being so, we cannot say how things really are, free from any admixtures and purified from the contaminations.

Philo seems to indicate that the mode depends not on commonplace observation but on something approaching scientific examination: 'anyone who goes into things more closely and looks at them in a purer light' will see that things affect us in a contaminated way. Sextus begins by stating that it is evident that external objects impress us in a mixed fashion; but a part at least of his illustrative matter draws upon scientific investigations rather than upon everyday experience.

To this extent the Sixth Mode is somewhat different from its predecessors, which generally rely only on common or garden observations. However, the scientific expertise which the mode invokes is not sophisticated or controversial professional knowledge – nor, more importantly, knowledge peculiar to ancient science or to any one school of ancient science. Rather, the mode relies on facts which are, as it were, only just beneath the skin. That there are membranes and liquids in the eye, say, is not a matter of commonsense experience, but nor is it a piece of disputable or outdated scientific speculation. The mode relies on science in a very minimal understanding of that term.

What are the contaminating admixtures? Sextus distinguishes two sorts of admixture, external and internal. The external examples are strange. 'The colour of our skin is seen as different *in* warm air . . .'; 'aromatic herbs are more pungent *in* the bath-house . . .'; 'a body *surrounded by* water is light . . .'. In each case Sextus appears to refer not to an admixture, but to a 'place' or background, and the examples seem to fit the Fifth Mode rather than the Sixth. Presumably Sextus expects us to make an inference from backgrounds to admixtures: if aromatic herbs are more pungent in the bath-house, they are so (we may like to infer) because the air of the bath-house 'mixes' with the aroma of the herbs, and the combination has the observed effect upon our olfactory apparatus. However that may be, Sextus' remaining example does explicitly refer to admixture: 'the same sound appears different *together with* clear air . . .'.

As for internal admixtures, Sextus discusses sight, hearing, smell and taste, but not touch. Although his remarks are concise, they contain some fairly complex arguments. We agree that there are 'membranes and liquids' in our eyes (and also, it must be added, that these are themselves coloured). When our eyes are discoloured, yellowed by jaundice or reddened by a suffusion of blood, then external objects appear yellowish or reddish to us. This too counts as an admitted fact. (As we commented in connexion with the First Mode, the alleged fact is a fiction, but it has continued as a serviceable philosophical example all the same.) The fact is to be explained by the hypothesis of 'admixture': green apples appear yellowish to people with jaundice because the impression made by the apples is mingled with or contaminated by the colour of the eyes themselves. But since in such pathological cases it is plain that the colour things appear depends not only on them but also on the colour of the eyes, then it is only reasonable to suppose that a similar admixture and contamination takes place in normal vision: the normal colour of eye-membranes and eye-liquids 'mixes' with the colour of external objects, and affects normal appearances.

The argument for hearing is less straightforward. Sounds appear different, Sextus observes, according to the nature of the region through which they pass. But the regions inside our ears are in some respects analogous to those outside: they contain winding passages, they are filled with turbid air. Hence the sound we hear will be affected by the region within our ears. This is a moderately plausible line of argument (and sounds certainly do seem to vary as our ears are variously affected). But what has it to do with 'admixtures'? Sextus appears to be talking of the way in which sounds can be distorted by the media through which they pass. He must interpret this distortion in terms of 'admixture' if it is to have any bearing upon the Sixth Mode, but it is not clear that 'admixture' comes into the picture. What can admix with a sound except another sound? And do the distortions which Sextus describes really occur by virtue of one sound's being interfered with by another? Philo (perhaps wisely) omits the example of hearing. He uses the example of sight, but in a way rather different from Sextus: we grasp colours 'together with air and light on the outside, and also together with the moisture in the eye itself' (§190). The external and the internal admixtures, separated by Sextus, are here combined. Philo does the same in the case of smell. In general, Philo's account of admixtures is neater and more convincing than Sextus': it perhaps represents an intelligent revision of his source.

Diogenes' text of the Sixth Mode is more than usually corrupt. We pass a few comments on some of his examples in Appendix E.

The Sixth Mode seems to have a structure different from that of the other modes. It might be expected to produce a set of oppositions each of the form:

(1.6) x appears F in admixture M
(2.6) x appears F^* in admixture M^*.

The Pyrrhonist might then urge that we cannot prefer M to M^* or *vice versa*. In fact there is no trace of any such 'oppositions' in our sources for this mode. And in any case the material that the mode assembles seems to guide us down a different path to scepticism.

The line of thought suggested by the material is, in general terms, this: Our impressions are contaminated by admixtures; we cannot filter out the contaminating agents; hence we cannot tell how things really are in themselves. In its simplest form, the mode will then consist of a sequence of observations of the form:

x appears F in admixture M.

Each observation in itself leads to scepticism, without needing an antithetical mate. For we know that the way x appears is affected by M, and that we cannot compensate for the effect of M. Hence we do not know how x really is.

A somewhat less simple argument may have been in the Pyrrhonist's mind. We incline to say such things as 'Honey tastes sweet' or 'The sea looks grey.' In fact, however, since all appearances involve admixture, we are only ever entitled to say such things as 'Honey mixed with saliva tastes sweet' or 'The sea mixed with opthalmic liquids looks grey.' The Sixth Mode would then in effect insist that all our reports of appearances should take the form:

Admixture M, which is $x + y + z + \ldots$, appears F.

We can say how admixtures appear; but we cannot distinguish the different effects of their constituents – we cannot say what effect x or y or z has upon the way M appears. This leads to a scepticism more profound than any we have so far reached. For according to the present argument, we cannot even say how things *appear*, let alone how they really are. 'How does honey taste?' 'I don't know: honey + saliva tastes sweet; but I've never tasted pure *honey*.'

This more advanced scepticism is not explicit in our texts, though it is at once suggested by their contents. Whether or not it was intended by the Pyrrhonists, the Sixth Mode is an argument-form of a different sort from its predecessors, and one that does not really fit into Sextus' classification.

The questionable part of the argument in the Sixth Mode is the step from contamination to doubt. It may well be true that our impressions are contaminated; but is it really true that we cannot filter out the contaminations and infer how things really are? Diogenes does not face the question: having listed some mixtures he concludes that 'we are ignorant of things in their own nature, as we are of oil in a perfume' (§85). Philo remarks (§192) that 'if there is no way in which we can see the invisible powers or perceive through the blends the particular character of each of the contributions, what remains but the necessity to suspend judgement?' But he does not argue for the antecedent of his conditional or attempt to prove that there *is* no way to see through the mixture.

Sextus is more helpful. In §127 he concludes that 'our senses do not grasp what external existing objects are accurately like'; and he at once adds, in §128, that 'our intellect will not do so either'. Our senses do not grasp things in uncontaminated form – and our minds cannot do so either, i.e. they cannot compensate for the contaminating factors. This is the second of the two passages in Sextus' presentation of the modes in which he mentions the intellect and considers the possibility of using it to decide the conflicts set by the modes. The other passage we have already noted: it occurs in §99 at the end of the Third Mode.

It is perhaps surprising that Sextus pays so little attention to the claims of intellect. It was a commonplace of ancient philosophy that our cognitive powers divide into two classes, the perceptual and the intellectual; and it is a natural thought that a weakness in the one class may be compensated for by a strength in the other. Consider the following passage from Hume:

> I need not insist upon the more trite topics, employed by the sceptics in all ages, against the evidence of *sense*; such as those which are derived from the imperfection and fallaciousness of our organs, on numberless occasions; the crooked appearance of an oar in water; the various aspects of objects, according to their different distances; the double images which arise from the pressing one eye; with many other appearances of a like nature. These sceptical topics, indeed, are only sufficient to prove, that the senses alone are not implicitly to be depended on; but that we must correct their evidence by reason. (*Enquiry concerning Human Understanding*, §117)

Hume, no enemy to scepticism, takes it as obvious that 'reason' or the intellect will determine the conflicts in perceptual appearances.

Sextus offers two arguments in §128 against the efficacy of the intellect. First, it will not serve us 'especially since its guides, the senses, fail it'. The intellect cannot reach any goal unless it is guided: its guides (its only guides, we must suppose) are the senses; thus if the senses fall down, the intellect has no way of achieving its end. This is the argument which Sextus used earlier in §99. It is, as it stands, wholly metaphorical; but behind the metaphor lies a strong thesis of empiricism about the mind, and it is presumably this thesis of which Sextus is reminding us. By 'empiricism about the mind' we mean the idea that the mind cannot function independently of experience. The mind, on this view, is essentially a capacity for manipulating ideas or concepts. It is not innately equipped with a set of concepts to manipulate: all its materials come to it through experience – and, in particular, through perceptual experience. The mind thus depends, for all its activities, on the senses.

Empiricism is an appealing doctrine. Traces of it can be found in the earliest period of Greek philosophical thought, and it appears in a celebrated fragment from a work by the fifth-century atomist Democritus who was aware of its sceptical potential:

> Democritus, when he had run down the senses (saying 'by convention is colour, by convention sweet, by convention bitter: in truth, atoms and void') then portrayed the senses speaking to the intellect as follows: 'Wretched mind, do you take your evidence from us and then overthrow us? Our overthrow is your fall.' (Galen, *On Medical Experience* XV 7 Walzer)

The intellect depends for its evidence on the senses (it is in this sense 'guided' by them); so if it then attempts to criticise, or to discriminate among, the senses, it undermines its own foundation.

Empiricism about the mind is conveniently expressed in the mediaeval slogan that 'there is nothing in the intellect which was not earlier in the senses'. The slogan derives from Aristotle, who more than once asserts the empiricist claim that the mind depends upon sense-experience. The same form of empiricism was also common to the Stoics and Epicureans. Plato, it is true, had rejected it, holding that the mind had independent access to truth, an access hampered rather than helped by the senses. But Platonism of this sort had no powerful supporters in the Hellenistic period, so that the Pyrrhonists could properly take it as a thesis of all their dogmatist opponents that the mind is dependent on the senses.

Yet even if empiricism is granted in its strongest form, it by no means follows that the mind is not capable of judging the deliverances of the senses; and neither Aristotle nor the Stoics, nor even the Epicureans, inferred that it was not. For the mind may depend for its materials on the senses, and yet have the power to judge those materials – to assess their mutual coherence and consistency, for example. Indeed, the intellect may well be conceived of precisely as a faculty for assessing and systematising the deliverances of the senses.

Consider the particular case of the Sixth Mode. What is honey really like? The intellect, let us allow, can make no answer to this question unless furnished with data by the senses – unless honey tastes in this and that way. Let us also allow that the taste of honey will vary according to the different admixtures with which it is contaminated. Nevertheless, it remains an open question whether the intellect can rationally determine the 'real' taste of honey on the basis of the various apparent tastes which form its materials. The intellect may consider the taste of honey + saliva, together with various other tastes of honey + x and of y + saliva. Thence, by applying some principles of similarity and difference, it may be able to determine the particular contribution made to the taste of any admixture by the constituent honey. Neither Sextus' metaphor of guides who slip nor the general thesis of empiricism about the mind implies that this is impossible

Sextus' second argument against the utility of the intellect is of a quite different nature. Just as the sense-organs are contaminated in their operations by their own properties, so the intellect 'produces some admixture of its own'. The admixture here is to be understood in ordinary physical terms: there is no question of any 'immaterial' contamination. All Sextus' main opponents were thoroughgoing materialists. They disagreed about the physiology of the intellect, but they all supposed that it had some physical nature and some physical location (perhaps in the heart or in the brain). As sight is to the eye, so thought is to the brain (or the heart or whatever). And just as the operations of sight are contaminated by the physical properties of the eye, so the operations of the intellect, it is only reasonable to suppose, are contaminated by the physical properties of the brain.

The physiology which Sextus assumes is, to say the least, antiquated, and his picture of 'admixtures' from the brain is quaint. But his point can be expressed without reliance on either of these questionable ideas. It is this: just as the way things appear to our senses depends in part upon the physical condition of our sense-organs, so the way things appear to our intellect depends in part upon the physical condition of our brains.

The truth of this idea, moreover, can be recognised even by philosophers who do not share the materialism common to the Hellenistic theorists. Plato himself thought that our intellects were hindered and diverted by our physical conditions. (This was precisely why he regarded death as a blessing: the philosopher, his mind freed by death from physical trammels, will be able to achieve a pure and uncontaminated grasp of the truth.) The most ardent opponent of a materialist conception of mind will grant that our intellects, as they in fact operate within us, are at the mercy of our bodily factors.

But how does this bear on the taste of honey? It is hard to see. There is, as so often in Sextus' arguments, a gap between the highly general reflexions about our human frailties and the particular issue over which we are invited to suspend judgement. It is not clear how the gap is to be bridged. Sextus suggests that when the intellect comes to assess the various sense-reports about honey it will somehow be contaminated by the physical constituents of the brain. Sextus' version of this point is bizarre; but most of us believe some less bizarre version of the thesis that the physical state of the brain has an effect on how we think of things. No doubt this thesis does have, potentially, *some* sceptical force, whatever theory of the mind–brain relation we may finally adopt. Still, to assess exactly what actual sceptical force it has is a difficult matter – and it requires far more reflexion than Sextus gives it.

10 Quantities

Sextus, *PH* I 129–34:

129   The seventh mode, we said, is the one depending on the quantities and preparations of existing objects – where by 'preparations' we mean compositions in general. That we are forced by this mode too to suspend judgement about the nature of objects, is clear.

For instance, the shavings from a goat's horn appear white when observed simply, without composition, but when combined in the actual horn are observed as black. And silver filings appear black on their own, but together with the whole impress 130 us as white. Bits of Taenarian marble when polished are seen as white, but appear yellowish in the whole mass. Grains of sand scattered apart from one another appear rough, but when combined as a heap affect perception softly. Hellebore produces choking when consumed as a fine powder, but not when grated coarsely. 131   Wine drunk in moderation fortifies us, but taken in greater quantity enfeebles the body. Food likewise shows different powers depending on the quantity; often, for instance, through being consumed in large amounts it purges the body by indigestion and diarrhoea. 132   Here too, therefore, we shall be able to say what the fine piece of horn is like, and what the combination of many fine pieces is like; what the small piece of silver is like, and what the combination of many small pieces is like; what the minute piece of Taenarian marble is like, and what the combination of many small pieces is like; and so with the grains of sand and the hellebore and the wine and the food – we can say what they are like relatively, but we cannot say what the nature of the objects is like in itself because of the anomalies in the appearances which depend on their compositions.

133   For in general, beneficial things seem harmful depending on their being used in immoderate quantity, and things which seem harmful when taken to excess seem to do no harm in minute quantities. The chief witness to this argument is what is observed in the case of medicinal powers: here the accurate mixing of simple drugs makes the compound beneficial, but sometimes when the smallest error is made in the weighing it is not only not beneficial, but extremely harmful and often poisonous.

134   In this way the argument from quantities and preparations confounds* the reality of external existing objects.

Hence this mode too would reasonably bring us round to suspension of judgement, since we cannot make declarations purely about the nature of external existing objects.

Diogenes IX 86:

Eighth is the mode depending on their quantities and qualities,* their being hot or cold, quick or slow, pale or coloured. For instance, wine taken in moderation fortifies us, while more of it enfeebles us; and similarly with food and the like.

Philo 184–5:

184   What of the quantities in preparations?

Whether the compounds harm or help depends on whether there is more or less: this is true in thousands of cases – and especially in the case of drugs made up according to medical
185 science. For the quantity in compounds is measured by formulae and rules which it is unsafe to fall short of or to exceed (less weakens their powers and more intensifies them, and both are harmful, the drug either being unable to act because of its weakness, or doing violent harm because of its extreme potency) and it vividly indicates how to test for its helpfulness or harmfulness by its qualities of smoothness or roughness and of density and compression or on the other hand of rarefaction and dilation.

The background to this mode is Epicurean. Plutarch, in his essay *Against Colotes* which we cited in connexion with the Second Mode, reports an argument from Epicurus' *Symposium*:

When Polyaenus says: 'Epicurus, do you deny the heating effects of wine?', he answers: 'Why should one assert universally that wine is heating?' A little later he says: 'It is apparent that, universally speaking, wine is not heating, but that a given quantity might be said to be heating for a given person.' And again, after mentioning the crowdings and dispersals of atoms and finding the cause in their mixings and alignings with other atoms as the wine mingles with the body, he adds: 'Hence one should not say, universally, that wine is a heating agent, but rather that such-and-such an amount is heating for such-and-such a constitution in such-and-such a condition and that such-and-such an amount is cooling for such-and-such a constitution. For in an aggregate such as this there are natures from which coldness might be constituted or which, when aligned with others, would effect a genuine cooling. Hence, deceived by this, some say universally that wine is cooling, others that it is heating.' (1109F–1110A)

These Epicurean reflexions later found their way into the sceptical tradition, where they were adapted to a new and wholly unEpicurean purpose.

The Seventh Mode exhibits certain oddities. First, the conclusion of the mode, as Sextus presents it, is somewhat different from the conclusions of the other modes. Secondly, Sextus' presentation of the mode appears to encompass two rather different forms of argument, while Diogenes and Philo appear to allude to a third form.

The double nature of Sextus' account is indeed hinted at in his title for the mode: it depends on 'quantities and preparations'. Sextus glosses the latter term by the word 'compositions', and it properly applies to compounds made up according to a recipe. Sextus does not make it plain that he is talking about two rather different things – in fact, he gives the impression that he takes the terms 'quantity' and 'preparation' to be virtual synonyms. But as we shall see, there really are two different lines of thought present in his version of the mode.

The first line of thought is presented in §§129–32. There we seem to have a standard argument based on conflicting appearances, thus:

(1.7a) x appears F in quantity Q

(2.7a) x appears F^* in quantity Q^*.

Now since

(3.7a) we cannot prefer Q to Q^* or *vice versa*

we end by suspending judgement as to what x really is.

Sextus' examples in fact fit that pattern only loosely. Under the notion of quantity we must allow him to include at least the following contrasts:

in large quantity	*versus*	in small quantity
in a lump	*versus*	divided up
combined	*versus*	dispersed
coarsely broken down	*versus*	finely broken down.

It is not obvious that these distinctions amount to the same thing, or even that they are usefully subsumed under a single head.

Sections 133–4 probably introduce a second argument. Although the passage begins with a phrase ('For in general . . . ') which appears to promise a generalisation of the previous argument, Sextus in fact turns to something quite different and we should take the phrase to be introducing a new set of considerations. These considerations turn upon the ways in which compounds are prepared, and in particular on the different proportions in which their ingredients are mixed. Thus we can set up a schema as follows:

(1.7b) x appears F when mixed in proportion P

(2.7b) x appears F^* when mixed in proportion P^*.

And this schema is plainly distinct from the former one.

No doubt the two schemata have something in common. Both, in a broad sense, deal with quantities. We might even try to amalgamate them by way of some such formulae as:

(1.7) x appears F in virtue of amount A

(2.7) x appears F^* in virtue of amount A^*.

We should then explain 'in virtue of amount A' as meaning, according to the circumstances of the particular example, either 'in quantity Q' or 'when mixed in proportion P'. But it is plain that these formulae merely give a spurious air of unity to a mode which is irredeemably two-faced.

Diogenes has material corresponding to the first of Sextus' two types of 'quantity'. Philo seems to have in mind rather the second of Sextus' two types. But both Philo and Diogenes refer in addition to *qualities*. Philo, in §185, talks of 'qualities of smoothness or roughness' and so on. Diogenes – but the text is uncertain – refers explicitly to the mode as depending on 'quantities and qualities'. In any case, Diogenes then certainly lists a number of qualities – 'hot or cold, quick or slow, pale or coloured' (§86). We do not know what to make of these allusions to qualities. The texts provide no illumination, and speculation is futile. It seems unlikely that the introduction of qualities is merely a silly mistake, for it occurs both in Philo and in Diogenes. But how and why qualities were introduced into the mode (by Aenesidemus?), we cannot say.

The second oddity about the Seventh Mode is the way in which Sextus states its conclusion. He says that 'we can say what they are like relatively, but we cannot say what the nature of the objects is like in itself' (§132). What he means is that we can say what things are like in given quantities but that we cannot say what things are like *tout court*. Now given that

Silver appears white in a large lump

whereas

Silver appears black in small shavings

we might expect to be told that we should suspend judgement as to how silver really is, contenting ourselves with avowals of the ways in which it appears. But Sextus quite explicitly allows us to say not only that silver *appears* white in large lumps but also that it *is* white in large lumps. And that is far more than he normally allows us.

Sextus is not merely being careless. Many of his examples actually demand such a conclusion, if only because they are ill conceived. Hellebore *is* fatal when pulverised but not when grated, wine *is* intoxicating when taken in large quantities but not when modestly imbibed. Heavy drinkers do not merely appear to be drunk, those who consume powdered hellebore really are dead.

What is the explanation, then, for Sextus' departure from his normal sceptical conclusion? Three possibilities suggest themselves, of which the third is the most interesting. First, Sextus may *mean* 'appears' when he *says* 'is'. Elsewhere he expressly announces that he sometimes uses the word 'is' in this off-colour sense (*PH* I 135), and he might be doing so here without mentioning the fact. Pyrrhonists do not quarrel about words (except when it suits them to do so), and the apparent difference between the conclusion of the Seventh Mode and those of the first six may be no more than apparent.

Secondly, the implicit concession in the Seventh Mode may be provisional. Sextus may mean that, as far as the Seventh Mode goes, we can indeed say that, for example, silver *is* white in lumps. But of course other modes will show that ultimately we cannot say even this much – we must in the end restrict ourselves to saying how silver *appears* in lumps. If that is what Sextus means, it is a pity that he did not make his meaning more plain. (We might also wonder why he did not think to make similar concessions in the case of the other modes.)

Thirdly, the concession may serve to indicate to us that the Seventh

Mode has a special target. It is not aimed at such dogmatic statements as 'Lumps of silver are white' or 'Large quantities of wine are heating.' Rather, it aims at statements such as 'Silver is white' or 'Wine is heating': it aims, in other words, at just those *universal* statements about substances which Epicurus thought should not be made. Why should a Pyrrhonist, or anyone else, see anything of importance in the difference between statements of those two kinds? The former statements are relatively everyday and can be made, or at least customarily are made, on the basis of casual observation. The latter statements go further: they are claims about a thing's nature, and making them demands more than simple observation.

A statement about what silver is – about what the stuff, silver, is, as opposed to what this or that lump of silver is – presupposes some scientific theory and advances beyond plain observation. There are passages in Sextus' works in which he poses as a defender of Common Sense and an opponent only of scientific and philosophical dogmatism. The Seventh Mode may be part of that pose. It aims for suspension of judgement not about ordinary matters but about what we should describe as scientific claims about the nature of things. Such an attack locates dogmatism not in the holding of beliefs as such but in the holding of a special class of belief – and that is a more restricted version of dogmatism than the one with which the earlier modes have been working.

The issue which the last paragraph introduces is thorny. It has been much debated in the recent learned literature, and we cannot discuss it here. Let it simply be said that there is evidence in the surviving texts that some sceptics were more radical than others. Some rejected all belief; others rejected only scientifico–philosophical beliefs. Both types of scepticism appear to have left traces in the text of Sextus. By and large the Ten Modes are designed to produce a radical scepticism. Perhaps the Seventh Mode is an exception, having originally been designed to achieve a more modest suspension of judgement.

Sextus' second line of thought, about proportions, is puzzling. No doubt 'the accurate mixing of simple drugs makes the compound beneficial' (§133), but how does that 'confound the reality of external existing objects'? Surely it simply points up the importance of getting the prescriptions right? If a compound mixed in proportion P cures us whereas one mixed in proportion P^* kills us, what sceptical moral can we draw? It is hard to see any obvious path to scepticism from these platitudes of the druggist's art.

Philo does not offer much help. What point he is making is obscure, but he appears to have in mind not the proportion of the ingredients within a compound drug but rather the amount of the compound itself. One aspirin will cure a headache, sixty will kill you – hence we cannot say whether aspirin is really lethal or salutary. If that is indeed Philo's point, then he is using the examples from Sextus' second argument as illustrations of the principle of Sextus' first argument, and the difficulty about Sextus' second argument remains untouched.

But it is not difficult to dream up sceptical arguments about recipes and mixtures. For example, it might be proposed that we cannot be sure of the effect of any one ingredient in a compound, since a change in the quantity of any ingredient affects the working of the compound as a whole. It is not possible, in other words, to isolate the properties of ingredients in compounds. This line of thought, which connects closely with the mode on admixtures, can be developed further, and conceivably it lies behind the façade of Sextus' text. But we confess that we cannot see it on the surface of the text – and we are wary of supposing that whenever Sextus' text contains an impenetrable piece of reasoning then his original source must have propounded a clear argument: sometimes, at least, the presence of a muddle in a text is a sign of nothing more than a muddle in the original author or source.

We turn, finally, to Sextus' first argument. Silver appears white in lumps, black in shavings. Thus even if we can say what colour silver is in certain given quantities, we cannot say what colour silver itself is. We know that Sextus' example of silver filings (and also the example of goat's horn) was used by Asclepiades, a leading doctor of the first century BC (Caelius Aurelianus, *On Acute Diseases* I 106). A recently published papyrus suggests that the example may be even older. An anonymous fragment which attacks philosophers and compares them unfavourably to lunatics contains the following snippet of information:

But even silver – and what could be more white than silver? – yet Thrasyalces says that it is black. (Oxyrhynchus Papyrus no. 3659)

We know nothing of Thrasyalces beyond the fact that he lived before Aristotle and was 'one of the old natural scientists'. It is possible that he argued that silver was black because shavings of silver are black, and that his paradoxical argument was later used for sceptical ends.

The sceptical use of the example relies on a tacit assumption. Sextus supposes, with some plausibility, that a lump of silver reveals the nature of silver no better – and no worse – than silver shavings do. The qualities of silver, and no doubt of other stuffs, vary from quantity to quantity. But mere quantity has no bearing on the essential nature of any stuff. Hence we cannot know what that essential nature is.

There is surely truth in this argument. But there are also at least two objections to it. First, it will work only against attempts to specify the nature of a stuff in terms of qualities which do as a matter of fact vary from quantity to quantity. Some qualities do indeed vary with quantity: Sextus' examples are correct, at least in the cases of silver, marble, and goat's horn. But we normally attempt to specify the nature of, say, silver, in terms of properties which are quantity-invariant. (The atomic number of silver does not vary from lumps to shavings – it is, precisely, the atomic number of *silver*.) Against qualities of this sort the Seventh Mode is powerless.

Sextus, however, need not have been perturbed by this objection. He does not, or at least he need not, claim that the Mode will work for *all* qualities; he does not, in other words, claim that for *every* quality F there will be an appropriate conflict of the form (1.7) and (2.7). It is enough that the mode works for *some* qualities – enough that it works, say, for colours and the like. Moreover, it seems possible that there will be some substances for which we can produce *no* quantity-invariant description: foodstuffs and drinks are perhaps like this. And in those cases Sextus may conclude, quite generally, that we cannot say what the nature of foodstuffs is.

Secondly, it is not clear why Sextus thinks that the Seventh Mode induces scepticism. Once again, there is a plausible alternative to scepticism, namely relativism. That, in effect, is the conclusion which Epicurus draws in the text from which our commentary on this mode began. Is wine a heating agent or a cooling agent? Neither: wine in certain quantities heats people of certain constitutions, and wine in certain quantities cools people of certain constitutions. That is all there is to be said on the matter. Again, is silver white or black? Neither: silver in certain quantities is white and in certain quantities black. That is all there is to be said on the matter.

A similar relativism was later espoused by John Locke in the course of his reflexions on 'secondary' qualities.

Pound an Almond, and the clear white *Colour* will be altered into a dirty one, and the sweet *Taste* into an oily one. What real Alteration can the beating of the Pestle make in any Body, but an Alteration of the *Texture* of it? (*An Essay concerning Human Understanding*, II viii 20)

Locke's argument is not impressive, but his conclusion is sound. Whole almonds look white and taste sweet, pounded almonds look greyish and taste oily. What colour and taste do almonds *really* possess? They do not really possess any colour or taste at all – their tastes and colours are relative to their 'quantity'. Sextus implies that silver really does have a natural colour but that we cannot say what it is. The relativist holds that silver has no colour at all: *bits* of silver have colours, depending on their size, but silver itself is without colour. That conclusion may sound as dramatic as the sceptical conclusion, if not more so: can we really maintain that silver is *colourless*? But the drama is illusory. The relativist maintains that silver is colourless only in the sense that there is no colour which every piece of silver possesses. Of course, every piece of silver possesses some colour or other, but there is no one colour which is possessed by every piece. In the same way we might say that coins are valueless: for there is no one value which is the value of every coin. But the valuelessness of coins, in this somewhat Pickwickian sense, is thoroughly compatible with the fact that every coin has a value.

The Seventh Mode does establish something. It establishes, for example, that silver is not white. But that conclusion is not a piece of scepticism, and the relativism which it embodies is not in the least daring.

11 Relativity

Sextus, *PH* I 135–40:

135   The eighth mode is the one deriving from relativity, by which
we infer that, since everything is relative, we shall suspend
judgement as to what things are independently and in their
nature. It should be recognised that here (as elsewhere) we use 'is'
instead of 'appears', implicitly saying: Everything appears
relative.

But this has two senses: first, relative to the subject judging
(for the external existing object which is judged appears relative
to the subject judging) and in another way relative to the things
observed together with it, as right is relative to left.

136   We have in fact already deduced that everything is relative,
both with respect to the subject judging (since each thing appears
relative to a given animal and a given human and a given sense
and a given circumstance), and with respect to the things
observed together with it (since each thing appears relative to a
given admixture and . . .* and a given composition and quantity
and position).

137   We can also infer specifically that everything is relative, in the
following way: Do relatives differ or not from things which are
in virtue of a difference? If they do not differ, then the latter are
relatives too. But if they do differ, then, since everything that
differs is relative (for it is spoken of relative to what it differs
from), things in virtue of a difference will be relative.

138   And according to the dogmatists, some existing things are
highest genera, others lowest species, and others both genera and
species. But all of these are relative. Everything, therefore, is
relative.

Further, some existing things are clear, others unclear, as they
themselves say, and what is apparent is a signifier, while what is

unclear is signified by something apparent – for according to them 'the apparent is the sight of the unclear' [Anaxagoras frag. 21a]. But signifier and signified are relative. Everything, therefore, is relative.

139 Further, some existing things are similar, others dissimilar, and some are equal, others unequal. But these are relative. Everything, therefore, is relative.

And anyone who says that not everything is relative confirms that everything is relative. For by his objections to us he shows that the very relativity of everything is relative to us and not universal.

140 So, since we have established in this way that everything is relative, it is clear then that we shall not be able to say what each existing object is like in its own nature and purely, but only what it appears to be like relative to something. It follows that we must suspend judgement about the nature of objects.

Diogenes IX 87–8:

Tenth is the mode based on setting things alongside one another* – e.g. light to heavy, strong to weak, bigger to smaller, up to down. Anything on the right, for instance, is not by nature on the right, but is thought of according to its relation to something else – if that is moved it will no longer be on the right.
88 Similarly both father and brother are relative; day is relative to the sun; and everything is relative to thinking. So things that are relative cannot be known in themselves.*

Philo 186–8:

186 Furthermore, everybody knows that pretty well nothing at all in the world is thought of in and by itself, but rather is assessed by juxtaposition with its contrary – e.g. small with big, dry with wet, hot with cold, light with heavy, black with white, weak
187 with strong, few with many. And similarly with what is a question of* excellence or defect: the beneficial is recognised by means of the harmful, the fine in opposition to the base, the just and in general the good by juxtaposition with the unjust and the bad. And the same holds for everything else in the universe: one would find on inquiry that it submits to decision in the same

way.* No one thing can be apprehended in itself, but rather seems to be recognised as a result of comparison with something else.

188   Now what is unable to testify adequately for itself, but requires advocacy from something else, is not firm enough to produce conviction. Here, then, is another way of testing those who make reckless agreements or denials on any subject at all.

Sextus' Eighth Mode turns explicitly to the topic of relativity. The Relativity Mode, which appears also in Philo and in Diogenes, is in many ways the most puzzling of the ten, and the most difficult to discuss. There are four main sources of puzzlement.

First, the relationship between Pyrrhonism and relativity is hard to determine. We have already seen how our sources are prone to assimilate relativism to scepticism, even though the two are incompatible with one another. This mistaken assimilation makes relativism the *conclusion* of sceptical argumentation. The Eighth Mode, on the other hand, proceeds *from* relativity to a sceptical conclusion. Scepticism and relativity thus stand in an ambivalent relation to one another.

Secondly, the notion of relativity is itself a complex one. The Greeks speak frequently of *ta pros ti*, 'things relative to something'; but behind that uniform nomenclature there stand several different accounts or theories of relativity. Different philosophical schools offered different analyses of *ta pros ti*. In order to understand and assess the Eighth Mode we must first determine which notion or notions of relativity it draws upon: there is no single, clear and agreed analysis to which we can appeal.

Thirdly, our three sources for the Relativity Mode differ strikingly from one another. Indeed, it is not even clear, in this case, that we have one mode presented in three different forms: the difference among our sources, which is signalled initially by their different names for the mode, suggests that we are in fact dealing with two or even three distinct modes.

Fourthly, Sextus himself has a curiously contorted attitude to the Relativity Mode. As we have seen, his taxonomy of the modes in §§38–9 assigns two seemingly incompatible places to relativity: on the one hand, the Relativity Mode is the eighth in order of the ten 'subordinate' modes; on the other hand, it is the 'most generic' mode under which all the rest are subsumed.

Because of those difficulties, our discussion of relativity must take a more circuitous course than our accounts of the other modes. We shall find it best to deal separately with Philo, Diogenes and Sextus. In each case our analysis of the text will be prefaced by a brief treatment of the type of relativity which we think it invokes. We should say in advance that we are by no means confident that we have discovered the right kind of relativity in each case.

First, Philo. We suggest that Philo has his eye on a Platonic account of relativity. Such an account, hints of which can be found in various passages in Plato's dialogues, is preserved in the one surviving fragment of a work *On Plato* by his pupil Hermodorus. The fragment is preserved in the *Commentary* on Aristotle's *Physics* by the sixth-century philosopher Simplicius. Simplicius says that he took the passage from Porphyry (third century) who had himself taken it from a book by Dercyllides, a thinker of the first century AD. (Much of our knowledge of early Greek philosophy depends on such complex transmissions of information.) According to Hermodorus, Plato

says that of the things that exist, some exist in their own right, like men and horses, others in relation to something else; and of the latter, some in relation to contraries – like good to bad – and others in relation to something; and of the latter, some determinate and others indeterminate. (Simplicius, *Commentary on the Physics* 248.2–5)

The information can be set out in a tree:

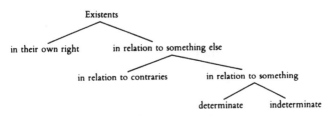

At *M* X 263–5 Sextus ascribes to 'the Pythagoreans' a related division of entities: things exist either 'in virtue of a difference' or 'in virtue of a contrariety' or 'in relation to something'. The three-fold Pythagorean division is not identical with the division which Hermodorus records; but scholars are no doubt right in supposing that it has a Platonic ancestry.

The peculiar feature of the Platonic division is its inclusion of a category of things 'in relation to contraries'. Philo's Relativity Mode appears to refer to the same category; for everything, according to Philo, 'is assessed by juxtaposition with its contrary' (§186). The fact, which is peculiar to Philo's account of the mode, suggests that the Platonic division is in the background here. We may add that Philo was himself well versed in Platonic thought.

The suggestion is not in itself sufficient for an interpretation of Philo. We need still to discover what type of relativity the Platonic analysis appeals to. Here Philo is helpful; for he speaks of something being 'thought of' or 'recognised' or 'apprehended' in relation to its contrary. We may infer that the notion of relativity is an epistemic one; that is to say, when Philo talks of one thing's being relative to another he means that one thing cannot be *known* or *recognised* without the other being known or recognised. Thus Fs are epistemically relative to Gs just in case Fs cannot be known unless Gs are known: good things, perhaps, are epistemically relative to bad things, inasmuch as you cannot recognise the good unless you can also recognise the bad. It seems clear that *Philo* has epistemic relativity in mind. We are inclined to think that *Plato* too had epistemic relativity in mind; but we shall not try to support that inclination, which is not strictly relevant to our present concerns.

Philo's argument in this mode is a simple one. He asserts, uncontroversially, that *some* things are relative in this epistemic sense. He then generalises the assertion and claims that *everything* – or at least everything 'in the universe' – is so relative. Finally he infers suspension of judgement about everything.

The generalisation is at first sight astounding. Philo offers no argument for it: he simply says that 'one would find on inquiry' that it is so. But how will we find that horses – to take one of the examples of things which allegedly exist 'in their own right' – are actually relative to something else? Speusippus, Plato's nephew and his successor as head of the Academy, had argued that in order to define anything you must know how it differs from everything else; and he inferred that you could not define anything without knowing everything. A Speusippan argument might possibly lie behind Philo's text. In order to recognise horses, say, you must be able to distinguish them from non-horses; for if you cannot tell a horse from a non-horse, how can you recognise that Dobbin is actually a horse? But in order to distinguish horses from non-horses you must know what non-horses are. Hence even horses are relative to their contrary: you cannot recognise horses without recognising non-horses. And so, in general, you cannot recognise Fs without being able to recognise their contraries, non-Fs.

We offer this Speusippan argument only by way of illustration. There is no evidence that Philo or his source had it in mind – and other arguments could certainly be invented. But we do suppose that some argument or other must lie behind Philo's generalisation. Philo's inference from the generalisation to scepticism relies upon a legal analogy: 'what is unable to testify adequately for itself, but requires advocacy from something else, is not firm enough to produce conviction.' Thus if x's testimony requires support from y, x is not to be trusted – and similarly if Fs can only be known by reference to Gs, Fs are not to be known.

Now the trouble with this is that the legal principle is indeterminately stated in Philo's text. First, Philo might mean that x's testimony is entirely worthless if it needs to refer to y. Such a principle – or rather, an analogous principle about knowledge – would certainly lead to scepticism; for if everything needs to refer to something else, and everything which needs to refer to something else is worthless, then everything is indeed worthless. And similarly, if everything requires reference to something else if it is to be known, and nothing which requires such a reference can be known, then everything is indeed unknowable. But the principle is absurd. For if we say that x's testimony needs y's support, we mean that x's testimony needs y's support *to make it trustworthy*. And x's testimony will therefore *be* trustworthy and possess value once it gets y's support.

Secondly, however, Philo might mean that if x's testimony is inadequate without reference to y, then x's testimony is worthless *on its own*. That principle is surely true – indeed, it seems to be a fairly obvious and trivial truth. But it is far from plain that this principle will lead to scepticism. After all, if x's testimony is untrustworthy by itself, then let x appeal to y and we shall know what to believe. Similarly, if Fs cannot be known apart from Gs, then let us refer to Gs and then we shall know Fs. A dogmatist could well allow that one thing cannot be known without reference to another: he would then be perfectly happy to *make* the appropriate reference and so claim knowledge.

Has Philo's sceptic any answer to a dogmatist who is content in that way with relative knowledge? He would perhaps have leaned on Agrippa and replied as follows: Suppose that Fs cannot be known apart from Gs. Then if you know Fs you already know Gs. But Gs themselves are, like everything else, epistemically relative. Hence if you know Gs you already know Hs. And so on – either the sequence $F, G, H, \ldots$ goes on *ad infinitum* or it returns on itself in a circle; and in neither case is knowledge of Fs possible. (We have discussed an argument of this form in connexion with the Fourth Mode.) Of course, there is no trace of any such Agrippan argument in Philo's text: we present it not as something which Philo actually had in mind, but rather as something which any sceptic would have thought of had he come across a dogmatist who claimed to be content with relative knowledge.

However that may be, it is clear that Philo's relativism is an epistemic relativism, and that his version of the Relativity Mode is idiosyncratic in that respect. We should observe, too, that Philo apparently employs the mode to show that we cannot have *knowledge* of things, and that too is different from the normal sceptical claim that we suspend judgement about things. We do not know whether Philo was conscious of the difference or aware that his appeal to *epistemic* relativity would leave him at a distance from suspension of *belief*.

Diogenes' version of the Relativity Mode is characteristically concise. A peculiarity of his account is the explanation of relativity in terms of change; what is to the right 'is thought of according to its relation to something else – if that is moved it will no longer be on the right'. A comparable reference to change is found in a Stoic account of relativity, and for that reason – which admittedly is not of invincible strength – we tentatively suggest that Diogenes' version of the mode rests upon the Stoic account.

The account is again given by Simplicius, this time in his *Commentary on Aristotle's Categories*. Discussing Aristotle's account of *ta pros ti* he observes that

the Stoics here enumerate two kinds rather than one; they talk about things which are in relation to something and about things which are somehow in relation to something. They contrast things which are in relation to something with things which are in themselves, whereas things which are somehow in relation to something they contrast with things which are in virtue of a difference. Things which are in relation to something include, they say, the sweet, the bitter, and the like; things somehow in relation to something include what is on the right, fathers, etc.; they say that things characterised by some form are in virtue of a difference . . . To put it more clearly, they say that things which are in relation to something are those which, being in a certain condition by virtue of their own character, refer to something else; whereas things which are somehow in relation to something are those things which, in addition to looking outside themselves, accrue or fail to accrue to something without any change or alteration in the things themselves. Thus when something is in a certain condition by virtue of a difference and refers to something else, that will just be in relation to something (e.g. possession, knowledge, perception). But when it is observed not in virtue of an internal difference but solely in virtue of its relation to something else, it will be a thing somehow in relation to something. Sons and people on the right require certain external things for their subsistence. That is why, even if no change takes place in themselves, a man may cease to be a father when his son dies and someone may cease to be on the right when what was next to him has changed position. But the sweet and the bitter do not become different unless their own properties participate in the change. So if without undergoing anything themselves they change in virtue of the relation of something else to them, clearly things somehow in relation to something have existence merely in a relation and not in virtue of some difference. (165.32–166.1; 166.15–30)

The passage contains several obscurities – which are not made any clearer by our unavoidably cumbersome English rendering of the technical terms. But it is clear that the Stoics are making use of a pair of distinct distinctions. First, they distinguish between 'things in themselves' (*ta kath' hauta*) and 'things in relation to something' (*ta pros ti*). Secondly, they distinguish between 'things in virtue of a difference' (*ta kata diaphoran*), and 'things somehow in relation to something' (*ta pros ti pōs echonta*). It is the *second* distinction with which we are concerned, for the reference to change occurs in the Stoic explanation of *ta pros ti pōs echonta*. Although Diogenes does not use the terminology of the second distinction, we suggest that he is using its concepts.

What sort of relativity is being invoked by this distinction? We suggest – once again tentatively – that the relativity is a form of ontological or existential dependence. Fathers are relative to children in the sense that fathers exist only if children exist; right-hand things are relative to left-hand things in the sense that right-hand things exist only if left-hand things exist. (The examples may not be wholly convincing, for we may wonder if fathers really are dependent on children in this way. But the principle which the examples are designed to illustrate is nonetheless reasonably plain.)

Diogenes' short list of examples seems to fit the Stoic analysis well enough, but it contains one curiosity which merits brief notice. He says that 'everything is relative to thinking'. What does this mean? It is tempting to construe it as expressing a form of 'idealism' which we associate with George Berkeley: everything exists 'in the mind' or 'in relation to the mind', since for a thing to exist is simply for it to be 'perceived' or thought of. But it would be rash to extract so remarkable a thesis from a single compressed sentence. Perhaps Diogenes is reflecting an argument to the effect that everything is a possible object of thought and all objects of thought are relative to – cannot exist without – thinking. Or perhaps his formulation is misleading and he means to offer not an *example* of relativity but a *generalisation* of the sceptics' claim: everything is relative to the thought of something else. We cannot tell.

The conclusion Diogenes invites us to draw is disappointing: 'things that are relative cannot be known in themselves'. That conclusion is no doubt true, but it seems wholly trivial: *of course* relatives are knowable, if at all, *as relatives* – how could they be known in any other way? No dogmatist will be moved by that claim. Once again, we must surely suppose that Diogenes is compressing his sceptical source, and that the Pyrrhonist whose views he is reporting offered some plausible-seeming argument for his sceptical conclusion. One such argument is this:

Everything is relative
Only non-relatives are knowable
Therefore nothing is knowable.

We cannot, of course, assert that Diogenes' source contained precisely that argument; but it is certainly an argument which a Pyrrhonist could well have employed here.

We offer three comments on the argument, two of them brief. First, Diogenes' sceptic, like Philo's, is certainly saying something about *knowledge*. But as we have already said, Greek sceptics officially concern themselves with belief rather than with knowledge. Thus even if Diogenes' argument were sound, it would not immediately license a Pyrrhonian conclusion, for it says nothing about suspension of belief.

Secondly, the argument yields a non-sceptical conclusion in another sense. A genuine sceptic about knowledge holds that we know nothing even though there are items which could in principle be known. Diogenes' argument implies that we know nothing *because there is nothing to be known*. Diogenes' conclusion thus differs from scepticism in just the same way as relativism differs from scepticism, and we have further evidence of the confusion which we examined in our discussion of the Fourth Mode.

Our third and longer comment concerns the second premiss of the argument: 'Only non-relatives are knowable.' It might seem absurd to ascribe such a proposition to Diogenes' putative sceptical source; for why should fathers and children, right hands and left hands, be deemed unknowable merely because they are relative? In fact, at least two lines of thought, distinct but connected, could have suggested the idea that relatives are unknowable.

The first line of thought associates knowledge with 'nature': the proper objects of knowledge, it is supposed, are the natures or essences of things; but relatives cannot form part of any nature; hence relatives are not objects of knowledge. The connexion between knowledge and natures is part of a complex of ideas which we cannot properly examine or document here. In outline, the thought is this: to know something is to know how it *really* is; but it is the inner nature of a thing which determines how it really is. Again, the contrast between what is natural and what is relative is frequently made, both in Sextus and in other authors. The underlying thought is perhaps this: if some property, *F*, is part of a thing's nature, then the thing cannot cease to be *F* without changing in its nature or ceasing to exist; but a thing can lose or acquire relative properties without changing in itself; hence relative properties cannot be part of the nature of anything.

The second line of thought suggesting that relatives are unknowable is short and simple: relatives do not really exist; hence they cannot be known.

The thesis that relatives do not exist is stated more than once by Sextus. The passage closest to our concerns is found in *M* VIII, where Sextus appears to be drawing on the Stoic conception of relatives:

Again, everything which exists is incapable of admitting any change or alteration without being affected – e.g. the colour white cannot become black unless it is converted and changed, and black cannot change into any other colour while staying black; and similarly the sweet cannot become bitter while subsisting unaffected and unaltered. Hence everything which exists does not admit change into something else without being affected in some way. But what is relative changes without being affected and even though no alteration occurs in it. For example, when a one-foot rule has a one-foot rule laid against it, it is said to be equal to it; but when it has a two-foot rule laid against it, it is no longer said to be equal but rather unequal. (*M* VIII 455–6)

The argument is no doubt mistaken (and Sextus' example of relative changes is ill-chosen). But it is not merely a piece of Pyrrhonian sophistry: it derives from a long tradition which worried about the status of relative things.

The view which the Pyrrhonists happily repeated was stated and criticised in a curious treatise by Polystratus, who was head of the Epicurean school in the third century BC.

It is silly to maintain that relatives have the same properties as things that have a nature of their own, or that the latter exist and the former do not. (It does not matter whether we refute the former view from the latter or the latter from the former.) It is also silly to think that, because what is greater and heavier or whiter and sweeter is greater than something and smaller than something (and heavier, and so on) and none of these is in its own right what it is in relation to something else, then stones and gold and the like, if they exist in truth, must be affected in the same way, so that they are not stones for all people and everywhere, and gold is gold relative to some people but relative to others has a contrary nature. Since this is not so, it is false to say that the former are merely thought of and do not exist. For what is the difference between maintaining this and saying falsely that beautiful and ugly things, because they are not the same for all people and everywhere, do not exist in truth? 'But my friend', someone will say, 'these are relative things, not things in their own right like the ones you mention.' Then would he not also say the same of the other things, because, even in the case of the body itself, some things benefit a healthy body, others a sick body, and among illnesses, some things benefit one illness and others another . . .? Similarly in the case of actions – for here too it is not the case that the same actions benefit everyone, but different actions benefit different people. Yet they are not all *falsely* believed to be such: they are such in virtue of the distinctness of the nature and properties of each. (*On Irrational Contempt for Popular Opinions* XXV–XXVII)

Polystratus' essay survives only on papyrus: the text is in several places uncertain, and our translation sometimes involves guesswork; but the general sense of the passage is unambiguous.

Polystratus is attacking some unnamed people who urged that *either* relatives and things with a nature of their own are indistinguishable *or else* the latter exist and relatives do not. The second option is, in effect, the one suggested by Sextus in *M* VIII. Polystratus insists that there really is a difference between relatives and things with a nature of their own, but he denies that relatives are therefore in any sense unreal or non-existent. Emetics, say, are relative things: a substance may be emetic for one person and not for another, and a change in the person may bring it about that the substance, itself unchanged, is for him no longer emetic. But it is foolish to infer that things are not *really* emetic or that emetics do not really exist. On the contrary, it is precisely the 'distinctness of the nature and properties' of substances that explain their relative powers: things really are emetic (or greater or heavier or sweeter), and what is more they are so in their natures, since it is their natures which determine them to have such and such an effect on such and such a person.

Polystratus' view is subtle, and it is surely correct. The Pyrrhonian attack on relatives as unreal has little to commend it: insofar as Diogenes' version of the Relativity Mode depends on this attack, it is weak.

We turn finally to Sextus, whose account of the Relativity Mode is the longest of the three and in some ways the most puzzling. First, let us ask what analysis of relativity it draws on. There is no clear answer to that question. But elsewhere, in *M* VIII 161–3, Sextus ascribes an analysis to the sceptics themselves. He uses Stoic terminology, distinguishing between 'things in virtue of a difference' (*ta kata diaphoran*) and 'things that are somehow in relation to something' (*ta pros ti pōs echonta*); but unlike the Stoics he makes no distinction between 'things somehow in relation to something' and 'things in relation to something', and we should not suppose that the sceptics' distinction is simply identical with the second of the two Stoic distinctions which we mentioned in connexion with Diogenes. The phrase *ta kata diaphoran* is used in the Relativity Mode in §137: it is plausible – but no more – to suppose that Sextus' version of the Relativity Mode makes use of the analysis which *M* VIII 161–3 ascribes to the sceptics.

The sceptics define 'things in virtue of a difference' as

those things which are conceived of in virtue of a reality of their own, and separately (e.g. white, black, sweet, bitter, and so on): we hit upon them naked and self-contained, without conceiving at the same time of something else.

As for 'things somehow in a relation to something', they are

those things which are conceived of in virtue of their relation to something else, and not grasped separately or in their own right – e.g. whiter, blacker, sweeter, more bitter, and everything of that sort.

It is presumably no accident that the examples of relatives are all expressed by way of comparative adjectives. Such adjectives are particularly suitable for indicating a certain sort of relativity; for sentences of the form '*x* is whiter' or '*x* is sweeter' are plainly elliptical for '*x* is whiter than *y*' and '*x* is sweeter than *y*'. ('Sugar is sweet but honey is sweeter' means 'Sugar is sweet but honey is sweeter *than sugar*.') Here the clause 'than *y*', whether explicit or suppressed, brings out the relativity of the sentence: to call something sweeter is to judge it in relation to something else.

The sort of relativity involved in the sceptics' account we shall call *semantic* relativity. We say that *F*s are semantically relative if sentences of the form '*x* is *F*' are elliptical for sentences of the form '*x* is *F* in relation to *y*'.

It should be clear that semantic relativity is different both from epistemic relativity and from ontological relativity. Thus sweet things, we might suppose, are epistemically relative to bitter things: you cannot recognise anything as sweet unless you are capable also of recognising bitter things. But the existence of sweet things does not imply the existence of bitter things, nor does '*x* is sweet' mean something of the form '*x* is sweet in relation to *y*'. Again, daytime, we may think, is ontologically relative to the sun: if the sun did not exist there would be no such thing as daytime. But you can recognise daytime without being able to recognise the sun, and 'It is daytime' is not elliptical for 'It is daytime in relation to the sun.' Finally, darker things are semantically relative; for '*x* is darker' is elliptical for, and so means, '*x* is darker than *y*'.

The interconnexions among the three sorts of relativity we have found in the ancient texts would be worth investigating more closely, and indeed each sort of relativity itself demands further elaboration. But our aim here is simply to show that the three kinds of relativity are indeed three *distinct* kinds.

Sextus' Relativity Mode is not only different from the modes found in Philo and in Diogenes: it is also quite different in structure from Sextus' other modes. For in the case of Relativity Sextus offers no illustrative material at all – he produces no dogmatic examples, he retails no anecdotes. Nor, more significantly, does he refer to conflicts of appearances. We should expect illustrations of the schema

(1.8) *x* appears *F* in relation *R*
(2.8) *x* appears *F** in relation *R**.

But we find no such schema in the text. Rather, Sextus begins by claiming that if everything is relative we shall suspend judgement as to what anything is really like. And he then proceeds to argue that everything is in fact relative.

His argument falls into two parts. The second part, §§137–9, consists of a sequence of six abstract arguments, the first five of which deal with relativity in respect of 'the things observed together', while the sixth concerns relativity in respect of 'the subject judging'.

The first five arguments all have the same structure, and we need only discuss the first of them. Sextus reasons thus. Suppose that there are non-relative things. Then either they differ from relatives or they do not. If they do not differ from relatives, then they are themselves relatives and not non-relatives after all. If they do differ from relatives, then again they are relatives; for they will differ *from relatives*, and anything which differs from some other thing is thereby relative to it. Hence, on either count there are no non-relatives.

The argument is sophistical. It is true that, say, horses differ from cows. It is also true that things that differ are semantic relatives; i.e. '*x* differs' is elliptical for '*x* differs from *y*'. But it does not follow from those two truths that horses are relative; that is to say, it does not follow that '*x* is a horse' is elliptical for '*x* is a horse relative to *y*'. In general, from the premises that Fs are G and 'G' is a relative term, we plainly cannot infer that 'F' is a relative term.

The sixth of Sextus' arguments is quite different in form. Let us imagine that a Pyrrhonist says 'Everything is relative.' A dogmatist, we may suppose, will disagree, and he will express his disagreement by saying 'Not everything is relative.' Now by his very disagreement, Sextus urges, the dogmatist confirms his opponent's opinion; for the disagreement shows that the relativity of everything is *itself* something relative. Since the dogmatist does not accept universal relativity, this universal relativity is itself only in force relative to the Pyrrhonist.

This argument, which has many parallels in Sextus' writings, is a variant of an argument form known technically as a *peritropē* or 'about turn'. The *peritropē* was, so far as we know, first used by Democritus: thereafter it was highly favoured by ancient philosophers of every persuasion. Expressed in its most general form, the *peritropē* goes like this: You maintain that P. Someone retorts that not-P. But his retort does an about turn, for it emerges that the thesis that not-P only serves to confirm the thesis that P.

In principle, about turn arguments are powerful; for if the negation of a thesis itself confirms the thesis, what stronger confirmation could be desired? And in fact many about turn arguments are sound. In particular, where not-P implies or entails P, the *peritropē* is sound. (Suppose someone says that some propositions are true, and an opponent maintains that, on the contrary, it is true that no propositions are true. Then the opponent has indeed done an about turn.) But the argument in §139, ingeniously paradoxical though it may be, is fallacious. The disagreement between the dogmatist and the Pyrrhonist does not show that universal relativity is itself relative to the Pyrrhonist (whatever that means) and thereby confirm the Pyrrhonist's opinion. It shows only that not everyone upholds universal relativity. In general, if two people disagree on some opinion, we cannot infer that the opinion holds (only) relative to one of them. If x maintains that P and y maintains that not-P, then one of them is mistaken – and that is all we can infer.

In the first part of his discussion, Sextus announces that 'We have in fact already deduced that everything is relative.' It is natural to take this to be a reference to the taxonomy of the modes in §§38–9, where Relativity was made the most general mode and all the particular modes were subsumed under it. But there are differences between §§38–9 and §136. In Chapter 3 we displayed the taxonomy of the earlier passage as follows:

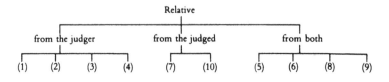

The taxonomy implicit in §136 can be set out in a comparable figure:

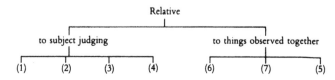

The bottom line of this figure is odd. No doubt the Ninth and Tenth Modes are omitted simply because Sextus has not yet discussed them. (But why, then, did he not place the Relativity Mode *tenth* in order, as Diogenes does?) The last three modes are mentioned out of order, for no reason that we can discern. (And the text is corrupt: between the references to the Sixth and Seventh Modes our manuscripts transmit a phrase which has not yet been satisfactorily explained – some suggestions are mentioned in Appendix E.)

The second lines of the two figures also differ: the earlier taxonomy contains three elements where the later one contains only two.

Sextus' procedure in §136 cannot be explained simply by a reference back to §§38–9. Rather, in order to understand what is happening here we must look ahead to the later sections in *PH* where Sextus presents the Five Modes of Agrippa. The third of these modes reads like this:

In the mode deriving from relativity, as we said above, the existing object appears to be such-and-such relative to the subject judging and to the things observed together with it, but we suspend judgement on what it is like in its nature. (*PH* I 167)

Now the two types of relativity distinguished here are exactly the same as the two distinguished in §§135–6 of the Eighth Mode. It is clear, then, that the phrase 'as we said above' in *PH* I 167 refers back to these paragraphs.

We are thus led to the following hypothetical explanation of Sextus' strange account of the Relativity Mode. We must surely suppose that in his sources for the Ten Modes Sextus found an Eighth Mode from relativity, and that this mode – like the Relativity Modes in Philo and in Diogenes – was broadly similar in style to the other nine. He decided, however, to eject this traditional material and to replace it by a version of Agrippa's Relativity Mode. He then explained the new Relativity Mode by a loose reference back to his earlier taxonomy and by the little set of six abstract arguments. (No doubt these arguments too were drawn from Agrippa.)

Why did Sextus decide to make this change to the original Aenesideman Modes? Why was he so concerned to establish that 'everything is relative'? How, after all, does that thesis connect with scepticism and with the other modes?

In Chapter 3 we remarked that the conflicts of appearances which the Ten Modes are designed to systematise have a common structure. We expressed this structure by the schemata:

(1) x appears F in situation S
(2) x appears F^* in situation S^*.

In the particular modes, the general qualifier 'in situation S' is replaced by 'to animals of kind K', 'in posture P', 'in quantity Q', and so on. Sextus, we suggest, also noticed this common structure (how could he have failed to?), and he chose to express it in terms of 'relations' rather than in terms of 'situations'. Thus instead of (1) and (2) he implicitly offered:

(1a) x appears F in relation R
(2a) x appears F^* in relation R^*.

Here the qualifier 'in relation R' functions in exactly the same way as our qualifier 'in situation S'. Sextus' claim in §39 that Relativity is the most general mode is thus a recognition of the common structure possessed by all the modes. His 'in relation R' is no less apt than our 'in situation S' – indeed, we prefer his locution to our own and we should have adopted it but for the confusions which any mention of relativity seems to introduce into the discussion of sceptical issues.

It may be objected that (1a) and (2a) speak of the relativity of *appearances*, whereas the Eighth Mode asserts that 'Everything *is* relative.' But that objection overlooks Sextus' explicit assertion in §135 that he is using the word 'is' in the sense of 'appears'. Thus when he says 'Everything is relative' what he actually means is 'Everything appears relative.' In §140, and again in his account of Agrippa's Relativity Mode, he repeats that the relativity in question is a relativity of *appearances*. Everything appears relative, and appearances are all relative.

And this, unlike the claim that everything *is* relative, is or ought to be an uncontroversial truth. For appearances *are* semantically relative. That is to say, '*x* appears *F*' should always be construed as elliptical for '*x* appears *F* in relation *R* [or: in situation *S*]'.

Sextus' account of his new Relativity Mode is thus fundamentally intelligible and coherent. The mode, as he says, is not on the same level as the other nine, and it cannot be presented and illustrated in the same way as they are. Rather, it provides a *general* description of the structure of all the Aenesideman Modes. The Aenesideman Modes collect oppositions of the form (1a) and (2a); we cannot prefer *R* to *R** or *vice versa*; hence we suspend judgement as to whether *x* is really *F* or *F**, contenting ourselves with the observation that *x* appears *F* in *R* and *F** in *R**.

Of course, Sextus' actual procedure is not beyond criticism, and he was perhaps not wholly clear in his own mind about what he was doing. He should not have *replaced* the original Relativity Mode with his own discussion of relativity, for that gives the false impression that the new discussion is simply a superior version of the old. And he should not have interpolated his new mode into the middle of the original sequence. He would have done better had he abandoned the original Relativity Mode altogether, thus reducing the Aenesideman canon to nine. Or, perhaps better still, he might have retained the original Relativity Mode and carefully distinguished it from his own new Relativity Mode. In either case, he could then have appended, at the beginning or the end of his account, his general reflexions on the structure of the modes.

In this and earlier chapters we have in effect distinguished three quite different ways in which questions of relativity impinge upon the modes. Since the matter is convoluted in itself and has been a source of considerable confusion in accounts of scepticism both ancient and modern, it may be helpful to recapitulate briefly.

First, then, relativity appears in some texts as a conclusion drawn from the undecidable conflicts of appearances. Sometimes, when *x* appears *F* in *S* and *F** in *S** and we have no way of preferring *S* to *S**, we may be inclined to infer that *x* is really *neither F nor F**: rather, *x* is *F* in *S* and *F** in *S**. This relativistic conclusion is, we have remarked, distinct from and incompatible with scepticism in its proper Pyrrhonian sense. Any Pyrrhonists who toyed with this sort of relativism were muddled.

Secondly, relativity appeared in the premises of the original Relativity Mode of Aenesidemus. One of Aenesidemus' ten sets of oppositions will have had the general form:

(1.8) x appears F in relation R
(2.8) x appears F^* in relation R^*.

Here the qualifier 'in relation R' is – or was intended to be – entirely on a par with the qualifiers 'to animals of kind K', 'in posture P', 'in quantity Q', and so on. The Pyrrhonists suggested that (1.8) and (2.8) induced suspension of judgement in just the same way as the other oppositions. This use of relativity is perfectly Pyrrhonian: traces of it are preserved, in variant forms, in Philo and in Diogenes.

Finally, relativity appears, as we have just seen, in Sextus' abstract characterisation of the Aenesideman Modes. Sextus is here borrowing material from the later Modes of Agrippa, and he implicitly uses sentences (1a) and (2a) to express the general structure of conflicts of appearances and to describe the general form taken by the Aenesideman arguments for suspension of judgement. This third use of relativity, like the second, is perfectly compatible with scepticism.

12 The Common and the Rare

Sextus, *PH* I 141–4:

141 As for the mode based on frequent or rare encounters (which we said was ninth in order) we shall set out some cases like the following.

The sun is actually a great deal more striking than a comet; but since we see the sun frequently and comets only rarely, we are struck by comets (so as actually to think it a divine sign) but not at all by the sun. However, if we conceive of the sun as appearing rarely and setting rarely, and as lighting up everything all at once, and suddenly plunging everything into darkness, then we shall consider the thing very striking.

142 Earthquakes, too, do not similarly upset people experiencing them for the first time and those who have grown accustomed to them. And how striking the sea is to someone who sees it for the first time! Further, the beauty of a human body when seen for the first time, and suddenly, excites us more than it would if it became a customary sight.

143 Also, what is rare is thought to be valuable, but not what is familiar and easily available. For instance, if we conceive of water as being rare, how much more valuable would it then appear to us than everything that seems valuable! Or if we imagine gold as simply strewn in quantity over the ground like stones, who do we think would find it valuable then, or worth locking away?

144 Since, therefore, the same objects seem now striking and valuable, now not, depending on whether they impress us frequently or rarely, we deduce that we will no doubt be able to say what each of these things appears to us to be like given the frequency or rarity of its impressing us, but we will not be able to assert baldly what each external existing object is like.

Because of this mode also, therefore, we suspend judgement about them.

Diogenes IX 87:

87   *Ninth* is the mode depending on what is habitual or strange or rare. For instance, earthquakes are not found surprising by people among whom they occur frequently; nor is the sun, because it is seen every day. (Favorinus makes the Ninth the Eighth, while Sextus and Aenesidemus make it the Tenth.* Sextus calls the Tenth the Eighth, and Favorinus calls it the Ninth.)

Sextus' Ninth Mode is not found in Philo: some will sympathise with Philo for omitting what might be thought to be the feeblest of the Ten Modes.

Diogenes presents the mode in a mutilated form and without any argumentative structure. He adds a confusing comment, which we have already discussed (above, p. 29), about the place of this mode in other authors.

As Sextus presents it, the mode can readily be formulated in the standard form. There are conflicting appearances of the appropriate variety, which we may express schematically as follows:

(1.9)   *x* appears *F* when encountered with frequency *f*

(2.9)   *x* appears *F** when encountered with frequency *f**

but:

(3.9)   we cannot prefer *f* to *f** or *vice versa*

so that we end up by suspending belief.

Sextus does not in fact restrict himself to examples of frequent and infrequent encounters. In some of his examples – earthquakes, the sea, the naked human body – the contrast is between a *first* encounter which surprises and *later* encounters when we no longer marvel. Novelty is not the same as infrequency nor familiarity as frequency. Sextus unwittingly runs two distinct contrasts together. Diogenes speaks of what is 'habitual or strange or rare'. It is possible that his two-fold comparison with the habitual is meant to make the distinction which Sextus ignores. The habitual contrasts both with the 'strange' or unfamiliar and with the 'rare' or infrequent.

Sextus' examples are limited to two types of ways in which things may appear: being striking as opposed to being unremarkable, and being valuable as opposed to having no value. These two pairs of properties are evidently distinct. Gold is valuable but it is not particularly

striking or remarkable. Earthquakes are no doubt striking but they will
hardly be regarded as valuable.

It is not clear whether Sextus wishes to restrict the scope of the Ninth
Mode to the properties of strikingness and valuableness – the text of
§144 is not determinate on the point. Certainly, it would not be difficult
to extend the mode to other properties. Democritus, for example,
remarked that 'of pleasures, the most uncommon give us the most joy'
(frag. 232), and that 'frequent toil becomes lighter by habituation' (frag.
241). These aphorisms could readily be worked up into illustrations of
the Ninth Mode. Or again, think how blue the sky appears on the first
day of a holiday in the Alps – and what a perfectly ordinary blue it
appears a week or so later. In general, familiarity breeds contempt, and
things appear in a different light once we get used to them.

Perhaps the sceptics chose to refer to remarkability and value because
those properties provide the most obvious and incontrovertible
examples of the effect of frequency or familiarity on appearances. Thus
a rhetorical handbook preserved among Cicero's works explains that:

no one is amazed by the rising and the passage and the setting of the sun, because
these things happen every day. But they are amazed by eclipses of the sun
because these happen rarely – and they are more amazed at eclipses of the sun
than at those of the moon, because the latter are more frequent. Thus our nature
shows that we are not to be stirred by common and customary things but are
moved by novelty and any remarkable occurrence. (*To Herennius* III xxii 36)

But if those reflexions are useful for the orator, it is not plain that they
advance the sceptic's position.

For it must seem obviously right to respond to examples of this sort
by a retreat into relativism. Surely, things are not striking or valuable
tout court: they are striking or valuable *to someone, in certain circumstances*,
and so on. Are earthquakes really striking or not? The question is
misconceived, and so, therefore, is the sceptical answer. It is a mistake
to say that we cannot tell whether earthquakes are really striking, for
there is nothing to tell here. The fact is that earthquakes are pretty
striking when you experience one for the first time but become
unremarkable (or so the sceptics invite us to believe) once you have
lived through three or four. Naked bodies are exciting the first time
you see them – they cease to excite (or so the sceptics purport to think)
when you have seen them on all the beaches of the Mediterranean. It is
silly to wonder whether or not they are *really* exciting 'in themselves' or
in their 'nature'.

That is not to say that the Ninth Mode shows nothing at all. On the contrary, if it is instrumental in establishing the relativity of values of certain types, then that is no small thing; it means that we cannot ask what is the *real* value of, say, gold or labour or the Mona Lisa. Relativism, as we have already remarked, is not always a trivial or an obvious fact. But we must again insist that relativism, far from being a form of scepticism, is actually incompatible with scepticism. Thus here again we think that the examples which the sceptics adduce do nothing towards establishing a sceptical conclusion or inducing a state of suspension of judgement.

The Ninth Mode has one further feature which requires brief comment. Sextus' examples are in many cases hypothetical rather than actual. 'For instance, if we conceive of water as being rare, . . . ': water in fact is not rare, so that Sextus cannot produce, as one half of a conflict, the proposition that:

Water appears valuable when rarely encountered.

Instead, he offers the hypothetical statement:

Water would appear valuable were it rarely encountered.

Now the appeal to hypothetical examples is a common procedure in philosophy, both ancient and modern. Sextus follows it elsewhere. For example, at *PH* I 34 he urges us not to assent to a sound-looking argument on the grounds that someone *might* later produce an equally plausible counter-argument; at *PH* III 233–4 he says that we should not allow that any given practice is wrong since that *might* be contested among people of whom we happen to be ignorant.

The use of hypothetical arguments, or 'thought-experiments' as they are sometimes called, is doubtless often legitimate and beneficial. But we may wonder whether the sceptic's appeal to them is well founded – and our doubt may actually be strengthened by Sextus himself, who appeals to hypothetical examples rarely and only when he has no actual examples to hand.

The legitimacy of Sextus' appeal to such examples depends in part upon their precise character. He says, in effect, 'It might be the case that . . . '. We can understand him in either of two ways. He might mean, strongly, 'It is plausible to hold that . . . ', and he might mean, weakly, 'It is possible, for all you know, that . . . '. The former case does not seem to pose any problems. If it actually *is* plausible to hold that, say, water would appear valuable to anyone who saw it rarely, then we may surely adopt that hypothetical 'appearance' and take it as one of our conflicting appearances. In effect, as we saw, that is just what Sextus does in the First Mode, where his claims about how things appear to animals are all introduced as being plausible or reasonable.

It is the second case which is the more interesting, for it is connected to a very common form of sceptical argument. Someone asserts that *P*. A sceptic remarks: 'But it is *possible* that *Q* – I mean, for all you know, it is actually the case that *Q*. And in fact, *P* and *Q* are incompatible.' To some philosophers this form of argument has seemed shabby – why, after all, should I recant my assertion that *P* simply because it *might* be the case that *Q*? If it actually *were* the case that *Q*, then of course I should have to recant; but a mere possibility does not demand a recantation.

In fact, there is surely something in the sceptic's argument. Consider the following three propositions:

(A) Sextus knows that he is in Alexandria
(B) For all Sextus knows, he is in Athens
(C) Sextus cannot be both in Alexandria and in Athens.

Surely these three propositions cannot all be true? For if (A) and (C) are both true, then (B) must be false: it is not true that for all Sextus knows, he is in Athens – he knows something, namely that he is in Alexandria, which excludes his being in Athens. And similarly, as the sceptic will argue, if (B) and (C) are true, then (A) cannot be true.

If that is correct, we can conclude that an appeal to hypothetical examples, even in the weak form of 'It is possible, for all you know, that . . .', may do some sceptical work.

But it will not do the particular sort of work which Sextus wants it to do. It may require us to recant a claim to *knowledge*, but it need not lead to our abandoning *belief*. For, as Sextus himself insists, we are led to abandon our beliefs by the *equipollence* of reasons on either side. When the Pyrrhonist claims that we cannot decide whether *x* is *F* or *F**, he does not mean merely that we cannot tell for sure: he means that nothing tips the balance one way or the other. Now such oppositions as

Grass appears green to us on earth
Grass may (for all we know) appear red on Mars

are unlikely to satisfy the requirement of equipollence. For the latter proposition, unlike the former, expresses a mere possibility: we may give it *some* weight – but the Pyrrhonist will find difficulty in making us give it a weight *equal* to that of its rival.

In short, the objection to Sextus' use of hypothetical examples is not that they cannot in principle induce suspension of judgement. Rather, it is that, at any rate in their weak form, they are unlikely to meet the condition of equipollence.

13 Customs and Persuasions

145 The tenth mode, which especially bears on ethics, is the one depending on lifestyles and customs and laws and belief in myth and dogmatic suppositions.

A lifestyle is a choice of a way of life or a way of acting practised by one person or many (for example, by Diogenes, or the Spartans).

146 A law is a written contract among citizens, transgressors of which are punished.

A custom or ordinary usage (there is no difference) is a common acceptance by a number of people of a certain way of acting, transgressors of which are not necessarily punished. For example, there is a *law* against adultery, but with us it is a *custom* not to have sex with a woman in public.

147 A belief in myth is an acceptance of matters that did not occur and are fictional – examples include the myths about Cronus which many people are led to credit.

A dogmatic supposition is an acceptance of a matter that seems to be established by abduction or proof of some kind, for example, that there are atomic elements of things, or homoeomeries, or least parts, or something else.

148 We oppose each of these sometimes to itself, sometimes to one of the others.

For example, we oppose custom to custom like this: some of the Ethiopians tattoo their babies, while we do not. The Persians consider it becoming to wear brightly-coloured full-length garments, while we consider it unbecoming. Indians have sex with women in public, while most other people think this shameful.

149 We oppose law to law like this: in Rome anyone who renounces his father's property does not repay his father's debts, but in Rhodes he does repay them in every case. Among the

Tauri in Scythia there was a law that strangers were sacrificed to Artemis, while among us killing a human at a religious rite is prohibited.

150   We oppose lifestyle to lifestyle when we oppose the lifestyle of Diogenes to that of Aristippus, or that of the Spartans to that of the Italians.

We oppose belief in myth to belief in myth when we say in one place that the mythical father of gods and men is Zeus, and in another that he is Ocean, citing

Ocean source of the gods and Tethys their mother.

[Homer, *Iliad* XIV 201]

151   We oppose dogmatic suppositions to one another when we say that some people declare that there is one element, other infinitely many; some that the soul is mortal, others immortal; some that human affairs are directed by divine Providence, others non-providentially.

152   We oppose custom to the others – for example to law, when we say that in Persia homosexual acts are customary, but in Rome they are forbidden by law; that among us adultery is forbidden, but among the Massegetae it is accepted by custom as indifferent* (as Eudoxus of Cnidus narrates in the first book of his *Journey round the World*); that among us it is forbidden to have sex with one's mother, but in Persia it is the custom to favour such marriages. In Egypt they marry their sisters, which among us is prohibited by law.

153   Custom is opposed to lifestyle: most men have sex with their own women in private, but Crates did it with Hipparchia in public. Diogenes went round in a sleeveless tunic, while we dress normally.

154   Custom is opposed to belief in myth: the myths say that Cronus ate up his own children, while with us it is the custom to provide for our children. And among us it is ordinary usage to revere the gods as good and as unaffected by evils, while they are represented by the poets as suffering wounds and envying one another.

155   Custom is opposed to dogmatic supposition: with us it is the custom to ask for good things from the gods, while Epicurus says that the divinity pays no attention to us; and Aristippus thinks that it is indifferent whether one wears women's clothes, whereas we think this shameful.

156　We oppose lifestyle to law: although there is a law that a free man of good family may not be struck, the all-in wrestlers strike one another, because that is the style of their way of life; and gladiators kill one another for the same reason, although murder is prohibited.

157　We oppose belief in myth to lifestyle when we say that the myths say that in Omphale's house Heracles

> carded wool and endured slavery
> [Homer, *Odyssey* XXII 423]

and did things which nobody would have done by choice even in moderation, whereas the style of Heracles' life was noble.

158　We oppose lifestyle to dogmatic supposition: athletes pursue glory as a good and take on for its sake a style of life full of exertion, while many philosophers hold the dogma that glory is a bad thing.

159　We oppose law to belief in myth: the poets represent the gods as committing adultery and indulging in homosexual acts, while with us the law forbids these things.

160　We oppose law to dogmatic supposition: Chrysippus says that it is indifferent whether one has sex or not with one's mother or sister, while the law forbids this.

161　We oppose belief in myth to dogmatic supposition: the poets say that Zeus came down and had sex with mortal women, while
162　the dogmatists consider this to be impossible; and Homer says that Zeus because of his grief for Sarpedon

> poured down upon the earth bloody drops of rain
> [*Iliad* XVI 459]

whereas it is a dogma of philosophers that the divinity is unaffected; and they deny* the myth of the centaurs, presenting the centaur to us as an example of unreality.

163　We could have taken many other examples for each of the above oppositions, but in a brief account these will suffice.

So, since so much anomaly has been shown in objects by this mode too, we shall not be able to say what each existing object is like in its nature, but only how it appears relative to a given lifestyle or law or custom, and so on. Because of this mode too, therefore, it is necessary for us to suspend judgement on the nature of external existing objects.

In this way, then, by means of the ten modes we end up with suspension of judgement.

Diogenes IX 83–4:

83   *Fifth* is the mode depending on lifestyles, laws, belief in myth, conventions due to custom* and dogmatic suppositions. This includes questions about what is fine and base, true and false, good and bad, about gods, and about the production and destruction of all the things that are apparent. For instance, the same behaviour is just for some and unjust for others, to some good and to others bad. Thus Persians do not regard it as strange to have sex with their daughters, while Greeks regard it as prohibited. The Massegetae, according to Eudoxus in Book I of his *Journey round the World*, have their wives in common; Greeks do not. The Cilicians used to take pride in being pirates; but not 84 the Greeks. Different people believe in different gods; some believe in divine providence and others do not. The Egyptians dispose of their dead by embalming, the Romans by cremation, the Paeonians by throwing them into lakes. Hence the suspension of judgement as to what is true.

Philo 193–202:

193   Are we not called by the following facts not to trust* too much to what is unclear – facts which pervade virtually the whole world and which have led* Greeks and foreigners alike on to the slippery slope of judgement? What are they? Lifestyles, of course, going back to our childhood, traditional customs and ancient laws, not a single one of which is agreed upon by everyone in the same form. Depending on country, nation or state – or rather even on village and individual home – men, 194 women and small children have completely different views: for instance what is base to us is fine to others, and similarly with what is becoming and unbecoming, just and unjust, impious and pious, legal and illegal, and again with what is blamed and praised, penalised and rewarded – and with the other cases where they hold contrary views.*

195   What need is there to make a long speech when I am drawn away by more pressing matters? Still, if someone not tempted by any more novel spectacle were willing to spend time on the

present topic and go into the lifestyles, customs and laws of different countries, nations, states, and localities – of subjects and rulers, the famous and the obscure, the free and the enslaved, lay people and experts, he would waste not one or two days, or even a month or a year, but his whole life, even if he enjoyed a long life-span; and nonetheless he would, without knowing it, leave many matters unscrutinised, unconsidered and unmentioned.

196   And so, since among different people these things are not just slightly different but utterly discordant, so as to compete and conflict, necessarily the appearances experienced will differ and
197   the judgements be at war with one another. This being so, who is so senseless and idiotic as to say steadfastly that such-and-such is just or intelligent or fine or advantageous? Whatever one person determines to be such will be nullified by someone else whose practice from childhood has been the contrary.

198   Myself, I am not surprised if the labile and heterogeneous mob, inglorious slaves of customs and laws instituted in any fashion, taught to obey them as masters or tyrants from the cradle up, and having their souls thrashed into submission and lacking the ability to grasp any great or imaginative thoughts, should believe whatever has once been handed down to them, or if, having left their minds without exercise, they should come out with assertions and denials which are unscrutinised and untried. But I *am* surprised that the majority of what are called philosophers, who do profess to hunt down the clear and the true in things, are divided into brigades and platoons and set down dogmas that are discordant – and often actually contrary to one another – not on some one chance point but on virtually everything, great and small, with which their investigations are concerned.

199   Some set up the world as infinite, others say it is finite; some make the universe uncreated and others represent it as created; some attach it to an irrational and spontaneous movement, with nothing to oversee and guide it, while others suppose that there is a wonderful providence, caring for both whole and parts, and a god who drives and steers it smoothly and safely. How could these people be having the same apprehensions of their subject-matter?

200   As for the appearances we get from inquiring about the good – do they not force us to suspend judgement rather than concur?

Some consider only the fine to be good and hoard it up in the soul, while others split the good up into many parts and extend it 201 as far as the body and external things. These people say that advantages due to good fortune are the body's guardians, and that health and strength, soundness and accuracy of the senses, and everything of that kind are the guardians of the sovereign soul. For the nature of the good, they say, has three levels, of which the third and outermost protects the second . . .* while the second forms a strong defence and fortification for the first.
202   Indeed, on this subject and on the different ways of life and the ends to which all actions should be referred, and on the thousand other topics in logic, ethics and physics – on all these there have been countless inquiries, but up to the present time agreement has not been reached in any one of them on the part of all the inquirers.

The Tenth Mode, according to Sextus, 'is the one depending on lifestyles and customs and laws and belief in myth and dogmatic suppositions' (§145). It is almost certain that these are the same as the five factors mentioned in Diogenes ('almost certain' because Diogenes' text in §83 is corrupt). Philo refers to 'lifestyles . . . traditional customs and ancient laws' in §193, and to 'dogmas' in §198. He does not mention 'belief in myths'. (But since he is writing a commentary on a Jewish text for Jewish readers, he would have good reason to omit this even if he did find it in his source.) Moreover, he appears to divide the material of Sextus' Tenth Mode into two independent parts: §§193–7 deal with lifestyles, customs and laws; §§198–202 deal with dogmas – and in §198 Philo seems to make a deliberate transition, as though he were turning to a new mode. So what our other sources present as a single mode probably figures as two modes in Philo. We cannot tell whether he is following an earlier Pyrrhonian source in this or rather has imposed his own form on the Pyrrhonian material.

This mode, Sextus says, 'especially bears on ethics' (§145). Diogenes reflects the same idea when he records that the mode 'includes questions about what is fine and base . . . ' (§83). Sextus' remark is ambiguous: he may mean either that the mode bears upon ethics more than upon any other topic, or that the mode bears upon ethics more than any other mode does. The use of the term 'ethics' requires a word of caution. Sextus is referring to the third of the three canonical parts of ancient philosophy, logic, physics, ethics; and he explains elsewhere that 'pretty well everyone has agreed in supposing that ethical study is concerned with the discrimination of what is good and bad' (*M* XI2). Ethics, then, is the study of value in general and not exclusively of *moral* value. Now much of the material in Sextus' version of the Tenth Mode is in fact ethical in this sense, and it is easy to see how the topics of lifestyle, custom and law will tend to produce oppositions of an ethical sort. (But the same is not true – at least not to the same extent – of mythical beliefs and dogmatic suppositions.) Thus Sextus could plausibly say that most of the matter falling under the Tenth Mode was ethical in nature. Again, the other modes have comparatively little to say about ethical issues. Such issues are, of course, included under the Relativity Mode, for that mode is comprehensive in its scope; and we have just met them in the Ninth Mode. But it remains plausible to assert that the Tenth Mode more than any other mode deals with ethical matters. Thus Sextus' remark in §145 is appropriate whichever way we construe it.

Sextus' presentation of the Tenth Mode is careful and elaborate. Each of the five elements of the mode – lifestyle, custom, law, myth, dogma – may be contrasted both with itself and with each of the other four. There are thus fifteen possible permutations, and Sextus runs through all fifteen in a reasonably systematic order. Comparing custom with custom produces the first set of oppositions; comparing law with law produces the second; and so on, until the fifteenth set is produced by comparing mythical beliefs with dogmatic suppositions. It is the availability of these permutations which explains why Sextus treats the Tenth Mode as a single mode rather than as five distinct modes, one for each element.

Sextus' illustrative examples are, as usual, traditional. He draws largely on the rich store of anthropological material which had been assembled by the Greeks from the days of Herodotus and before. His sources are more numerous and more varied than in the other modes, ranging from Homer at one end (§150, §157, §162) to Roman law at the other (§149, §152). But he does not refer to the most celebrated 'opposition' in ancient literature. Herodotus relates how the Persian king, Darius,

summoned those Greeks who were present and asked them for how much money they would be willing to eat their fathers when they died. They said that they would not do such a thing for any price. Darius then summoned the Callatian Indians, who eat their parents, and asked them, in the presence of the Greeks who learned what was said through an interpreter, for how much money they would be prepared to burn their fathers in a fire when they were dead. They shouted out and begged him not to blaspheme. These, then, are their laws; and Pindar, I think, is right when he says that law is king of everything. (*Histories* III 38).

Law conflicts with law, custom with custom.

One feature of Herodotus' story is worth a moment's reflexion. The Greeks and the Indians are *shocked* by one another's practices: each seems not merely strange but actually offensive to the other. Many of Sextus' illustrations of cultural diversity are similarly shocking – indeed, it is hard to avoid the suspicion that he relishes the outrageousness of some of the notions he reports. But there is perhaps a certain tension in the Tenth Mode as a result of this: on the one hand, Sextus supposes that his stories will lead us to recognise the doubtful status of our own beliefs and practices, and will thus induce suspension of judgement. On the other hand, to the extent that he shocks his readers he is unlikely to achieve his sceptical goal; for the sense of shock may reinforce rather than weaken existing prejudices.

The material in Diogenes is of the same nature as that in Sextus, although only one of his illustrations has an exact counterpart in Sextus' version of the mode. (Both Diogenes §84, and Sextus §151, refer to disagreements of dogma over the providence of the gods.) Sextus observes that 'We could have taken many other examples for each of the above oppositions' (§163), and in his discussion of the 'ethical part of philosophy' in *PH* III he uses some of the material with which Diogenes illustrates the mode (and he also reuses much of his own illustrative material).

Philo's presentation of the mode is somewhat different in style. He offers no examples at all to illustrate differences in lifestyle and custom. (Perhaps he was too fastidious to repeat the mildly salacious stories he found in his sources.) But when he turns to consider dogmas, and to oppose one dogma to another, he does produce a handful of illustrations, one of which (the disagreement over providence) is also found in Sextus and Diogenes. Philo professes to find differences of doctrine among 'the majority of what are called philosophers' more striking (and more shocking) than differences of lifestyle or habit on the part of 'the labile and heterogeneous mob'. It is this fact which makes his account of the Tenth Mode so different in tone from the accounts in Sextus and in Diogenes; more importantly, as we shall see, it enables him to give an idiosyncratic turn to the sceptical conclusion he wants to draw.

But why draw any sceptical conclusion at all? No doubt the various oppositions which the Pyrrhonists collect are intriguing: they require some explanation, and no doubt they point some moral. But is there any reason to think that the moral is a sceptical one? Aristotle thought not. Here is his response to the oppositions in the special case of justice:

> Of political justice part is natural and part legal – natural being what has the same force everywhere and does not depend on being thought to be so or not, and legal being what originally makes no difference one way or the other but does make a difference once it is laid down – e.g. that the ransom is one mina, that a goat and not two sheep should be sacrificed, and also laws passed for particular cases (e.g. to sacrifice for Brasidas) and decrees. Some people think that all justice is of this latter sort because what is natural is unchangeable and has the same force everywhere (in the same way as fire burns both here and in Persia) while they see that what is just changes. But that is not so – although it is so in a sense: with the gods it is not so at all, but with us there are indeed things just by nature, and yet everything just is changeable, but nonetheless there are some things that are just by nature and some that are not. As to what sorts of things, among those that can be otherwise, are so by nature, and what sorts are not, but only legal and by agreement (both being equally changeable) – that is clear. (*Nicomachean Ethics* 1134b18–33)

Aristotle holds that some practices are just by nature. Some people, he says, propound an argument to the contrary: 'Whatever is such-and-such by nature is unchangeably such-and-such, i.e. is such-and-such in all places and at all times; but nothing just is unchangeably just; therefore nothing just is just by nature.' Aristotle allows that all just practices are changeable; but he denies that changeability implies non-naturalness.

Aristotle's opponents are not sceptics but conventionalists. They do not argue that we cannot tell what is really just: rather, they deny that there is anything more to justice than what the laws or the conventions of a society lay down. Nonetheless, their argument was adopted, to different ends, by the Pyrrhonists (the contrast between the dependability of fire and the inconstancy of values is repeated by Sextus at *PH* III 179–82 and at *M* XI 69–78). And Aristotle's rejection of their argument incorporates a rejection of scepticism. For Aristotle claims that it is 'clear' what practices are naturally or really just and what are not.

The Pyrrhonists, of course, would not have shared Aristotle's confidence: given the oppositions in practices and the disputes among thinkers, it is simply *not* clear what is naturally just and what is not. Now we might well grant the Pyrrhonists that much, but still wonder why the oppositions should lead us to suspend judgement. Diogenes is characteristically brief: 'Hence the suspension of judgement as to what is true' (§84). Sextus, uncharacteristically, is not much more expansive:

'since so much anomaly has been shown in objects by this mode too, we shall not be able to say what each existing object is like in its nature, but only how it appears relative to a given lifestyle or law or custom, and so on' (§163). How does Sextus intend us to reach this *impasse*?

Consider the first of Sextus' illustrations, when he opposes custom to custom: 'some of the Ethiopians tattoo their babies, while we do not' (§148). Here we have two different and opposing customs. But where is the 'anomaly'? Whence does scepticism derive? Clearly the opposition of *customs* is not itself an antithesis of 'appearances' of the sort which the modes collect. Rather, the opposition of customs is cited as *evidence* for an antithesis of appearances. Given the general claim that the Tenth Mode is concerned especially with ethics, it is not hard to construct a relevant antithesis. In §148 Sextus expects us to realise that

Tattooing babies appears good to Ethiopians
whereas
Tattooing babies appears bad to Greeks.

The 'appearances' are appearances of *value*, and Sextus' general point is that the same practices appear to have opposite values in different cultures.

Let us use the term 'persuasion' as a generic word covering lifestyles, customs, laws, myths and dogmas. Then we can represent the structure of the Tenth Mode, in the familiar way, as follows:

(1.10) x appears F to those of persuasion P
(2.10) x appears F^* to those of persuasion P^*

And since

(3.10) we cannot prefer P to P^* or *vice versa*

it follows that

(4) we suspend judgement as to whether x is F or F^*.

Sextus does not produce any concrete instance of this schematic argument. He does not even produce a concrete instance of (1.10) or (2.10). Rather, his illustrative material is the evidence from which we may construct antitheses of appearances, and so reach scepticism. (Here his procedure is the same as it was in the First Mode.)

Philo's account of the mode gives some support to this interpretation of Sextus. Having referred to differences in lifestyles, customs and laws, he infers that 'since among different people these things are not just slightly different but utterly discordant, so as to compete and conflict, necessarily the appearances experienced will differ and the judgements be at war with one another' (§196). Again, after referring to various doctrinal differences among the philosophers, he asks 'How could these people be having the same apprehensions of their subject-matter?' (§199). Philo's intentions here are not entirely plain; but a plausible interpretation of his remarks is that he is explicitly inviting us to construct antitheses of the form (1.10) and (2.10) from the material given to us in the Tenth Mode.

However, even granted that we have antitheses of the familiar form, why should we end up in a state of scepticism? Sextus gives us no reason; he does not mention, let alone justify, step (3) in the argument. No doubt he felt that it would be superfluous to do this. Step (3) in the Tenth Mode is no different in principle from the analogous step in the other modes, and Sextus has already produced a variety of arguments for the 'undecidability' of the conflicts which the modes assemble. If we want to be assured that step (3) is true, we need only turn back to one of the earlier modes and extract the relevant arguments from it.

Philo, on the other hand, introduces something novel. Indeed, each part of Philo's mode (or perhaps rather, each of Philo's two modes) hints at arguments which we have not yet met.

In §197, having inferred that 'the appearances experienced will differ', Philo continues: 'This being so, who is so senseless and idiotic as to say steadfastly that such-and-such is just or intelligent or fine or advantageous? Whatever one person determines to be such will be nullified by someone else whose practice from childhood has been the contrary.' In this sentence we find an intimation at least of an argument which sceptics of every age have welcomed. It runs roughly as follows: 'Differences in appearances can be seen to correlate strongly with differences in cultural background. That being so, the best explanation of why x appears F to y is that y was brought up in such-and-such a persuasion. But if appearances can be explained by this sort of hypothesis, we cannot properly reach beyond appearances to any underlying reality.'

The Presocratic philosopher Xenophanes, whom later Pyrrhonists claimed as an intellectual ancestor, was perhaps the first thinker to put forward a sceptical argument of this sort.

> If cows and horses or lions had hands
> or could draw with their hands and make statues as men do,
> horses would draw likenesses of the gods
> similar to horses, cows to cows, and they would create statues
> in the same form as they themselves each had.
>
> (frag. 15)

And there is a moral here for humans; for

> Ethiopians say that their gods are snub-nosed and dark,
> Thracians that they are blue-eyed and red-haired.

(frag. 16)

The sceptical point is clear: our ideas about the gods are explained not by any facts about *the gods*, but rather by certain facts about *ourselves*; and if this is so, we will suspend judgement in matters of theology.

In general, suppose that x appears F to y. How is this to be explained? *One* possible explanation is, of course, that x really *is* F. But in some cases at least another explanation is more plausible. If the way x appears varies systematically with the lifestyles or customs or habits of different people, then x's appearing F (and F^* etc.) may best be accounted for by the various features of these different lifestyles; and if this is the case, we shall suspend judgement about the reality of x's being F.

This is a powerful form of argument. How effective particular instances of it may be will of course depend on the nature of those instances. But what you *value* does often seem to depend to a large extent on your social and cultural background. Scepticism is not the only conclusion to be drawn from sociological facts of this sort: there are other possible explanations. But scepticism is often a very plausible conclusion.

In §202 Philo introduces a further consideration. On various philosophical and theoretical issues, he asserts, 'there have been countless inquiries, but up to the present time agreement has not been reached in any one of them on the part of all the inquirers'. The Pyrrhonists habitually harp on the fact of disagreement and dispute, and sometimes they seem to suggest that this fact in itself is enough to induce suspension of judgement. This is an unappealing suggestion, for disagreement may be due to prejudice or ignorance or irrationality, and the mere fact of dispute should not in itself drive us to doubt. But Philo's suggestion is more subtle and more persuasive. The disputes are not disagreements among the 'labile mob' – they involve intelligent philosophers. They are not temporary or juvenile – they remain despite 'countless inquiries'. Numerous intelligent investigators, working over many years in many societies, have failed to produce any agreed results. In such circumstances the rational person will surely suspend judgement.

This form of argument is also of considerable power, and many instances of it are surely sound. In Philo's day scepticism was the rational position with regard to most areas of philosophy and science.

In our day it is still the rational position on many philosophical points and in large areas of science where dispute remains endemic.

Philo's arguments are, in principle, good. They differ in character from most of the Pyrrhonist arguments that we have so far considered, for they advocate scepticism piecemeal. They cannot pretend to show that on *every* issue suspension of judgement will follow; rather, they show that on any issue of a determinate type (an issue where appearances depend upon cultural background, or an issue where the experts have long disagreed) scepticism is the reasonable person's response. How broad a scepticism such arguments will produce is an empirical question.

Ethical scepticism has never lacked support, and it has always thrived on the sort of considerations which the Pyrrhonist produces in the Tenth Mode. But contemporary scepticism characteristically differs from ancient scepticism in several important ways.

First, contemporary philosophers who discuss moral scepticism regularly contrast it with something they call 'objectivism'. Thus in his recent book on *Ethics*, J. L. Mackie begins by asserting, under the heading 'Moral Scepticism', that 'there are no objective values'. An objectivist holds that values, and in particular moral values, really exist in the world – people and actions really are cruel and kind, mean and generous, and so forth – whether or not we are sensitive to them or react to them in the appropriate way. We may be concerned about values or indifferent to them; we may care about some values but not about others; we may act on them in pertinent or in grossly inept ways: they are there all the same, they are not brought into being by our decisions or our actions.

Both ancient and modern sceptics abandon objective values, but they do so in different and incompatible ways. For modern sceptics about value, the belief that things or people are objectively good or bad is simply *wrong*. Thus Mackie calls his scepticism an 'error theory', because it claims that the belief in objective values is an error, a commitment to what is false. We do not have to proceed as far as Mackie's arguments to see that he has already parted company with the Pyrrhonists. In their terms he is a negative dogmatist. Ask any moral question – e.g. 'Is incest really wrong?' – and the modern sceptic will answer: 'No – objectively speaking there is nothing wrong with incest, for there are no objective values at all.' From the point of view of the Pyrrhonist, who will answer the same question with a sceptical shrug to indicate his suspension of belief, that reply is profoundly unsceptical.

For the Pyrrhonist way of dealing with beliefs about value is just the

same as their way of dealing with any other sort of belief. They point
out that appearances conflict, and they claim that there is as much to
be said on one side of the conflict as there is on the other: and so they
suspend judgement about value. The Tenth Mode works in exactly
the same fashion as the other modes. The Pyrrhonist, unlike the
modern sceptic about values, does not move from the pre-sceptical
belief that incest is wrong to the belief that it is not really bad after
all. Rather, he moves from the belief that it is wrong to a state of
mind in which he has no beliefs at all on the subject. No doubt he
will continue to have *feelings* on the subject: incest may continue to
appear bad to him. But he will regard that appearance as indeed
nothing more than an appearance, and he will no longer assent either
to the proposition that incest is bad or to the proposition that it is
not.

There are, we must now admit, a few traces in the ancient texts of
one version of the modern position. In Sextus' longest account of
ethical scepticism, in *M* XI, we find arguments which rest on the
claim that there is no value shared by and common to everyone:
different people have different views as to what is good, bad, and
indifferent. (These arguments seem to go back to Aenesidemus (see
M XI 42–4), though they have left no mark on the Tenth Mode.) But
instead of concluding, as the Tenth Mode does, in suspension of
judgement about what is really good or bad or indifferent, the arguments of *M* XI urge us to shed our concern for any *common* good and
limit ourselves each to our own *private* good.

> If someone should deny that anything is by nature more an object of choice
> than of avoidance or of avoidance than of choice (since everything that
> happens to one is relative and is set up as an object now of choice and now of
> avoidance, depending on different occasions and circumstances), then he will
> live happily and free from anxiety. (*M* XI 118)

We cannot simply dismiss this text, but neither should we take it as
evidence of a *rapprochement* between Pyrrhonism and modern error
theories of value. The occurence of the word 'relative' should sound a
warning: Sextus is here guilty of conflating relativism and scepticism.
M XI obtrudes relativism into an otherwise coherently sceptical text,
and we should treat it as a temporary aberration on Sextus' part.
Moreover, the conflation, as we have seen, occasionally appears elsewhere in ancient scepticism, and it has no special connexion with
scepticism about values.

A second difference between ancient and contemporary ethical scepticism emerges from one of the two arguments which Mackie deploys against objectivism. It is

the argument from queerness. This has two parts, one metaphysical, the other epistemological. If there were objective values, then they would be entities or qualities or relations of a very strange sort, utterly different from anything else in the universe. Correspondingly, if we were aware of them, it would have to be by some special faculty of moral perception or intuition, utterly different from our ordinary ways of knowing everything else. (*Ethics*, p. 38)

According to the modern sceptic, there is a fundamental difference between values and the subject-matter of the sciences. Were values objective, then, they would be unaccountably – indeed incredibly – *strange* items. Modern scepticism thus depends on a *contrast* between ethics and the sciences, and it is essentially a *local* scepticism. The ancient Pyrrhonist, on the other hand, regards ethics as entirely parallel to the other 'parts of philosophy': for him, there is no contrast, and the subject-matter of ethics does not seem peculiar. In consequence his scepticism is *global*.

This is an important difference. In modern philosophy, ethical scepticism tends to be treated as a special subject. On the one hand, moral philosophers usually regard moral scepticism as a fundamental issue within their discipline, whether or not they have any concern for general epistemological questions. They discuss the status of ethical belief in a way that is largely independent of discussions of belief in general. On the other hand, epistemologists who discuss the general status of belief and knowledge do not usually regard scepticism about values as a central part of their studies; indeed, they rarely pay attention to ethical beliefs at all. (Descartes' *First Meditation*, which set the pattern for modern discussions of scepticism, makes no mention of values or of ethics.) In short, moral scepticism and general scepticism are usually treated as though they were independent areas of philosophical inquiry.

This separation of interests is not a feature of ancient scepticism. It is true that Sextus has self-contained accounts of 'the ethical part of philosophy' both in *PH* (at III 168–279) and in *M* (Book XI); and the Tenth Mode is in some sense especially concerned with ethics. But the treatment of 'the ethical part of philosophy' is an integral part of a single sceptical attack which is coherent in method, in mode of argument and in upshot. And the Tenth Mode, while especially concerned with ethics, is so only as a matter of degree. Ethical scepticism in the ancient world was essentially part of a larger philosophical design.

The third difference between ancient and contemporary moral scepticism is the most striking and the most important. For the reactions of the sceptics to their scepticisms are radically different. Typically, a contemporary sceptic will regard his position as wholly compatible with the entertainment of determinate, even passionate, moral convictions. While maintaining, on the theoretical level, that animal vivisection, say, is objectively neither good nor bad, he may be found, on the practical level, an ardent opponent of the institution. 'There are no *objective* values', he will say, 'but I hold fast to *my own* values, and these are the marks by which I judge and determine my conduct.'

Some contemporary philosophers suppose that my values are 'my own' in a peculiarly strong sense. If we cannot find values 'in the world', they think, then the only alternative is to invent or create them. Mackie puts the point well:

> But if there is no objective moral truth to be discovered, is there nothing left to do but to describe our sense of justice? At least we can look at the matter in another way. Morality is not to be discovered but to be made: we have to decide what moral views to adopt, what moral stands to take . . . the object of the exercise is to decide what to do, what to support and what to condemn, what principles of conduct to accept and foster as guiding or controlling our own choices and perhaps those of other people as well. (*Ethics*, p. 106)

Each of us, in a valueless world, decides what is to be valuable, and values are thus the products of our own creative capacities.

This view is often presented as a stern encouragement to moral endeavour. If we must create our own values and invent right and wrong, then we have a Herculean task before us. The ethical objectivist need only recognise the values that are placed in front of him: we must make our own values. The manufacture of values is a serious undertaking, and since the values we invent will be our own we shall be committed to them in the strongest possible way.

There may well seem to be something paradoxical in all this. Certainly, the ancient Pyrrhonists would have found it hard to comprehend a self-styled scepticism which both insists that nothing has any objective worth and also seriously commits itself to a set of values.

In *M* XI 112–14, Sextus explains that unhappiness is always due to 'disturbance' (*tarachē*), and that disturbance is itself caused by 'intensity' (*suntonia*). To achieve happiness we must attain a state of tranquillity (*ataraxia*, 'non–disturbedness'), and this we shall reach if we cease to pursue and avoid things with intensity. Now intensity too has a cause; it comes about, Sextus claims, because we 'believe in addition' that the objects of our pursuits and avoidances are good or bad. Wanting, say, a large salary or a post in the civil service, I believe in addition that such a salary or such a post is in itself a good thing. Fearing poverty or unemployment, I believe in addition that these states are bad. And it is my additional beliefs which account for the intensity of my strivings, and hence for my disturbance. Abandon the beliefs and I cease to be disturbed.

Ethical scepticism thus produces, not a passion to create values, but a calm acceptance of, and detachment from, whatever happens. Not believing that things are good or bad, the Pyrrhonist finds that he ceases to worry – or at any rate, ceases to worry with any intensity – over what he achieves or what happens to him. That way happiness lies.

Sextus, we should note, does not hold that a Pyrrhonist is reduced to a state of total anaesthesia. He is human and he experiences human passions; if he is struck, he feels pain; if he is praised he glows with pleasure. Again, he will positively pursue pleasure and positively avoid pain. There are certain inescapable facts about the human animal, and these facts ensure that not even an advanced Pyrrhonist will reach a state of complete contentment.

> We do not . . . deem the sceptic to be undisturbed in every way. We say rather that he is disturbed by things that force themselves on him; we agree that at times he is cold and thirsty and is affected in that kind of way. But in these cases ordinary people are afflicted by two sets of circumstances: by the affects themselves and no less by their thinking that these circumstances are evil by nature; while the sceptic, by shedding the further opinion that each of these things is in its nature bad, gets off more moderately even in these cases. This, therefore, is why we assert that the sceptic's aim is to be untroubled in matters of opinion, and to be only moderately affected in matters forced on him. (*PH* I 29–30)

Sceptics, then, will at least be better off than dogmatists. For they will not pursue and avoid things in the conviction that they are good or bad, and thus they will be free from the disturbance which these convictions produce.

How plausible is Sextus' claim? We might be inclined to think that scepticism would produce anxieties of its own. If I do not know whether a decent salary is good or bad, may not that very ignorance make me worry? If I knew that a decent salary was in fact a good thing, then no doubt I should worry, striving to maintain my position and fearing lest I lost it; and the Pyrrhonist escapes *these* worries. But does he not fall into the equally unenviable condition of being tormented by his ignorance and uncertainty?

This is not a trivial question; for the aim and purpose of ancient scepticism (of scepticism as a whole, not only of its ethical part) was to achieve *ataraxia* or tranquillity:

> The causal origin of scepticism is, we say, the hope of being tranquil. For men of talent, disturbed by the anomaly in things, and puzzling over which of them they should rather assent to, came to investigate what is true in things, and what false, thinking that by determining that issue they would gain tranquillity. (*PH* I 12)

But the men of talent were deceived; they could not determine what was true and what false:

> Beginning to philosophise in order to decide about the appearances and to apprehend which were true and which false, so as to gain tranquillity, they fell into equipollent disagreement which they could not decide. So they suspended judgement, and their suspension of judgement was by chance attended by tranquillity on matters of opinion. (*PH* I 26)

The desire for tranquillity spurs investigation. But investigation turns up nothing but disagreements – and disagreements which are 'equipollent': there is as much to be said for the one side as for the other, and no reason to choose between them. Thus the investigation ends in suspension of judgement – and the desired tranquillity follows 'by chance'.

Is the Pyrrhonist tormented by his ignorance? No, says Sextus. He gives no reason, but he reports as a fact (we should no doubt say an apparent fact) that suspension of judgement is 'by chance attended' by tranquillity. Tranquillity follows suspension of judgement 'as a shadow follows a body' (*PH* I 29; cf Diogenes IX 107). And the Pyrrhonists found a pleasing analogy:

> What is said to have happened to the painter Apelles befalls the sceptic too. They say that Apelles was painting a horse and wanted to represent in his picture the foam at the horse's muzzle. He was so unsuccessful that he gave up and hurled at the picture the sponge he used to wipe the paints off his brush. The sponge touched the picture and produced a representation of the foam. (*PH* I 28)

In the same way the investigator abandons his search for knowledge, throws in the academic sponge – and to his surprise achieves tranquillity.

Tranquillity results from suspension of judgement about any issue. Ideally the Pyrrhonist will suspend judgement about all issues, or at least all issues which trouble him – for he will only be motivated to investigate topics where he cares what the true answer is. In the special case of values, the suspension of judgement which results from his investigations will produce an inner detachment of a striking kind. The Pyrrhonist will continue to act, indeed for most of the time he will act like other people. For he is affected in the ways that everybody is, by hunger, thirst and so on. And he receives, and reacts to, appearances of value, just as he does to appearances of any other kind. If he has been brought up in Greece, it will appear to him, with some force, that incest is bad; and his Greek upbringing will ensure the appropriate reaction. (At least, it will do so as long as he is in Greece: when he goes to Egypt it may be a different matter.) But he regards these appearances as no more than appearances, and he suspends judgement about the reality behind them.

If the Pyrrhonist's outward behaviour is generally indistinguishable from that of other people, is not his scepticism ultimately as much of a charade as those modern scepticisms we briefly described in Chapter 1? The answer to this depends in part on what the sceptic is sceptical about. In theoretical matters, suspension of judgement may perhaps leave the sceptic in pretty much the same state as the dogmatist: whether you are committed to, or suspend judgement about, the existence of atoms and void need not affect your attitude to other things. But in practical matters there is a real difference. The Pyrrhonist who suspends judgement is, in his inner indifference to any reality behind the appearances of value, a very different kind of person from the rest of us. For his reaction to the appearances of value is just that – a reaction. He accepts things as good or bad in an entirely passive way: he does not question, or regard as suitable objects of deliberation or of concern, his own ethical beliefs and dispositions. He reacts to incest with horror because he is a Greek. But he can regard this as no real *concern* of his. His upbringing and dispositions are simply part of the appearances; just as he suspends judgement as to whether incest really is good or bad, so he is bound to suspend judgement as to whether his own responses to it are well founded or not. To ask whether he *ought* to respond in the way he does would be to ask the kind of question to which the sceptic thinks that there can be no answer. In practical matters, then, the sceptic is led to suspend judgement on, and thus to be detached from, and indifferent about, his own dispositions to act. So, even if his behaviour is externally indistinguishable from the dogmatist's, his inner state is totally different.

Sextus, of course, is aware of this: in fact it is for him a positive recommendation for scepticism. For it is precisely in such detachment and tranquillity that, according to him, happiness lies: the detached inner state is scepticism's purpose and goal.

Not everyone will agree with Sextus on either point. First, we may well find such tranquillity a strange, or even a repellent, conception of what it is for a human being to be happy. Sextus, of course, is not recommending tranquillity as a desirable goal that we should try to achieve. Rather, he is saying that if we are sceptics we shall, as a matter of fact, find ourselves in a state of tranquillity, and that when we attain it we shall recognise that it was what we were striving for. But, for our part, we do not find this a plausible saying.

Some people, no doubt, will find happiness in a Pyrrhonian tranquillity. Most of us, moreover, think from time to time that 'the world is too much with us' and welcome a degree of inner detachment in some parts of our lives. But in allowing that, we do not embrace Sextus' ideal of perpetual tranquillity and total detachment. We would, we suspect, find such a state profoundly boring; and we might also regard it as ignoble. Intensity and engagement are no doubt disturbing, but they are also rewarding – they add, at the lowest estimate, an edge and a zest to life. Human happiness, for some of us at least, requires activity and participation, even at the price of anxiety and disappointment. To adapt an ancient metaphor, we do not want merely to be unconcerned spectators at the Olympic Games: we want to take part.

Secondly, it is not clear that we must follow Sextus on the more general issue, and see the point of scepticism in the happiness that is alleged to result from it. For we may well think that scepticism neither has nor needs any such point. If many or most of our beliefs have no justification, then to become aware of this is surely worthwhile for its own sake. We do not need any incentive beyond the one which Socrates had – the hope of discovering the limits of our knowledge and the extent of our ignorance. It is striking that, however much the Pyrrhonists rejected the goals and aspirations of their dogmatist opponents, they did not think to reject the assumption, shared by all the schools of ancient philosophy, that philosophising must have a further goal, and that its goal must be the philosopher's own happiness.

It is in their failure to reject this basic assumption that we find a final difference between ancient and modern scepticism. A modern sceptic does not regard it as a reasonable demand on his sceptical philosophising that it should contribute to his well-being: he does not think that philosophy *ought* to make him happy, and he does not think that it *will* make him happy – he may indeed suspect that sceptical inquiry is more likely to result in depression, or even in neurosis, than in tranquillity or well-being.

The earlier differences we have found between ancient and modern scepticism have perhaps shown the former to be the more compelling and the more significant philosophy. About this final difference we are more likely to be ambivalent. It is easy, on the one hand, to feel the force of the ancient demand. For why should I philosophise at all if I shall be no happier for it? If there is no way in which philosophy makes my life more satisfactory, then the pursuit of it may seem either perverse or trivial. Pursuing an occupation which leads merely to depression is surely perverse. And there must be something to the thought that philosophy is a trifling game or an empty academic exercise if the philosopher thinks it has no serious bearing on the rest of his life. All the ancient schools, whatever they took human well-being to consist in, were agreed that philosophy would be a footling occupation if it did not make the philosopher's life better.

On the other hand, we can also feel the force of the modern notion. The sceptic who demands that his inquiries result in happiness is surely making an unrealistic demand on the world. As a matter of fact, we do not have much reason to think that scepticism is any way at all, never mind the best way, to achieve happiness. And there seems something peculiarly unsceptical about assuming that sceptical inquiries will have the result which the sceptic most desired before he started out on them. Moreover, if we believe that intellectual pursuits are good in themselves, we shall feel it neither perverse nor trivial to follow out our philosophical inquiries regardless of their effect on our state of well-being.

Both positions here, the ancient and the modern, are plausible. To the extent that we feel ambivalent as to which to prefer, we find them equally plausible – equipollent. On the one hand, we can hardly step outside our own modern philosophical assumptions, which are bound to exert pressure on us and make us view the ancient aspiration of seeking happiness through scepticism as wrong-headed. On the other hand, the reader who has followed, with sympathy, the ancient sceptics up to this point will probably have acquired some feeling for and some susceptibility to the ancient point of view. So in studying scepticism we may come to illustrate it: insofar as we find it hard to find grounds for preferring ancient to modern scepticism or *vice versa*, we are led to suspend judgement as to which of them is nearer the truth.

Appendix A
Philo and Diogenes on the Modes

(1) Diogenes Laertius, *Lives of the Philosophers* IX 78–88

78   What the statements of the Pyrrhonists are, then, is a kind of record*
of what appears or is in any way thought of, a record in which
everything is set alongside everything else and is found in the comparison to contain a great deal of anomaly* and disturbance, as Aenesidemus says in his outline introduction to Pyrrhonism. To arrive at the
oppositions inherent in inquiries they would first demonstrate the
modes in which things convince us, and then use the same modes to
destroy our conviction about them. For they say that things are
convincing when there is accord in perceiving them, or when they
never – or at any rate rarely – change, or they are familiar or determined
79 by law or pleasing or unsurprising.* So they used to display* cases of
equal plausibility from among things contrary to those which convince
us.

The puzzles they produced arising from the discordances* in what
appears or is thought of were organised in ten modes in respect of which
objects appear in various ways. These are the ten modes he* sets out.

First is the mode depending on the differences among animals with
regard to pleasure and pain and harm and advantage. Through this it is
inferred that different appearances are produced by the same things, and
that suspension of judgement follows conflict of this kind. Some
animals are produced without copulation, like fire-creatures, the
Arabian phoenix and worms; others after intercourse, like humans and
80 the rest. And some have one kind of constitution, others another.
Hence they differ in their perception too – hawks, for example, have
very keen sight and dogs very keen smell. It is reasonable, therefore,
that the sense-appearances presented to animals with different kinds of
eyes should themselves be different. Vine-shoots are edible by goats but
bitter to humans, hemlock nourishes quails but is fatal to humans, and
manure is edible by pigs but not by horses.

Second is the mode depending on the natures and customs and constitutions* of humans. For instance, Demophon, Alexander's
81 waiter, used to feel warm in the shade and shiver in the sun. Andron of Argos, according to Aristotle, used to travel through waterless Libya without drinking. One person devotes himself to medicine, another to farming, another to trade. The same things harm some and benefit others. Hence judgement should be suspended.

Third is the mode depending on the differences among the channels of perception. An apple, for instance, is experienced as yellow to sight, sweet to taste, and fragrant to smell. The same shape is observed as different depending on the differences in the mirrors. So it follows that what appears is no more such-and-such than so-and-so.

82 *Fourth* is the mode depending on conditions and common variations*: for example, health and disease, sleeping and waking, joy and sorrow, youth and old age, confidence and fear, need and repletion, hate and love, heating and chilling. Depending on breathing, depending on having one's channels blocked. So things experienced appear different depending on their kind of condition. For not even mad people are in a state which is contrary to nature – why them rather than us? For even we see the sun as stationary. When Theon of Tithorea, the Stoic, went to bed he used to walk about in his sleep. (And Pericles' slave on the roof-top.)

83 *Fifth* is the mode depending on lifestyles, laws, belief in myth, conventions due to custom* and dogmatic suppositions. This includes questions about what is fine and base, true and false, good and bad, about gods, and about the production and destruction of all the things that are apparent. For instance, the same behaviour is just for some and unjust for others, to some good and to others bad. Thus Persians do not regard it as strange to have sex with their daughters, while Greeks regard it as prohibited. The Massegetae, according to Eudoxus in Book I of his *Journey round the World*, have their wives in common; Greeks do not. The Cilicians used to take pride in being pirates; but not the
84 Greeks. Different people believe in different gods; some believe in divine providence and others do not. The Egyptians dispose of their dead by embalming, the Romans by cremation, the Paeonians by throwing them into lakes. Hence the suspension of judgement as to what is true.

Sixth is the mode depending on mixtures and shares; it shows that nothing appears purely in itself, but together with air, with light, with moisture, with solid body, heat, cold, movement,* evaporations and other forces. For instance, purple shows a different colour in sunlight, moonlight and lamplight. Our skin-colour has a different appearance
85 at mid-day – and so does the sun.* A stone which in the air it takes two men to lift* is easily moved in water: either it is heavy and made light by the water, or it is light and weighed down by the air. So we are ignorant of things in their own nature, as we are of oil in a perfume.

Seventh is the mode depending on distances, kinds of position, places and occupants of places. According to this mode, things that seem big appear small, square things appear round, level things appear to have projections, straight things appear bent, pale things appear coloured. For instance, the sun, depending on its interval from us, appears a foot across.* Mountains appear airy* and smooth from a
86 distance, but rugged from close at hand. Again, the sun as it rises has a quite different appearance from the sun at its zenith. The same body* has a different appearance in a thicket and on open ground. A picture appears different depending on its kind of position, and a dove's neck depending on the way it turns. So, since it is not possible to perceive these things apart from places and positions,* it is not known what their nature is.

Eighth is the mode depending on their quantities and qualities,* their being hot or cold, quick or slow, pale or coloured. For instance, wine taken in moderation fortifies us, while more of it enfeebles us; and similarly with food and the like.

87 *Ninth* is the mode depending on what is habitual or strange or rare. For instance, earthquakes are not found surprising by people among whom they occur frequently; nor is the sun, because it is seen every day. (Favorinus makes the Ninth the Eighth, while Sextus and Aenesidemus make it the Tenth.* Sextus calls the Tenth the Eighth, and Favorinus calls it the Ninth.)

Tenth is the mode based on setting things alongside one another* – e.g. light to heavy, strong to weak, bigger to smaller, up to down. Anything on the right, for instance, is not by nature on the right, but is thought of according to its relation to something else – if that is moved
88 it will no longer be on the right. Similarly both father and brother are

relative; day is relative to the sun; and everything is relative to thinking. So things that are relative cannot be known in themselves.*
These are the ten modes.

(2) Philo, *On Drunkenness* 169–205

169 Anyone priding himself on his deliberations or on an adequate capacity to choose and avoid things should be reminded of the following considerations. If it were always the case that the same unvarying appearances were produced from the same things, then no doubt we should of necessity admire as unerring and incorruptible those two standards, perception and thought, which are established in us by nature, and we should not be in two minds and suspend judgement on anything, but rather should credit things as soon as they appear, and so choose some things and conversely reject others.

170 But since we find that we are actually affected* differently by them, there is nothing firm we can say about anything; for what appears is not stationary, but undergoes changes of many kinds and many forms. For where the appearance is not fixed, the judgement on it cannot be fixed either. The reasons for this are many.

171 First of all, there are countless differences among animals, not just in one respect but in nearly all – differences in their production and constitution, in their diet and way of life, in what they choose and avoid, in the activities and motions of their senses, in the peculiarities of the countless ways in which they are affected both in body and in soul.

172 Quite apart from the judging subjects, look at some of the objects of judgement, such as the chameleon and the octopus. The chameleon, so they say, changes its colour and assimilates itself to the ground over which it usually crawls; the octopus assimilates itself to the rocks in the sea around which it clings. Perhaps nature, in order to preserve them, has given them this ability to turn into many colours as a talisman or antidote against capture.

173 Have you never seen a dove's neck changing in the rays of the sun into a thousand different shades of colour? Is it not magenta and deep blue, then fiery and glowing like embers, and again yellow and reddish, and all other kinds of colours, whose very names it is not easy to keep in mind?

174 And indeed they say that among the Geloan Scythians there is found a most amazing animal. It is rare, but it does exist, and they call it the reindeer. In size it is no smaller than an ox, and it is very like a deer in the

shape of its head. The story goes that it regularly changes the colour of its coat to match the landscape and the trees and in general whatever its background may be, with the result that, owing to the similarity of colour, it escapes the notice of anyone looking for it, and is hard to hunt down for this reason rather than because of any bodily strength.

175   These facts and others like them are clear warrants that things are inapprehensible.

Next there are the diversities of every kind that are found not just
176   among animals in general but among humans themselves. It is not only that they judge the same things differently on different occasions – different people judge them in different ways, receiving pleasure and displeasure in opposite ways from the same objects.* What some find displeasing, others enjoy; and on the other hand, what some accept and are drawn to as attractive and appropriate, others spurn utterly as alien and hostile.

177   For instance, I have often been in the theatre and watched the effect of one and the same melody produced by the performers on stage, or by the musicians. Some of the audience are so carried away that they are excited and join in and involuntarily shout their appreciation. Some are so unmoved that as far as this goes you would think them no different from the lifeless seats they are sitting on. Others again are so alienated that they actually get up and leave the show and even block their ears* with both hands lest any echo of the music should linger there and produce displeasure in their fastidious and easily annoyed souls.

178   But why mention facts like these? Each single one of us on his own, paradoxical as it is, undergoes thousands of shifts and changes in both body and soul, now choosing and now rejecting things which themselves change not at all but retain the same natural constitution.

179   People do not usually have the same experiences when healthy and ill, when waking and sleeping, when young and old. Someone standing still gets appearances different from those of someone in motion, and the same goes for people who are confident or fearful, sad or joyful, loving or on the contrary hating.

180   But what need is there for long and wearisome speeches on the subject? In a word, every motion of body and soul, whether natural or unnatural,* becomes a cause of that unstable movement of apparent things which produces in us conflicting and discordant dreams.

181   The instability of appearances depends in no small measure on the positions, the intervals and the places in which things are located.

182   Do we not see fish in the sea appearing larger than they are in reality when they swim with their fins stretched out? Oars too,
183   however straight they are, come to look bent under water. Distant objects produce false appearances and usually deceive our minds: lifeless things are on occasion assumed to be living and living things on the contrary to be lifeless; again, stationary things are taken to be moving and moving things to be stationary, approaching things to be receding and departing things to be advancing, extremely long things to be very short and angular things to be round. And plain sight produces a thousand other distortions which no-one in his senses would endorse as being firm.

184   What of the quantities in preparations?

Whether the compounds harm or help depends on whether there is more or less: this is true in thousands of cases – and especially in the
185   case of drugs made up according to medical science. For the quantity in compounds is measured by formulae and rules which it is unsafe to fall short of or to exceed (less weakens their powers and more intensifies them, and both are harmful, the drug either being unable to act because of its weakness, or doing violent harm because of its extreme potency), and it vividly indicates how to test for its helpfulness or harmfulness by its qualities of smoothness or roughness and of density and compression or on the other hand of rarefaction and dilation.

186   Furthermore, everybody knows that pretty well nothing at all in the world is thought of in and by itself, but rather is assessed by juxtaposition with its contrary – e.g. small with big, dry with wet, hot with cold, light with heavy, black with white, weak with strong,
187   few with many. And similarly with what is a question of* excellence or defect: the beneficial is recognised by means of the harmful, the fine in opposition to the base, the just and in general the good by juxtaposition with the unjust and the bad. And the same holds for everything else in the universe: one would find on inquiry that it submits to decision in the same way.* No one thing can be apprehended in itself, but rather seems to be recognised as a result of comparison with something else.

188   Now what is unable to testify adequately for itself, but requires advocacy from something else, is not firm enough to produce conviction

Here, then, is another way of testing those who make reckless agreements or denials on any subject at all.

189   And why should this be surprising? Anyone who goes into things more closely and looks at them in a purer light will recognise that no one thing affects us according to its own simple nature; all of them contain the most elaborate mixtures and blends.

190   For a start, how do we grasp colours? Surely together with air and light on the outside, and also together with the moisture in the eye itself. In what way are sweet and bitter assessed? Independently of the flavours, whether natural or unnatural, in our own mouths? Hardly. Well, do the smells from burning incense present us with the natures of these substances in a simple and pure form, or rather as blends of themselves and of the air – and sometimes of the fire which melts the substances and of the workings of our nostrils?

191   From these cases we infer that we grasp not colours, but the blend produced from the objects and light; not smells, but the mixture brought about by the effluence from the substances and the hospitable air; not flavours, but what is produced by the incoming thing tasted and the moist substance in our mouths.

192   Since things are this way, people who persist in making ready agreements or denials about any subject at all deserve to be condemned for their simple-mindedness or rashness or pretentiousness. For if the simple powers of things are inaccessible, and only mixed powers, with contributions from several factors, are open to view, and if there is no way in which we can see the invisible powers or perceive through the blends the particular character of each of the contributions, what remains but the necessity to suspend judgement?*

193   Are we not called by the following facts not to trust* too much to what is unclear – facts which pervade virtually the whole world and which have led* Greeks and foreigners alike on to the slippery slope of judgement? What are they? Lifestyles, of course, going back to our childhood, traditional customs and ancient laws, not a single one of which is agreed upon by everyone in the same form. Depending on country, nation or state – or rather even on village and individual home

194   – men, women and small children have completely different views: for instance what is base to us is fine to others, and similarly with what is becoming and unbecoming, just and unjust, impious and pious, legal and illegal, and again with what is blamed and praised, penalised and rewarded – and with the other cases where they hold contrary views.*

195   What need is there to make a long speech when I am drawn away by more pressing matters? Still, if someone not tempted by any more novel spectacle were willing to spend time on the present topic and go into the lifestyles, customs and laws of different countries, nations, states, and localities – of subjects and rulers, the famous and the obscure, the free and the enslaved, lay people and experts, he would waste not one or two days, or even a month or a year, but his whole life, even if he enjoyed a long life-span; and nonetheless he would, without knowing it, leave many matters unscrutinised, unconsidered and unmentioned.

196   And so, since among different people these things are not just slightly different but utterly discordant, so as to compete and conflict, necessarily the appearances experienced will differ and the judgements be at
197   war with one another. This being so, who is so senseless and idiotic as to say steadfastly that such-and-such is just or intelligent or fine or advantageous? Whatever one person determines to be such will be nullified by someone else whose practice from childhood has been the contrary.

198   Myself, I am not surprised if the labile and heterogeneous mob, inglorious slaves of customs and laws instituted in any fashion, taught to obey them as masters or tyrants from the cradle up, and having their souls thrashed into submission and lacking the ability to grasp any great or imaginative thoughts, should believe whatever has once been handed down to them, or if, having left their minds without exercise, they should come out with assertions and denials which are unscrutinised and untried. But I *am* surprised that the majority of what are called philosophers, who do profess to hunt down the clear and the true in things, are divided into brigades and platoons and set down dogmas that are discordant – and often actually contrary to one another – not on some one chance point but on virtually everything, great and small, with which their investigations are concerned.

199   Some set up the world as infinite, others say it is finite; some make the universe uncreated and others represent it as created; some attach it to an irrational and spontaneous movement, with nothing to oversee and guide it, while others suppose that there is a wonderful providence, caring for both whole and parts, and a god who drives and steers it smoothly and safely. How could these people be having the same apprehensions of their subject-matter?

200   As for the appearances we get from inquiring about the good – do they not force us to suspend judgement rather than concur? Some consider only the fine to be good and hoard it up in the soul, while

others split the good up into many parts and extend it as far as the body
201 and external things. These people say that advantages due to good fortune are the body's guardians, and that health and strength, soundness
and accuracy of the senses, and everything of that kind are the guardians
of the sovereign soul. For the nature of the good, they say, has three
levels, of which the third and outermost protects the second . . .* while
the second forms a strong defence and fortification for the first.

202   Indeed, on this subject and on the different ways of life and the ends
to which all actions should be referred, and on the thousand other topics
in logic, ethics and physics – on all these there have been countless
inquiries, but up to the present time agreement has not been reached in
any one of them on the part of all the inquirers.

203   So is it not fitting that the Mind should be represented as suffering
from ignorance* when its two daughters, Deliberation and Assertion,*
have cohabited and slept with it? For it is said that 'he did not know
204 them when they lay down, or when they rose up' [Genesis XIX 33, 35].
It seems that the mind does not apprehend either sleep or waking, or
rest or motion, clearly and steadfastly. Even when it thinks it has
205 deliberated excellently, it is found to be extremely bad at deliberating
and the issue of things is unlike its expectations. And when it has
resolved to endorse some view as true, it reaps the condemnation
passed on recklessness, since what it formerly was convinced of as most
secure appears untrustworthy and infirm. So, since things usually turn
out contrary to what one presumed, it is safest to suspend judgement.

Appendix B
The Eight Modes against Causal Explanation
(Sextus, *PH* I 180–5)

180 Just as we hand on the modes of suspension of judgement, so some people also set out modes in accordance with which we bring the dogmatists to a halt by raising puzzles about their particular causal explanations – we do this because they pride themselves on these especially. Aenesidemus, indeed, hands down eight modes in accordance with which he thinks he can refute and declare unsound every dogmatic causal explanation.

181 Of these, the *first*, he says, is the mode in accordance with which causal explanations, which are all concerned with what is unclear, have no agreed confirmation from what is apparent.

According to the *second*, some people often give an explanation in only one mode, although there is a rich abundance enabling them to explain the subject of investigation in a variety of modes.

182 According to the *third*, they assign causes that display no order to things that take place in an ordered way.

According to the *fourth*, when they have grasped how apparent things take place, they consider that they have apprehended how non-apparent things take place. But perhaps unclear things are brought about similarly to apparent things, perhaps not similarly but in a special way of their own.

183 According to the *fifth*, just about all of them give explanations according to their own hypotheses about the elements, not according to any common and agreed approaches.

According to the *sixth*, they often adopt what is concordant with their own hypotheses but reject what opposes them, even when this has equal credibility.

184 According to the *seventh*, they often assign causes which conflict not only with what is apparent but also with their own hypotheses.

According to the *eighth*, often when what seems to be apparent is just as puzzling as what is being investigated, they rest their teaching about what is puzzling upon what is just as puzzling.

185 He says that it is not impossible that some should fail in their causal explanations in virtue of some mixed modes dependent on those just described.

Appendix C
The Five Modes of Agrippa (Sextus, *PH* I 164–9)

164 The later sceptics hand down the following five modes of suspension of judgement:

> first, the mode deriving from dispute,
> second, the mode throwing one back *ad infinitum*,
> third, the mode deriving from relativity,
> fourth, the hypothetical mode,
> fifth, the reciprocal mode.

165   According to the mode deriving from dispute, we find that undecidable dissension about the matter in question has come about both in ordinary life and among philosophers. Because of this we are not able either to choose or to disqualify anything, and we end up with suspension of judgement.

166   In the mode deriving from infinite regress, we say that what is brought forward as a warrant for the matter in question needs another warrant, which itself needs another, and so *ad infinitum*, so that we have no point from which to begin to establish anything, and suspension of judgement follows.

167   In the mode deriving from relativity, as we said above [I 135–6], the existing object appears to be such-and-such relative to the subject judging and to the things observed together with it, but we suspend judgement on what it is like in its nature.

168   We have the mode from hypothesis when the dogmatists, being thrown back *ad infinitum*, begin from something which they do not establish but claim to assume simply and without proof in virtue of a concession.

169   The reciprocal mode occurs when what ought to be confirmatory of the object of investigation has need of warrant from the object of investigation; then, being unable to take either to establish the other, we suspend judgement about both.

Appendix D
The Two Modes (Sextus, *PH* I 178–9)

178 They also hand down two other modes of suspension of judgement. Since everything apprehended is thought to be apprehended either by means of itself or by means of something else, they are thought to introduce puzzlement about everything by suggesting that nothing is apprehended either by means of itself or by means of something else.

That nothing is apprehended by means of itself is, they say, clear from the dispute which has occurred among natural scientists over, I suppose, all objects of perception and of thought – a dispute which is undecidable, since we cannot use either an object of perception or an object of thought as a standard, because anything we may take has been disputed and so is not credible.

179 And for the following reason they do not concede either that anything can be apprehended by means of another thing. If that by means of which something is apprehended will itself always need to be apprehended by means of another thing, they throw one back on the reciprocal or the infinite mode; and if one should want to assume that that by means of which another thing is apprehended is itself apprehended by means of itself, this is met by the fact that, for the above reasons, nothing is apprehended by means of itself.

Appendix E
Textual Notes

The following notes do not discuss all the difficulties in our texts, nor do they give a full critical account of the passages they do discuss. The notes refer to the passages asterisked in the translation: we comment on all the points at which we have decided to differ from the editions we normally follow; in addition, there are a few comments on other contentious passages

I Sextus

'MM' refers to the text of the *PH* printed in J. Mau's revision of H. Mutschmann's Teubner edition.

§38 'and* is in some circumstance': we reject MM's ἤ (a conjecture by Mutschmann), and retain καί (the reading of the Greek MSS and by implication of T, the mediaeval Latin translation).

§41 'some from earth,*': most scholars think that there is a lacuna in the text, though the MSS do not indicate one. Kochalsky suggested ‹like earthworms›', comparing Lactantius, *Inst. div.* VII vii 9; Fabricius preferred mice, and Bury grasshoppers.

§41 'some from donkeys,*': we retain the received text, as does MM, but it is doubly odd. (i) Surely dung-beetles come from dung, not from donkeys? (ii) Surely a reference to donkeys is out of place here? They should appear later in the sentence, alongside bulls and horses. Origen, *c.Cels.* IV 57, says that γίνεται ... ἐκ βόος μέλισσα καὶ ἐξ ἵππου σφὴξ καὶ ἐξ ὄνου κανθαρίς. (Koetschau prints κάνθαρος, a marginal variant for ·κανθαρίς, comparing IV 58: ἐξ ὄνου δὲ κανθάρων.) The Suda, s.v. κάνθαρος, and a scholiast to Aristophanes, *Peace* 82, report that dung-beetles come from the dung of donkeys. Perhaps there were originally two stories: the dung-beetle is generated from dung, the blister-beetle (κανθαρίς) from the flesh of dead donkeys. The source of the Suda and the scholiast may have conflated the two stories, failing to distinguish κάνθαρος from κανθαρίς. As for Sextus, his note may simply be careless. Alternatively, the text may be corrupt. The easiest way to remove both oddities, (i) and (ii), is to suppose that he reported the same story as the Suda and the scholiast, and that he wrote τὰ δ' ἐξ ὄνων ‹κοπροῦ›.

§56 'some in forests,*': the point is out of place, for it is what animals eat, not where they eat, that is in question. Perhaps we should change ὑληνόμα to ὑληφάγα ('some on wood').

§56 'or even* fatal': we read ἤ καί (after T), which is more pointed than καί (MSS, MM).

§65 'appropriate nature . . .* the affects': the MSS read τῶν κατὰ τὴν οἰκείαν φύσιν ἀρετῶν τῶν περὶ τὰ πάθη; MM prints ‹καὶ› τῶν περὶ τὰ πάθη (after T). Neither reading makes much sense. Heintz proposed ‹καὶ› τῷ περὶ τὰ πάθη, which is little better. The following sections of the text indicate that 'internal reason' is dependent on *four* capacities (see esp. §72). Hence the corrupt phrase §65 must describe *two* capacities. Mau, in the Appendix to MM, therefore suggests that Sextus may have written something like: τῇ ἀντιλήψει ‹καὶ παραμυθίᾳ τῶν οἰκείων παθῶν, τῇ δὲ ἀναλήψει› τῶν κατὰ τὴν οἰκείαν φύσιν ἀρετῶν [τῶν περὶ τὰ πάθη]. There is no need to posit so complicated a corruption. The required sense could be expressed by e.g. . . . ἀρετῶν ‹ καὶ τηῃ παραμυθίᾳ › τῶν περὶ τὰ πάθη.

§69 'who is particularly hostile*': we retain πολεμοῦντα (MSS, T). The received text is exactly right: 'even though Chrysippus in general was extremely hostile to animals, still . . .'. MM's συμπολεμοῦντα, Diels' προσέχοντα, and Bury's ὁμιλοῦντα are all wrong.

§72 'in this respect,*': with T and three of the MSS we read κατὰ τοῦτο. Other MSS have κατὰ τούτου.. Heintz's κατὰ τοῦτον, accepted by MM, is unnecessary.

§77 'and show*': retaining ὑποδεικνύειν – there is no need for the old conjecture ἀποδεικνύειν, accepted by MM.

§78 'having before* shown': retaining the inelegant ἔμπροσθεν which MM excises.

§85 'which the dogmatists provide*': MM follows Heintz in excising this clause. Heintz's arguments are frail, and the words have point: see above, p. 61.

§94 'given the purpose of our treatise,*': here we follow the first Teubner edition in which Mutschmann excised τοῦ τρόπου and construed the clause with ἐκεῖνο λεκτέον. MM accepts Heintz's defence of τοῦ τρόπου, attaching the clause to μὴ διατρίβωμεν. The reading is intelligible but extraordinarily clumsy.

§94 'it has these qualities alone,*': Heintz excises μόνας, and is followed by MM. But μόνας is intelligible in itself, and it is supported by §99 (although there it must be said that μόνας, which MM prints, is Bekker's conjecture).

§95 'in flutes . . . instruments*': we translate the MSS text, retaining ἐν (excised by MM) and omitting MM's supplement ἐμπνεομένου.

§97 'from among the qualities in the apple*': MM follows Heintz in excising this clause, for no good reason.

§97 'the objects perceptible by them*': the MSS, and T, give τῶν κατ' αὐτὰς αἰσθητῶν; where αὐτάς can only refer to τὰς ποιότητας. We can make nothing of this, and propose κατ' αὐτά for κατ' αὐτάς, taking αὐτά to refer to τὰ αἰσθητήρια.

§99 'if it is possible*': the MSS give ἐνεχώρει, which is ungrammatical. MM prints εἰ ἐνεχώρει, perhaps after T. We prefer Heintz's εἰ ἐγχωρεῖ.

§104 'the existence or non-existence of the objects*': we retain αὐτοῖς (MSS), sc. τοῖς ὑποκειμένοις. MM prints αὐταῖς (Apelt), sc. ταῖς φαντασίαις. But the question of the existence of *the appearances* is never raised by Sextus, nor is it relevant here.

§112 'in different conditions,*': the MSS divide between ἄλλως and ἄλλων. With MM we prefer ἄλλως. The decision between a sigma and a nu determines the overall interpretation of the mode: see p. 83.

§117 'credit from the other*': reading τὴν ‹ἐκ› θατέρου πίστιν with Heintz, a conjecture supported by numerous parallel passages. The MSS reading, retained by MM, means 'waiting for the other to be credited'.

§121 'by these modes too*': we read διὰ τούτους τοὺς τρόπους (MSS, T). MM accepts Bekker's conjecture, διὰ τούτου τοῦ τρόπου. For διά + acc. see §§99, 144, 163 (cf §89); for the plural τρόπους see p. 102.

§134 'the argument from ... confounds*': we read συγχεῖ (MSS), with MM. T gives *continet* = συνέχει. Heintz supports this reading and accordingly takes λόγος to mean 'proportion'.

§136 'and ...*': MM prints καὶ τόνδε τὸν τρόπον (MSS), but this makes no sense. Pappenheim changes τρόπον to τόπον; but it is strange to have only two of the three parts of the Fifth Mode referred to, and referred to discontinuously. Kayser excises the whole phrase. For the problems with Sextus' procedure here see p. 142.

§152 'by custom as indifferent*': the meaning is plain enough, but we do not see how to extract it either from ἀδιαφορίας ἔθει (MSS, T) or from ἐν ἀδιαφορίας ἔθει (MM).

§162 'they deny *': MM marks a lacuna after ὅταν.

II Diogenes

'Long' refers to the text printed by H.S. Long in the Oxford Classical Text series.

§78 'a kind of record*': we retain μνήμη (MSS) – Galesius' μήνυσις (accepted by Long) is unnecessary.

§78 'a great deal of anomaly*': ἀνωμαλίαν (Long, after Kühn) for ἀνωφέλειαν (MSS) is supported by *PH* I 12; but ἀνωφέλειαν makes tolerable sense and may possibly be correct.

§78 'or unsurprising*': we propose καὶ τὰ ‹μὴ› θαυμαζόμενα. *Surprising* things do not persuade, and the reference here must be to the Ninth Mode (in Sextus' numbering).

§78 'they used to display*': we prefer ἐδείκνυον (F) to ἐδείκνυσαν (Long).

§79 'the discordances*': for συμφωνίας (MSS, Long) we propose διαφωνίας, which gives the required sense. (Elsewhere we translate διαφωνία by 'dispute'.)

§79 'the ten modes he* sets out': the MSS reading τοὺς δέκα τρόπους καθ' οὓς τίθησιν is certainly corrupt. It is simple to expunge καθ' οὓς (so Long), which will have been carelessly repeated from the preceding sentence. But who, then, is the subject of τίθησιν? Some suggest

Aenesidemus, the last Pyrrhonist to have been named by Diogenes. But Diogenes' account of the modes does not copy Aenesidemus (see §87). Others think of Pyrrho, whose life Diogenes is writing. But Pyrrho's biography ends in §70 and Diogenes is now giving a general account of Pyrrhonism. Either Diogenes is writing carelessly (a not implausible supposition) or else there is further corruption in the text. Nietzsche proposed καὶ Θεοδόσιος for καθ᾽ οὕς (for Theodosius see Diogenes IX 70 and the Suda, s.v.) – perhaps Diogenes wrote καὶ Θεο.

§80 'the natures and customs and constitutions*': the main MSS read φύσεις καὶ ἔθνη καὶ συγκρίσεις. Long, following Menagius, prints φύσεις καὶ τὰς ἰδιοσυγκρισίας (cf *PH* I 81). But συγκρίσεις is perfectly apt, and ἔθνη may be a corruption of ἔθη (some MSS actually read τὰ ἔθη). With some qualms we read φύσεις καὶ ἔθη καὶ συγκρίσεις. (ἔθη is not wholly apposite: ἤθη would be better.)

§82 'common variations*': we read κοινὰς παραλλαγάς, taking παραλλαγάς in the sense of 'changes'. For κοινάς the chief MSS have κοινῶς (so Long); but if we read κοινῶς we are obliged to suppose falsely that παραλλαγάς is a wider term than διαθέσεις.

§83 'conventions due to custom*': we read ἐθικὰς συνθήκας with Menagius. The MSS have τεχνικὰς συνθήκας, which is nonsense. Long prints τὰς ἐθνικὰς συνθήκας, which is little better. (Long attributes this reading to Menagius; but Menagius does not suggest τάς, and the word ἐθνικάς which is found in his commentary is plainly a misprint for ἐθικάς.) συνθήκας is not entirely appropriate: perhaps Diogenes wrote συνηθείας.

§84 'with solid body, heat, cold, movement,*': so the MSS (and Long). But the sequence is doubly odd: we expect an opposite to be paired with στερεῷ, and κινήσει is not easy to understand. Perhaps the text should read σὺν στερεῷ ‹κενῷ›, θερμότητι ψυχρότητι, [κινήσει].

§84 'and so does the sun.*': we read καὶ ὁ ἥλιος, with most MSS – the text is abrupt but intelligible. Two MSS read καὶ ὁ ἥλιος ἀλλοῖος μὲν ὑπὸ τῇ ἕῳ, ἀλλοῖος δὲ ὑπὸ τῇ μεσημβρίᾳ φαίνεται. That probably represents a scribe's intelligent attempt to make the text smoother. Scholars generally suppose that καὶ ὁ ἥλιος is corrupt: Menagius suggested καὶ ὑπὸ δείλην, M. Casaubon ἀλλοῖον ὑπὸ τὴν δύσιν; Long prints Kühn's conjecture καὶ ‹ὅτε› ὁ ἥλιος ‹δύνει›. The sense would then be: 'Our skin has a different appearance at mid-day and in the evening/at sunset/when the sun sets.'

§85 'it takes two men to lift*': we retain κουφιζόμενος (MSS, Long), but with qualms. (We must understand 'is lifted by two men' to mean 'takes two men to lift'.) Perhaps κουφιζόμενος is a careless anticipation of the κουφιζόμενος which occurs a few words later in the sentence: Diogenes may have written something like οὐ φερόμενος or μόλις κινούμενος.

§85 'a foot across.*': most MSS read πόρρωθεν; there is a variant τετράγωνος.

Neither word makes sense. Kühn proposed πόρρωθεν ⟨μικρός⟩; Menagius' διπόδης is better, but Diogenes surely wrote ποδιαῖος. For the philosophical commonplace of the sun's appearing a foot across see e.g. Heraclitus, frag. 3; Aristotle, *An.* 428b2, *Somn.* 458b28.

§85 'Mountains appear airy*': ἀεροειδῆ (MSS) will do – the word means 'cloudy-coloured' (cf [Aristotle] *Col.* 794a4) and that is how mountains look at a distance. (See also the Louvre papyrus, quoted above, p. 107.) But the text remains unsatisfactory, since we expect a contrast for ἀεροειδῆ. Perhaps read ἐγγύθεν δὲ ⟨ἑτερόχροα⟩ καὶ τραχέα.

§86 'The same body*': an opaque illustration – read χρῶμα for σῶμα?

§86 'places and positions,*': perhaps add ⟨καὶ ἀποστημάτων⟩.

§86 'quantities and qualities,*': some MSS read ποσότητας (so Long), others ποιότητας. Cobet proposed ποσότητας καὶ ποιότητας, and we follow him. Although the mode is officially about quantities, Diogenes (like Philo) also refers to qualities in his account of it. This is puzzling (see above, p. 122); and although Cobet's text does not remove the puzzle, it makes the words θερμότητας κ.τ.λ. somewhat less surprising.

§87 'Sextus and Aenesidemus make it the Tenth.*': in *PH* Diogenes' Ninth Mode is again Ninth – it is Diogenes' Fifth Mode which is tenth in *PH*. Hence Hirzel suggested ⟨τὸν πέμπτον⟩ δέκατον. He may be right; but see above, p. 29.

§87 'one another*': we opt for ἄλληλα (the MSS also present ἄλλα (so Long) and ἄλλας).

§88 'known in themselves.*': Long's *apparatus* is unintelligible; but whether ὡς καθ' αὑτά or καθ' αὑτά is read makes no difference to the sense.

III Philo

'CW' refers to the text printed in the standard edition of Philo's works by I. Cohn and P. Wendland.

§170 'actually affected*': retaining καὶ κινούμενοι (MSS). CW follows pseudo-Herennius, who omits καὶ. (On 'Herennius' see p. 199. His relation to Philo is still uncertain, and his text requires re-editing: in such circumstances we have preferred to put little weight on his reported readings.)

§176 'from the same objects.*': we accept Mangey's conjecture, ⟨ἐκ⟩ τῶν αὐτῶν.

§177 'block their ears*': we again follow Mangey in reading προσαποκλειομένους (CW prints the MSS' reading προσαποσειομένους, which makes little sense).

§180 'whether natural or unnatural,*': the MSS read κατὰ φύσιν τε αὖ [or αὐτή or αὕτη], which CW prints. But αὖ is barely intelligible (it is apparently not found in ps.-Her.), and we follow von Arnim in excising it.

§187 'with what is a question of*': we accept Wendland's conjecture κἂν τοῖς ὅσα (καὶ ὅσα, CW).

§187 'in the same way.*': Wendland's τρόπον seems right (τύπον MSS, CW). τρόπον here might have – or suggest – the semi-technical sense of 'mode'.

§192 'the necessity to suspend judgement?*': we retain the MSS' ἀναγκαῖον, needlessly excised by CW.

§193 'not to trust*': reading προσπιστεύειν (MSS). CW accepts Turnebus' προπιστεύειν, but the prefix προ- has no point here ('trust them before' *what?*) – and ps.-Her. writes πιστεύειν. As for προς-, that may háve no semantic force; if it *is* to be pressed for sense, we may understand: 'trust what is unclear in addition to what is clear'.

§193 'which have led*': ἐπαγαγόντα (MSS) is satisfactory; CW prefers ἐπάγοντα (ps.-Her.).

§194 'where they hold contrary views.*': CW prints the MSS text, ὅσα ἄλλα ἐναντία ταῦτα νομίζουσι. But this is hard to understand. Mangey's ταὐτά for ταῦτα gives the wrong sense (the point is not that people think opposites to be the same). Wendland conjectures τοιαῦτα for ταῦτα; we prefer to excise ταῦτα.

§201 'the second ...*': the MSS read τῆς δευτέρας καὶ ὑπειλούσης (FGH) or ἀπειλούσης (U). But ὑπειλούσης is a non-word, and ἀπειλούσης makes no sense. CW prints Turnebus' ὑπεικούσης, the Loeb editor suggests ὑπ' εἶλαρ οὔσης. Neither proposal is convincing, and we can think of nothing better. (Ps.-Her. simply omits καὶ ὑπειλούσης.)

§203 'from ignorance*': omitting ἐπιστήμης, as Cohn suggests.

§203 'and Assertion,*': συναινέσεως is Mangey's correction of συνέσεως (MSS).

Glossary

ἀγωγή	lifestyle
ἀναλογισμός	abduction [We take this term from C. S. Pierce: his use of it does not correspond exactly to Sextus' use of ἀναλογισμός, but the terms are close and Sextus' technical word needs a technical translation.]
ἀνωμαλία	anomaly
βέβαιος	firm
διάθεσις	condition [see p. 82]
τὰ κατὰ διαφοράν	things which are in virtue of a difference [see p. 135]
διαφωνία	dispute
δόγμα etc.	dogma, etc [see p. 1]
δοκεῖ	seems, is thought to be
ἐπικρίνειν	decide
τὰ ἐκτός	external (existing objects)
(ὑποκείμενα)	
ἐπέχειν	suspend judgement
ἐποχή	suspension of judgement [see p. 44]
ζητεῖν	investigate
ἰσοσθένεια	equipollence [see p. 24]
καταλαμβάνειν	apprehend
κρίνειν	judge
κριτήριον	standard [see p. 89]
οἰκεῖος	appropriate

πάθος   affect [πάθος is the noun from πάσχειν, 'to be affected'; it can often be translated as 'feeling' or 'emotion', but neither of those English terms is accurate in the context of *PH*. We have, with some reluctance, settled on the word 'affect': in archaic English this word answers exactly to πάθος, and it is also used in modern psychology in a related sense.]

περιπίπτειν   impress

περίστασις   circumstances [see p. 82]

πίστις   credibility, warrant

πιστός   credible

πρός τι   relative [see Index of Topics]

σκέψις   inquiry

ταραχή   disturbance

τρόπος   mode, way [see p. 21]

ὑπάρξις   reality

ὑπαρκτός   existent

φαίνεσθαι   appear [see p. 23]

τὸ φαινόμενον   what appears, what is apparent

φαντασία   appearance

Bibliography

This bibliography (which limits itself, with one or two exceptions, to books and articles written in English) is intended first to provide some introductory reading on ancient scepticism, and secondly to list a few items which bear on particular issues discussed or mentioned in our various chapters.

Sextus' two surviving works, the *Outlines of Pyrrhonism* and *Against the Mathematicians*, are available in English translation (with facing Greek text) in the Loeb Classical Library (edited by R. G. Bury, in four vols., 1933–49). Diogenes Laertius' *Lives of the Philosophers* is published in the same series (edited by R. D. Hicks, two vols., 1925): the life of Pyrrho is in the second volume.

The best short introduction to Hellenistic philosophy, both to scepticism and to the dogmatic philosophies which formed its background, is:

A. A. LONG: *Hellenistic Philosophy* (London, 1974)

There is a brief guide by

D. SEDLEY: 'The Protagonists', in *Doubt and Dogmatism* [see below, M. Schofield *et al.*]

The best full-length books on ancient scepticism are

V. BROCHARD: *Les Sceptiques grecs* (Paris, 1923²)

and

M. DAL PRA: *Lo scetticismo greco* (Bari, 1975²)

In English see

C. L. STOUGH: *Greek Skepticism* (Berkeley–Los Angeles, 1969)

There are collections of papers in

M. SCHOFIELD, M. F. BURNYEAT, J. BARNES (eds.): *Doubt and Dogmatism* (Oxford, 1980)

M. F. BURNYEAT (ed.): *The Skeptical Tradition* (Berkeley–Los Angeles–London, 1983)

There are selective bibliographies in Long's *Hellenistic Philosophy*, and in *Doubt and Dogmatism*. A comprehensive bibliography of modern work on ancient scepticism is included in:

G. GIANNANTONI (ed.): *Lo scetticismo antico*, Atti del Convegno organizzato dal centro di studio del pensiero antico del C.N.R., Roma, 5–8 nov. 1980 (Naples, 1982)

On Pyrrho see

A. A. LONG: 'Timon of Phlius: Pyrrhonist and Satirist', *Proceedings of the Cambridge Philological Society* 24, 1978, 68–91

E. FLINTOFF: 'Pyrrho and India', *Phronesis* 25, 1980, 88–108

On the sceptical Academy see

G. STRIKER: 'Sceptical Strategies', in *Doubt and Dogmatism*

M. FREDE: 'Stoics and Sceptics on Clear and Distinct Ideas', in *The Skeptical Tradition*

and the detailed scholarly study of

J. GLUCKER: *Antiochus and the Late Academy*, Hypomnemata 56 (Göttingen, 1978)

For Aenesidemus see

J. M. RIST: 'The Heracliteanism of Aenesidemus', *Phoenix* 24, 1970, 309–19

On the sceptical doctors see

L. EDELSTEIN: 'Empiricism and Scepticism in the Teaching of the Greek Empiricist School', in his *Ancient Medicine* (Baltimore, 1967)

M. FREDE: 'The Method of the So-Called Methodical School of Medicine', in J. Barnes, J. Brunschwig, M. F. Burnyeat, M. Schofield (eds.), *Science and Speculation* (Cambridge–Paris, 1982)

And for Sextus himself consult

K. JANÁČEK: *Sextus Empiricus' Sceptical Methods* (Prague, 1972)

A. A. LONG: 'Sextus Empiricus on the Criterion of Truth', *Bulletin of the Institute of Classical Studies* 25, 1978, 35–49

D. K. HOUSE: 'The Life of Sextus Empiricus', *Classical Quarterly* 30, 1980, 227–38

The classic work on the rediscovery of Sextus (see Chapter 1) is

R. H. POPKIN: *The History of Skepticism from Erasmus to Spinoza* (Berkeley–Los Angeles–London, 1979[2])

See also

C. SCHMITT: 'The Rediscovery of Ancient Scepticism in Modern Times', in *The Skeptical Tradition*

On the relations between ancient and modern scepticism see

A. NAESS: *Scepticism* (London, 1968)

M. F. BURNYEAT: 'Idealism and Greek Philosophy: What Berkeley Missed and Descartes Saw', *Philosophical Review* 91, 1982, 3–40

On the modes or 'tropes' (Chapter 3) see

G. STRIKER: 'The Ten Tropes of Aenesidemus', in *The Skeptical Tradition*
– a paper which also contains a clear discussion of the connexions between relativism and scepticism.

On the ancient notion of 'appearances' or *ta phainomena* consult

M. F. BURNYEAT: 'Conflicting Appearances', *Proceedings of the British Academy* 65, 1979, 69–111

For the Hellenistic debate over the status of non-human animals (Chapter 4) see
A. TERIAN: *Philonis Alexandrini de animalibus*, Studies in Hellenistic Judaism 1 (Chico CA, 1981)

On the relation between the Epicureans and the sceptics (mentioned in Chapters 5, 8 and 10) see
D. FOWLER: 'Sceptics and Epicureans', *Oxford Studies in Ancient Philosophy* 2, 1984, 237–67
(this is a critical notice of M. Gigante's book, *Scetticismo e Epicureismo*)

The Louvre papyrus, which we mention in Chapter 8, has been most recently edited and discussed by
F. LASSERRE: 'Un papyrus sceptique méconnu (P. Louvre Inv. 7733 R^0), in J. Binger *et al* (eds.), *Le Monde Grec – hommages à Claire Préaux* (Brussels, 1975)

On Aenesidemus' Eight Modes against Causal Explanation (again Chapter 8), and other sceptical attacks on causation, see
J. BARNES: 'Ancient Scepticism and Causation', in *The Skeptical Tradition*

There is currently a debate about the scope of ancient Pyrrhonism (briefly mentioned in Chapter 10): see
M. F. BURNYEAT: 'Can the Sceptic Live his Scepticism?, in *Doubt and Dogmatism* and in *The Skeptical Tradition*
J. BARNES: 'The Beliefs of a Pyrrhonist', *Proceedings of the Cambridge Philological Society* 29, 1982, 1–29 and *Elenchos* 4, 1983, 5–43
also
M. F. BURNYEAT: 'The Sceptic in his Place and Time'
and
M. FREDE: 'The Sceptic's Two Kinds of Assent and the Question of the Possibility of Knowledge', both in *Philosophy in History*, ed. R. RORTY, J. B. SCHNEEWIND, Q. SKINNER (Cambridge, 1984)

And for about turn arguments (Chapter 11) see
M. F. BURNYEAT: 'Protagoras and Self-Refutation in Later Greek Philosophy', *Philosophical Review* 85, 1976, 44–69

Finally, on the sceptical arguments about value (Chapter 13) see
J. ANNAS: 'Doing Without Objective Values: Ancient and Modern Strategies', in M. Schofield and G. Striker (eds.), *The Norms of Nature* (Cambridge, 1985)

Index of people referred to

I Ancient

More information on many of these people can be found in *The Oxford Classical Dictionary* or *Die Kleine Pauly*. All authors are Greek, except those marked (L) for Latin.

Page references in **bold type** indicate that the reference occurs within one of the modes.

ACADEMICS. Adherents of the philosophical school founded by Plato (q.v.) in the Academy gymnasium. Generally used for followers of the sceptical Academy (sometimes called Middle or New Academy) founded by Arcesilaus (q.v.) *See also* PLATONISTS, -ISM: 1, 14, 15, 17, 45, 48, 49, 72
Alleged differences from Pyrrhonists: 14

AENESIDEMUS of Cnossus. First-century BC sceptical philosopher who abandoned the Academy (q.v.) as it became more dogmatic, and established a more radical scepticism invoking the name of Pyrrho (q.v.). Also had puzzling interest in Heraclitus (q.v.): 15, 16, 18, **20** = **172**, 21, 22, 26, 27, 28, 30, 44, 50, 62, 108, 123, 143, 144, 145, **147** = **174**, 164

AGRIPPA. Pyrrhonist philosopher of uncertain date, some time between Aenesidemus (q.v.) and Sextus (q.v.). Nothing is known of him except that he invented (or codified) the Five Modes: 22, 29, 50, 62, 89, 90–2, 94, 102–3, 133, 142–3, 182; quoted: 182

ALCIBIADES of Athens. Fifth-century BC politician, famous for his wild lifestyle: 60

ALEXANDER of Aphrodisias. Late second-century AD Peripatetic philosopher and influential commentator on Aristotle's works: 11, 71

ALEXANDER the Great. His conquest of the Punjab, which Pyrrho may have accompanied, took place in 327–325 BC: 10, 12

ANAXAGORAS of Clazomenae. Philosopher-scientist active in Athens in the mid fifth century BC. Quoted: **129**

ANDRON of Argos. Otherwise unknown: **55**, **57** = **173**, 61

ANONYMOUS (1) author of verse tragedy. Quoted: 55

AULUS GELLIUS (L) *c* AD 130–180. Author of *Attic Nights*, a collection of short essays on a variety of historical, literary and philosophical topics. Quoted: 28, 96

CAELIUS AURELIANUS (L). Fifth-century AD medical writer, who translated the second-century AD medical writer Soranus: 125

CALLATIAN INDIANS. Possibly mythical people alleged by Herodotus (q.v.) to dispose of their dead by eating them: 157–8

CARNEADES of Cyrene, 214–129/8 BC. Head of the sceptical Academy and its most famous controversialist, who argued particularly against the Stoics (*see* CLITOMACHUS): 1, 14

CASSIUS. Celebrated Roman doctor of the early first century AD, described by Galen as a Pyrrhonist in philosophy: 16

CELSUS (L). First-century AD author of *On Medicine*: 16

CHRYSERMUS. Otherwise unknown doctor, follower of Herophilus (q.v.): 55

CHRYSIPPUS of Soli, *c.* 280–207 BC. Third head of the Stoic school, and its most influential and extensive author, particularly famous for his logic: **36**, **47, 48, 153**

CICERO (L) 106–43 BC. Roman politician and amateur philosopher, writing from an Academic viewpoint: 6, 14, 15, 104

CICERO, PSEUDO- Author of *Ad Herennium* (no connexion with 'Herennius'), a rhetorical treatise usually dated to the early first century BC, wrongly ascribed to Cicero. Quoted: 148

CILICIANS. Inhabitants of present-day southern Turkey: **154** = **173**

CLITOMACHUS (originally HASDRUBAL) of Carthage. Pupil of Carneades; wrote down over 400 books of his arguments, but emphasised that Carneades did not commit himself to believing any of them and that he had no idea what Carneades did believe, if anything: 1

CRATES of Thebes, *c.* 365–285 BC. Cynic philosopher who took pride in rejecting social conventions. *See* HIPPARCHIA: **152**

DEMOCRITUS of Abdera. Fifth century BC. First major defender of atomism. His views on knowledge sound sceptical, but it is uncertain how this fitted with his metaphysics: 12, 116, 141, 148; quoted: 12, 116, 148

DEMOPHON. Alexander the Great's waiter: **54**, **56** = **173**, 58

DERCYLLIDES. First-century AD scholar and commentator on Plato: 131

DIOGENES of Sinope. Third century BC. First cynic philosopher ('cynic' derives from the Greek word for 'dog') who publicly rejected most social conventions: **151, 152**

philosopher. Regarded by sceptics as a half-hearted predecessor, because he produced highly speculative ideas as well as sceptical comments on the difficulty of attaining knowledge: 12, 161; quoted: 12, 161–2

II Modern

Information on most of these philosophers can be found in *The Encyclopedia of Philosophy*, ed. P. Edwards (4 vols., New York, 1973)

Index of Topics